Edward I's Conquest of Wales

Edward I's Conquest of Wales

Sean Davies

Pen & Sword
MILITARY

First published in Great Britain in 2017 by
PEN & SWORD MILITARY
An imprint of
Pen & Sword Books Ltd
47 Church Street
Barnsley
South Yorkshire
S70 2AS

ISBN 978-1-47386-166-4

A CIP catalogue record for this book is available from the British Library.

Typeset by Concept, Huddersfield HD4 5JL.
Printed and bound in Great Britain by TJ International Ltd. Padstow, PL28 8RW

Pen & Sword Books Ltd incorporates the imprints of Pen & Sword Archaeology,
Atlas, Aviation, Battleground, Discovery, Family History, History, Maritime,
Military, Naval, Politics, Railways, Select, Social History, Transport, True Crime,
and Claymore Press, Frontline Books, Leo Cooper, Praetorian Press,
Remember When, Seaforth Publishing and Wharncliffe.

For a complete list of Pen & Sword titles please contact
PEN & SWORD BOOKS LIMITED
47 Church Street, Barnsley, South Yorkshire, S70 2AS, England
E-mail: enquiries@pen-and-sword.co.uk
Website: www.pen-and-sword.co.uk

Contents

List of Plates

Timeline

1264	Battle of Lewes.
1265	Agreement of Pipton.
	Battle of Evesham.
1267	Treaty of Montgomery.
1270	Edward leaves England on crusade.
1272	Death of Henry III, accession of Edward I.
1273	Llywelyn fails to perform fealty to Edward's officers.
	Arguments over the building of the castles of Dolforwyn and Cefnllys.
1274	Edward returns to England after his crusade.
	Dafydd ap Gruffudd and Gruffudd ap Gwenwynwyn plot to kill Llywelyn.
	Edward cancels meeting at Shrewsbury where Llywelyn was to perform homage.
1275	Refusals by Llywelyn to travel to England to perform homage.
	Llywelyn marries Eleanor de Montfort by proxy.
	Eleanor captured by Edward's men on her way to Wales.
1276	Unofficial war throughout the march of Wales.
1277	Edward's first Welsh war.
	Treaty of Aberconwy imposes humiliating terms on Llywelyn.
	Llywelyn does homage to Edward in Westminster.
1281	Reginald de Grey appointed as Justice of Chester.
1282	Rising against English rule in Wales.
	Edward's second Welsh war (ends in 1283).
	Killing of Llywelyn ap Gruffudd.
1283	Dafydd ap Gruffudd's capture and execution.
1284	Statute of Rhuddlan.
1287	Revolt of Rhys ap Maredudd.
1290	Death of the 'Maid of Norway' draws Edward deeper into affairs in Scotland.
1294	War between England and France over Gascony.
	Revolt of Madog ap Llywelyn begins in Wales.
1295	Battle of Maes Moydog.
	Capture of Madog and the end of the revolt.
1301	Edward of Caernarfon endowed with the royal lands in Wales, becomes known as Prince of Wales.

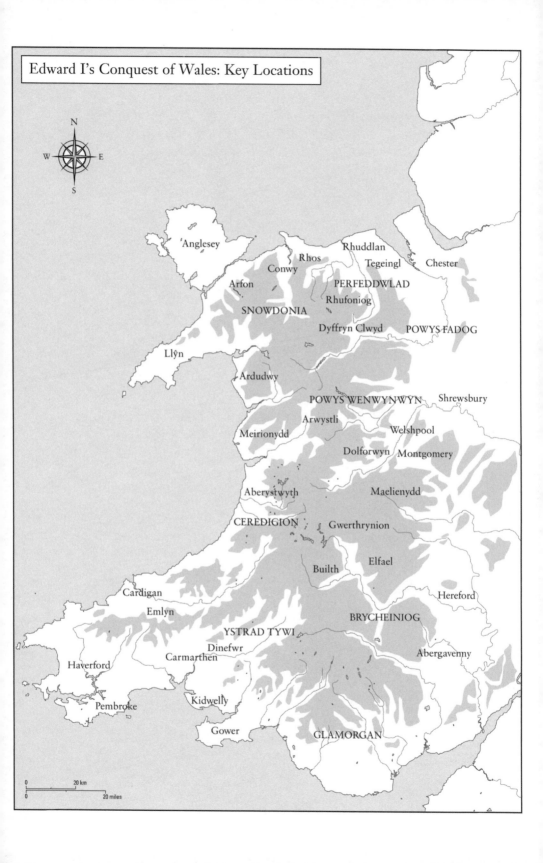

Edward I's Conquest of Wales: Key Locations

Anglesey

Rhuddlan

Rhos

Conwy

Tegeingl

Chester

Arfon

PERFEDDWLAD

Rhufoniog

SNOWDONIA

Dyffryn Clwyd

POWYS FADOG

Llŷn

Ardudwy

POWYS WENWYNWYN

Shrewsbury

Arwystli

Welshpool

Meirionydd

Dolforwyn

Montgomery

Aberystwyth

Maelienydd

CEREDIGION

Gwerthrynion

Elfael

Builth

Cardigan

Hereford

Emlyn

BRYCHEINIOG

YSTRAD TYWI

Dinefwr

Abergavenny

Haverford

Carmarthen

Pembroke

Kidwelly

Gower

GLAMORGAN

0   20 km
0   20 miles

Chapter 1

The Red and the White Dragons

On a blustery day in 1056, King Edward the Confessor of England stared west across the river Severn, awaiting a meeting with his troublesome neighbour Gruffudd ap Llywelyn, King of Wales:

> Ambassadors were sent from both sides and then they negotiated from opposite banks of the Severn, Edward being at Aust Cliff, Gruffudd at Beachley. The nobles went to and fro between them in boats, and after many exchanges of messages, the question was long debated which of them ought to cross over to the other. It was a difficult crossing owing to the roughness of the water, but that was not the ground of the dispute. Gruffudd alleged his precedence, Edward his equality: Gruffudd took the ground that his people had gained all England, with Cornwall, Scotland, and Wales, from the giants, and affirmed himself to be their heir in a direct line: Edward argued that his ancestors had got the land from its conquerors. After a great deal of quarrelsome contention Edward got in a boat and set off to Gruffudd. At that point the Severn is a mile broad. Gruffudd seeing him and recognising him cast off his state mantle – for he had prepared himself for a public appearance – went into the water up to his breast and throwing his arms lovingly about the boat, said: 'Wisest of kings, your modesty has vanquished my pride, your wisdom has triumphed over my foolishness. The neck which I foolishly stiffened against you you shall mount and so enter the territory which your mildness has today made your own.' And taking him on his shoulders he seated him upon his mantle, and then with joined hands did him homage. This was an admirable beginning of peace, but, after the Welsh manner, it was only kept till they felt able to do mischief.[1]

The apparently irreconcilable perceptions of rights of precedence between Wales and England, the red dragon and the white, were already centuries old in 1056, dating back to the innumerable skirmishes, raids, battles and conquests that accompanied the slow death of Roman Britain in the fifth century and beyond. They remained evident in the 1270s and 1280s when they were at the heart of the conflicts between King Edward I and Prince Llywelyn ap Gruffudd, clashes that would lead to the ultimate conquest of Wales. One of the clearest expressions of the Welsh position at that time was made by the prince: 'The king knows well that the rights of [Llywelyn's] principality are totally separate from the rights of his kingdom, although Llywelyn holds his principality under his royal power.'[2]

To trace the origins of the differing interpretations of English and Welsh regal rights, we need to take ourselves back to the fifth-century world of the British elite, nobles who saw themselves as the successors of Roman civilisation and the Roman right to rule. Their ability to exercise such rule was challenged by the influx of various peoples and tribes, most famously the Angles and Saxons; their British rivals would cut through any tribal distinctions by referring to the Germanic newcomers as *Saeson* ('Saxons'). An early ninth-century Gwynedd source, the *Historia Brittonum*, gives one of the more florid accounts of the rivalries between the two peoples. The source describes the supposed actions of a fifth-century British leader, Vortigern, as he struggled to deal with the Anglo-Saxons. At one point he attempted to construct a citadel in Snowdonia, but whenever work was started it collapsed and disappeared overnight. A boy – here the son of a Roman consul called Ambrosius, but who became Merlin in later historical traditions – was brought to the spot to be offered as a blood sacrifice by Vortigern's 'wise men'. Instead, he explained why the construction problems occurred:

'There is,' said he, 'a pool; come and dig:' they did so, and found the pool. 'Now,' continued he, 'tell me what is in it;' but they were ashamed, and made no reply. 'I,' said the boy, 'can discover it to you: there are two vases in the pool;' they examined, and found it so: continuing his questions, 'What is in the vases?' they were silent: 'There is a tent in them,' said the boy; 'separate them, and you shall find it so;' this being done by the king's command, there was found in them a folded tent. The boy, going on with his questions, asked the wise men what was in it? But they not knowing what to reply, 'There are,' said he, 'two serpents, one white and the other red; unfold the tent;' they obeyed, and two sleeping serpents were discovered; 'consider attentively,' said the boy, 'what they are doing.' The serpents began to struggle with each other; and the white one, raising himself up, threw down the other into the middle of the tent and sometimes drove him to the edge of it; and this was repeated thrice. At length the red one, apparently the weaker of the two, recovering his strength, expelled the white one from the tent; and the latter being pursued through the pool by the red one, disappeared. Then the boy, asking the wise men what was signified by this wonderful omen, and they expressing their ignorance, he said to the king, 'I will now unfold to you the meaning of this mystery. The pool is the emblem of this world, and the tent that of your kingdom: the two serpents are two dragons; the red serpent is your dragon, but the white serpent is the dragon of the people who occupy several provinces and districts of Britain, even almost from sea to sea: at length, however, our people shall rise and drive away the Saxon race from beyond the sea, whence they originally came.[3]

While the fact that the clashes between the peoples were often bitter and brutal is beyond dispute, modern DNA studies have established that this was not a war of racial extermination. The movement of people from continental Europe to Britain was limited, the Anglo-Saxon conquest of the island being very much the victory of a military and cultural elite. The cultural victory proved wholescale, though, through the effects of imitation of that elite and the desire of the native population to win patronage; the scale of this imperial triumph is indicated by the mere handful of Brythonic ('Welsh') words that have survived in the English language. The connection between political mastery and cultural control is clearly revealed by Bede's enormously influential *Ecclesiastical History of the English People*, a great 'national' history telling the story of the successes of God's chosen people following their conversion to Christianity. For the author, it was an inconvenient truth that many of the Anglo-Saxons' British opponents were already Christians, including Cadwallon of Gwynedd who came close to eradicating the ruling dynasty of Bede's Northumbria. Cadwallon's eventual death at the hands of Oswald at the battle of Heavenfield (*c.*633) is depicted as a great victory for the English people and the Christian faith, but the reality of shifting political alliances was far more complex. The platform for Cadwallon's campaign that took him to the shadow of Hadrian's Wall had been laid by his alliance with Penda, an Anglo-Saxon, pagan leader of Mercia with a curiously Brythonic-sounding name ('Pen-da' translates as 'good leader'). Meanwhile, Oswald's campaign had started from his adopted home, the Gaelic kingdom of Dál Riata in Argyll. He enjoyed backing from King Domnall Brecc and the clerical community of Iona, as well as from the Brythonic kingdom of Rheged, the heart of which was in the region of Carlisle.

Cadwallon's defeat was symbolic of the retreat and decline of Brythonic political power, and the independence of Brythonic leaders in the island would eventually be restricted to the lands that would become Wales. Offa's Dyke helped give that retreat physical form, although it should be stressed that we know very little about the date or purpose of the earthwork that runs along much of the length of Wales' eastern border and that has traditionally been attributed to the late eighth-century Mercian leader Offa. The kings to the west of that dyke faced pressure from both Anglo-Saxon and Hiberno-Scandinavian rivals in the succeeding centuries, external forces that impacted on the potential development of a single kingdom of Wales. A long tradition began of the submission of less powerful Welsh kings to more imposing Anglo-Saxon kings from Mercia and Wessex, as particularly seen under King Athelstan (d. 939). According to the twelfth-century writer William of Malmesbury, *c.* 930 Athelstan summoned nearly all the kings of Wales to gather at his court in Hereford, the border city itself a great symbolic location in the wars between the peoples. There Athelstan is said to have imposed humiliating terms on them, including an enormous annual tribute of 20lbs of gold, 300lbs of silver, 25,000 oxen and large numbers of hounds and hawks. In the years that followed, the mighty Anglo-Saxon king repeatedly underlined his authority by compelling the Welsh kings to attend his courts and witness his charters. This state of affairs has been seen as the catalyst for the composition of the famous Welsh poem *Armes Prydein*, a song of defiance that envisaged a grand alliance against Athelstan made up of the Welsh, Scots, Irish, the Danes of Dublin and the Britons of Strathclyde, Brittany and Cornwall.[4]

The kings of the Britons

Many in England may have seen the situation under Athelstan as the natural order of things. It is possible that many in Wales also acknowledged this, but the existence of *Armes Prydein* shows that an alternative narrative existed and it is also clear that there were kings to the west of Offa's Dyke with far greater ambitions. Such men did not then call themselves 'kings of Wales'; the label 'Welsh' came from the language of the Anglo-Saxons where it meant 'foreigner' or 'outsider'. While the old Brythonic population at times referred to themselves as the *Cymry* – which could be translated as 'compatriots' or 'people of the same region' – their most powerful and successful leaders were called in the native chronicles 'kings of the Britons'. The first man known to receive such an epithet was Anarawd ap Rhodri Mawr (d. 916) and the title was also accorded to Hywel Dda (d. 950), Maredudd ab Owain (d. 999), Llywelyn ap Seisyll (d. 1023), Gruffudd ap Llywelyn (d. 1063) and Bleddyn ap Cynfyn (d. 1075).[5] The title itself implies a connection to the history and mythology that saw the kings of the Britons as the descendants of the Trojans; as the rightful rulers of the whole island following their conquest of it from the giants, they were superior to any Anglo-Saxon overlord. These leaders used propaganda associated with such mythology to fuel their own rise to superiority over the other, less powerful 'kings' of Wales.

The man who would bring this policy to fruition was the remarkable Gruffudd ap Llywelyn. Not only was he the first, last and only native king to rule all the lands that comprise modern Wales, he took things further, reversing the trend of the westward expansion of English control and reclaiming

'Welsh' land to the east of Offa's Dyke that had been in Anglo-Saxon hands for centuries. Such reconquered land ran almost the entire length of Wales' eastern border and contained many inhabitants who would have considered themselves 'Welsh' by language, culture and inclination. The resurgence in Welsh power since the days of Athelstan was remarkable and had been helped by divisions in the Anglo-Saxon state, partly caused by the impact of the Vikings. The key to Gruffudd's success was an unshakeable alliance with the leaders of Anglo-Saxon Mercia, who were prepared to suffer territorial losses in the west in return for the support of the Welsh against their rivals from Wessex: Harold and the rest of the Godwine dynasty.

Gruffudd's 1056 meeting with Edward the Confessor, described at the beginning of this chapter, was preceded by two years of border warfare that started with the exile of Earl Ælfgar, the heir to Mercia, at the instigation of the Godwines. Ælfgar gathered a Hiberno-Scandinavian fleet which he brought to the mouth of the Wye for a rendezvous with his ally, Gruffudd. In the course of these events, Gruffudd killed his last remaining native rival, the king of south-east Wales, before the allies embarked on an attack up the Wye valley that ended with the destruction of the strategically and symbolically key town of Hereford. After more border skirmishing, Ælfgar was returned to his earldom and, eventually, Gruffudd was able to win recognition of his position as King of Wales from the English state. While the Anglo-Saxon Chronicle merely noted that 'Gruffudd swore oaths that he would be a loyal and faithful under-king to King Edward', from the nature of their agreement it is clear that any submission made by Gruffudd was nominal; he offered no dues, gave no hostages and would not perform any military service for the Anglo-Saxon king, while the deal was accompanied by major territorial gains in favour of the Welsh king. The fact that Gruffudd is said to have done homage is, of course, significant, but his loosely defined position as an under-king within the British Isles is more akin to the nature of the relationship that would develop between the kings of England and Scotland than to the more sub-servient relationship between the kings of Wales and Athelstan. Within Wales itself, Gruffudd was described in almost imperial terms. The Welsh chronicle called him 'the foremost of the Britons' and the 'head, shield and defender' of his race. The *Life of St Gwynllyw* described him as 'valiant king of all Wales', while in the Book of Llandaff he was called 'King Gruffudd, sole and pre-eminent ruler of the British'. Perhaps even more significantly, his status was clearly acknowledged in external sources from England, Ireland and France, and even by the late eleventh-century German chronicler Adam of Bremen.

This enhancement of Welsh power and prestige is unlikely to have ever sat comfortably with Harold Godwine and he had a further, more pressing, reason for breaking the power of Wales; fracturing Gruffudd's alliance with his Mercian rivals was the only way to open a path towards the English throne. The death of Ælfgar, which is thought to have occurred in late 1062, gave Harold his opportunity; he launched a lightning strike on Gruffudd's Christmas court at Rhuddlan, then set about planning a major spring and summer campaign that would crush the fledgling kingdom of Wales. Harold's plan would, in many ways, serve as a blueprint for any future English leader seeking to reduce the native Welsh. He sowed dissension and won native support by nurturing members of the rival dynasties that Gruffudd had humbled and displaced in his rise to the kingship. Harold gathered a fleet in Bristol which he used to effect landings at key coastal locations, quickly winning over the leading men in the various localities whose allegiance to the north Walian Gruffudd was brittle. Meanwhile, Harold's brother Tostig, the earl of Northumbria, led a mounted force along the north Wales coast, the invasion route to this part of the country having been opened by the disruption in Mercia that followed Ælfgar's death. The Godwine brothers would eventually join forces, catching Gruffudd in a pincer movement. In the meantime, however, our sources indicate that the Welsh king mounted a vigorous resistance, retreating to the wildest parts of his lands – most probably a reference to Snowdonia – and engaging the invaders in guerrilla warfare. But Harold and Tostig were outstanding commanders, capable of handling the tough opposition and challenging conditions. Their methodical, relentless campaign ground down the Welsh in a manner that left a lasting impression on future generations. The twelfth-century writer John of Salisbury said that:

> When [Harold] perceived the mobility of the foreigners, he selected for the mission soldiers who fought in the same way, since he resolved that they were to engage in battle practice in light armament, assaulting in rawhide boots, chests covered by hardened straps and hides, throwing up small light shields against the missiles, and at one time hurling javelins, at another employing swords against the enemy. His troops would stick close to the enemy's fleeing footsteps in order that they might hold fast 'foot to foot and spear to spear' and might repulse shield with shield. And so he devastated everything along the way to Snowdon and ... he captured their kings and presented their heads to the king who had sent him. And killing every male he could find, all the way to pitiful little children, he pacified the province with the edge of a sword.[6]

John's contemporary Gerald of Wales included in his book the *Description of Wales* an outline of the way a potential conqueror should approach the reduction of the country. It included a description of methods undertaken by some of the most successful Anglo-Saxon leaders in Wales that concluded with Harold's final campaign against Gruffudd:

> Then, last of all, and by far the greatest, came Harold. He advanced into Wales on foot, at the head of his lightly clad infantry, lived on the country, and marched up and down and round and about the whole of Wales with such energy that he 'left not one that pisseth against a wall'. In commemoration of his success, and to his own undying memory, you will find a great number of inscribed stones put up in Wales to mark the many places where he won a victory. This was the old custom. The stones bear the inscription: HIC FUIT VICTOR HAROLDUS. It is to these recent victories of the English over the Welsh, in which so much blood was spilt, that the first three kings of the Normans owe the fact that in their lifetime they have held Wales in peace and subjection.[7]

When faced with such overwhelming, relentless opposition, Gruffudd's key supporters deserted him and he was eventually betrayed and murdered by his own closest associates, who delivered his head to Harold.

The end of the kingdom of the Britons

It is only with hindsight that the seminal nature of the change that then took place in the country can be seen, and I have argued elsewhere that the events of these years marked the end of the kingdom of Wales and the beginning of what would become the principality of Wales.[8] Harold installed in Gruffudd's place the former king's half-brothers, Bleddyn and Rhiwallon. Their ambition was to recreate the dominion enjoyed by Gruffudd, but the reality of their situation was very different. The brothers had lost the extended eastern borderlands that had been won by Gruffudd, including Tegeingl, the territory of modern-day north-east Wales between the Clwyd and Dee that had been at the heart of Gruffudd's rule. Rival Welsh dynasties that Gruffudd had crushed or vanquished in south-east and south-west Wales were now back in control of their families' traditional heartlands and the leaders of these dynasties were themselves called kings. If Gruffudd had used propaganda regarding the superiority of the 'kings of the Britons' to the Anglo-Saxons to advance his 'imperial' position within Wales, the nature of Bleddyn and Rhiwallon's submission to Harold and Edward the Confessor would have hamstrung their ability to tap into such a source of soft power. The Anglo-Saxon Chronicle describes their accession thus:

> In autumn King Gruffudd was killed on 5 August by his own men because of the fight he fought against Earl Harold. He was king over all the Welsh, and his head was brought to Earl Harold, and Harold

brought it to the king, and the figurehead of his ship and the ornaments with it. And King Edward entrusted the country to the two brothers of Gruffudd, Bleddyn and Rhiwallon, and they swore oaths and gave hostages to the king and the earl, promising that they would be faithful to him in everything, and be everywhere ready on water and on land, and likewise would pay such dues from that country as had been given before to any other king.[9]

The taking of hostages and the promise of unlimited military service is indicative of the nature of this submission, while the reference to the payment of 'such dues as had been given to any other king' may even hark back to the onerous settlement enforced by Athelstan in the tenth century. It is also notable that the Anglo-Saxon Chronicle never describes Bleddyn or Rhiwallon as king, a fact that stands in stark contrast to the same source's acknowledgement of Gruffudd's exalted status.

Rhiwallon (d. 1069) and Bleddyn (d. 1075) would restore Gruffudd's alliance with Mercia and follow policies aimed at throwing off the shackles of the 1063 agreement, but they would never come close to recreating the kingdom of Wales that had been ruled by their half-brother. The arrival of the Normans complicated matters, their restless, expansionist military presence adding another factor into the bloody dynastic politics that would tear Wales apart in the final quarter of the eleventh century, destroying any remaining vestige of a kingdom of Wales. By the 1090s, many of the most attractive, richest lowlands of the country had fallen permanently into Anglo-Norman hands, forming the so-called march of Wales, ruled by ambitious men whose lordships were geared for conflict and who had the legal backing of marcher custom to further extend their dominions by making war on the Welsh. Any future clash between England and Wales would not be a contest between nations; Wales was now a fractured, divided land made up of a bewildering array of semi-independent marcher lordships, English royal lands, and territories held by a variety of competing native Welsh dynasties.

The word 'territories' for the Welsh lands is deliberately chosen; to many of the Welsh themselves they would have been described as 'kingdoms', but such a term was becoming increasingly anachronistic. Bleddyn was the last native leader to be given the exalted title 'King of the Britons' in the native Welsh chronicle, although it was an epithet awarded to one other man: the king of England, William the Conqueror. When the king of Deheubarth (south-west Wales), Rhys ap Tewdwr, was killed in battle by the Normans in 1093, the Welsh chronicle bemoaned the fact that 'then fell the kingdom of the Britons', while John of Worcester stated that 'from that day kings ceased to rule in Wales'. A century later Gerald of Wales would have no hesitation in telling the Pope that 'Wales is a portion of the kingdom of England, and not a kingdom in itself'.

The continued use of the term 'king' by Welsh leaders in the twelfth century became a fact that was used by the Anglo-Normans to mock them and their now-unrealistic ambitions. For example, the chronicler Jordan Fantosme (fl. 1170–80) said of a group of Henry II's knights that there was not one of them who 'did not consider himself less than a Welsh king'. As well as the obvious limitations of such 'kings' in terms of political and military power, this mockery was related to a changing notion of what defined a barbarian in twelfth-century Europe. In the early middle ages, the term had been reserved for the pagan raiders and invaders of the lands of the old Roman Empire, but now it was being used to describe societies on the fringe of the continent's dominant civilisations, including the Magyars, Slavs, Scandinavians, Scottish, Irish and Welsh. Some of the characteristics of the societies of such people were thought to include the predominance of pastoral over agriculture, little urban development, unsophisticated economies and little scope for fine art. Differences in military, religious and cultural practices added to the mix, meaning that these 'fringe' societies tended to be viewed with 'condescension, suspicion, scorn and dread'.[10] While some such differences can be acknowledged between lands in the heart of Europe and those on the edge, the highlighting of such otherness was also, of course, used to help justify conquest and related atrocities and oppressions.

Geoffrey of Monmouth

It was within this context that Geoffrey of Monmouth's *History of the Kings of Britain* was composed (*c.* 1136), the book that would prove the key work in the transmission of the legend of King Arthur to the wider European world. The author, a Welsh cleric in the service of the Anglo-Normans, wished to defend his compatriots' heritage and culture, stressing their ancient claims to rule the land, having a story that stretched back to survivors from Troy, who conquered Britain from the giants. Geoffrey's pseudohistory embraced the story of Roman Britain, plus Arthur and the other 'kings of the Britons' who ruled after the legions withdrew. These kings were seen as the champions of the Roman legacy as they battled the Germanic, 'barbarian' invaders – the future kings of England. Even so, Geoffrey had no truck with any near-contemporary claims of Welsh leaders to be 'kings of the Britons'; in his work, the last man to hold such a title was Cadwaladr the Blessed (d. 682), the grandson of the Cadwallon who fell at Heavenfield. According to Geoffrey, it was Cadwaladr's death in the seventh century that led the 'Britons' to take on the name 'Welsh'. While presenting this story of the historical ascendancy of 'British' kings, Geoffrey is also the first known source for the legend of the division of Britain between the sons of Brutus, Locrinus, Albanactus and Camber, with Locrinus – the eldest, who ruled 'England' – acknowledged as the superior king over the other two, who ruled 'Scotland' and 'Wales'. This vision of three kings in Britain with the superior ruler in London would ultimately be accepted and promoted by Welsh princes in the thirteenth century. The Scots, though, would reject this tale that gave England supremacy, denying any Trojan heritage and promoting their own mythology that based their claims to the Scottish crown on Scota, the daughter of an Egyptian Pharaoh from the time of Moses.

The fact that the notion of Welsh supremacy, or even equality, could not be countenanced by Geoffrey is understandable in the aftermath of the reign of Henry I (1100–35). According to the Welsh chronicles he was 'the man who had subdued under his authority all the island of Britain' and the man 'against whom no-one could be of avail save God himself'.[11] He dominated the Anglo-Normans and Welsh of south Wales, while overawing the other native rulers of the country by his influence and with two major royal expeditions, in 1114 and 1121. In 1114 the Welsh chronicles said that he intended 'to exterminate all the Britons completely, so that the Britannic name should never more be remembered'.[12]

The princes of Wales

Throughout this time, Gruffudd ap Cynan (d. 1137) of Gwynedd proved to be the great survivor. The head of an ancient dynasty who returned to Wales from Irish exile after the death of Bleddyn, Gruffudd's patient work of consolidation would pave the way for his descendants to prosper. The Anglo-Norman civil war that followed Henry I's death was the catalyst for a substantial recovery of native Welsh power, focused on the competing dynasties that ruled in Gwynedd, Powys and Deheubarth. Each of those regions would enjoy periods as the most powerful of the native Welsh 'kingdoms', but the Gwynedd dynasty would eventually stake its claim to leadership of Wales, with its leaders using the title Prince of Wales. The first man known to have used this epithet was Gruffudd's son Owain Gwynedd (d. 1170), a leader who struggled against Henry II for many years as the latter sought to recover the dominant position held in Wales by Henry I. As part of that struggle, Owain had tried to use the title 'King of Wales', but it became evident that such an epithet had lost any credibility. In diplomatic negotiations with Henry's rival, Louis VII of France, Owain adopted the title 'Prince of Wales' in an attempt to raise himself above his country's other 'kings'; in Roman law a prince was an independent, sovereign ruler and Owain's use of the epithet is known to have annoyed Henry II.[13]

Although the title 'prince' was an assertion of independence, it was also becoming clear that the nature of Welsh submission to English kings was now more defined than it had been in Anglo-Saxon times. It typically involved a formal oath of allegiance (fealty), which was often backed up by the Welsh ruler acknowledging that he held his lands from the king before becoming his vassal in a formal ceremony of homage. English kings were keen to make all the Welsh 'kings' and 'princes' do this on an individual basis; but Owain Gwynedd and his descendants would seek to secure the oaths of lesser Welsh leaders themselves, and to see that the prince of Gwynedd was the only Welsh leader to make submission to the English king. Inherent even in this model, of course, was the ultimate overlordship of the king of England. As has been seen, the nature and extent of such overlordship had fluctuated over the centuries, but by the late twelfth century government generally was growing in scale and sophistication and, with more stone buildings being built, treaties and other documentation had a greater chance of preservation and survival. Such factors would work to the benefit of England, where both government and ruling dynasties were more stable than in Wales. Even if a dominant English position in Wales was reversed by a later Welsh leader, English rulers would prove reluctant to enshrine the achievements of the Welsh in any sort of formal treaty; Professor Beverley Smith eloquently described Henry III's 'predilection for evasion' in such circumstances.[14] The 'official' position regarding the state of power between the two peoples would be preserved in the English archives, and interpreted according to the interests of the English government.

Llywelyn the Great

Gwynedd's pretensions to the leadership of native Wales had collapsed with the struggle for succession and civil war that followed Owain Gwynedd's death in 1170, but the ambitions of the region revived under Owain's grandson, Llywelyn ap Iorwerth (often referred to as Llywelyn 'the Great'). His 1201 deal with King John is the first surviving formal written treaty between a Welsh prince and an English king, a treaty that recognised Llywelyn's title and land, plus the right to use Welsh law to settle disputes in his territories. In 1205 Llywelyn was married to John's illegitimate daughter, Joan, but the Welshman's growing power and pretensions brought him into conflict with his new father-in-law. The loss of Normandy in 1204 played a part in refocusing John's attention on Britain, and in 1211 he launched two major expeditions against Gwynedd. The first was unsuccessful, but the second was devastating; John's meticulously planned campaign crossed the river Conwy and reached into the heart of Snowdonia, allowing him to impose humiliating terms on Llywelyn. In the opinion of Professor Rees Davies: 'The reign of

King John was a formative period in Anglo-Welsh relations ... In his campaigns of 1211–12, John had laid the ground-plans of a military conquest and settlement of the country which it only remained for Edward I to copy and put fully into operation.'[15]

John's ambitions were, of course, thwarted by the baronial opposition that led to Magna Carta. Llywelyn played a major role in these events, emerging as the undoubted leader of the native Welsh polity and joining the wider opposition to the king. As a consequence, in the minority of John's son, Henry III, Llywelyn was able to win an acceptance of his conquests, along with other major concessions from the English state, his position acknowledged in a truce agreed under the Treaty of Worcester (1218). But the question of whether this deal would hold when Henry matured and England got stronger remained, and Llywelyn's achievements were nibbled away at in the later years of his reign. The memories of this, and the need for a more formal treaty of recognition of the rights of Wales, would be taken on board by the next generation of leaders in Gwynedd.

While the clashes between the princes and the English monarchy tend to attract most attention, arguably of more significance was the fraught relationship between the expansionist leaders of Gwynedd and the marcher lords of Wales. The opposing sides contended for the homage, or lands, of the minor Welsh nobility, while the conquests of Gwynedd made its leaders an alternative source of lordship for the Welsh communities in even the most settled marcher territories. The marches of mid-Wales would prove to be the key battleground, and the Mortimer family the main enemies of the lords of Snowdon. They had settled at Wigmore in the early Norman period and soon began a long-running struggle with the native Welsh lords of neighbouring lands for control of the territory of Maelienydd and Gwerthrynion. The nearby family of de Braose had a similar background, initially settling at Radnor but pushing into New Radnor and Elfael; in the mid-thirteenth century, marriage brought these de Braose interests to the Mortimers. In Maelienydd in the early 1220s, Hugh Mortimer targeted the removal of the native Welsh lords between Builth and Montgomery. Llywelyn would not stand idly by, telling Mortimer that he had taken the homage of those lords and that he would defend them. In many ways it could be said that some of the defining issues at stake in the conquest of Wales were thereby laid out.[16]

Chapter 2

English and Welsh Military Institutions

Geography and weather

Because of its high mountains, deep valleys and extensive forests, not to mention its rivers and marshes, [Wales] is not easy of access.[1]

So wrote Gerald of Wales in the twelfth century, and the difficulties of geography, weather and transport in the country can, at times, seem almost as frustrating to the modern-day commuter or tourist as to the medieval general. But while it is easy to generalise about the difficulties of campaigning in Wales, it is also important to be specific when looking at individual events, noting that large sections of the country were open to external attack and that – by the time of Edward I – much of that land was already lost to native Welsh political control.

Gwynedd

Perhaps the most obvious place to begin is the dynastic and political heartland of the princes of Wales, Gwynedd. If the description of Wales at the start of this chapter can be applied to any one place in particular it is the mountainous citadel of Snowdonia, the eastern approaches of which are protected by the treacherous, tidal waters of the river Conwy. This was the final, strongest redoubt of the Welsh, a natural fortress that would require a major military commitment to breach. Yet, despite the huge defensive strengths of this region, there were weaknesses inherent in the heartland of Gwynedd itself. The mountainous interior butts into the coast to the north and west, meaning that any enemy with naval dominance could land a force on the coastline. Although paths inland into the vertiginous mountains were then limited and defensible, this vulnerability was most obvious when it came to Anglesey, the bread basket of Snowdonia; the island itself is all but flat and would repeatedly prove an inviting target to sea raiders, as well as a potential staging point for an invader seeking a back-door route into Snowdonia.

Moving east of the Conwy, the area known as the Perfeddwlad stretched from the eastern banks of the Conwy to the Dee. There were four distinct territorial units in this region, each of which was called a *cantref*: Rhos, Rhufoniog, Dyffryn Clwyd and Tegeingl. These were key lands that the rulers of Gwynedd saw as part of their domain and that they would look to secure. Historical geographer Glanville Jones believed that native rulers deliberately kept large tracts of this region under-developed in order to increase its defensibility, citing in particular the heavy, poorly drained woods of the Conwy valley and the large expanses of marshland near the coast. Very few English rulers managed to penetrate west of the Conwy, and it was only the more successful kings who were able to control the westerly half of the Perfeddwlad, the territory between the Conwy and the Clwyd; the latter river with its extensive marshlands was another tricky barrier facing any invader from the east.

Heading east past the Clwyd to the Dee and the modern-day Wales–England border, the *cantref* known as Tegeingl had more heavily wooded, defensible territory, with an additional shield provided by the Clwydian range of hills and mountains, stretching from Prestatyn in the north to Llandegla in the south. Potential invasion routes into north-east Wales included the Alyn valley, the Dee valley and the narrow, badly drained, heavily wooded coastal path. If none of these options was exactly inviting, they were also not truly intimidating and the proximity of the region to the great port of Chester and the English midlands left it vulnerable.

Moving south from the heartland of Gwynedd along the western coast, Traeth Mawr just below Cricieth is the first of a series of treacherous tidal estuaries that need to be negotiated. Below this comes the hazardous Mawddach estuary and marshlands, the crossing of which takes a traveller into the southern barrier of Gwynedd, Meirionydd and the Cader Idris range. Although not quite as formidable as Snowdonia, this is also a difficult area to traverse, as described by Gerald of Wales:

> Meirionydd is the rudest and roughest of all the Welsh districts. The mountains are very high, with narrow ridges and a great number of very sharp peaks all jumbled together in confusion. If the shepherds who shout to each other and exchange comments from these lofty summits should ever decide to meet, it would take them almost the whole day to climb down and up again.[2]

Beyond this challenging landscape to the south lies yet another major water barrier, the Dyfi estuary. To the east of Meirionydd stand more mountains, those of the Berwyn range which – very roughly speaking – form a square bounded by Llangollen in the north-east, Corwen in the north-west, Oswestry in the south-east and Bala in the south-west. The name given to the most important hill pass that traverses this range is indicative of its importance and the use it was put to in the days of conflict between England and Wales; it is called Ffordd y Saeson, which translates as 'the English Way'.

*   *   *

It can be seen that the native leaders of north Wales had formidable natural defences to fall back upon, although it was rare for the rulers of all these regions – which included parts of Powys – to be allies facing a common enemy to the east. Under the more powerful of the princes of Gwynedd in the late twelfth and thirteenth centuries, there were times when they did control much of this region and Glanville Jones contended that they then made deliberate moves to strengthen the natural defences of their domain with strategically placed stone castles, used to control vulnerable entry points to specific areas; this theory is discussed below.

The middle march

The ambitions of the princes of Gwynedd for a wider dominion in Wales naturally took them into the mountain massif of central Wales, land also contested by the rulers of Powys and the marcher lords. The old Welsh kingdom of Rhwng Gwy a Hafren ('between Wye and Severn') – roughly equating with modern Radnorshire, but also stretching south of the Usk to the Brecon Beacons – was the key area of contention. Professor Rees Davies noted that here 'mountains and moor were at their most daunting and uninviting',[3] but there were welcoming eastward-running valleys that could serve as invasion routes. Montgomery would prove an ideal base for invaders from England to probe up the Severn valley and beyond, giving the option of striking into north-west or south-west Wales. Further south, Builth in the Wye valley was keenly contested between Welsh leaders and the English and would be crucial to Gwynedd's ambitions of pushing deeper into Brycheiniog ('Breconshire') and on into south Wales.

South Wales

South-east Wales lacks a truly formidable natural defence to a threat from the east; the rich lowlands of Gwent were the first to fall to permanent Anglo-Norman political control, and Glamorgan soon followed. The wild valley uplands and hinterlands of the south-east long remained under native Welsh rule, but this was largely because the Anglo-Norman aristocracy would have gained little through conquest, preferring instead to exercise suzerainty over the Welsh lords, many of whom proved loyal and served in the Anglo-Norman armies in Wales and far beyond.

Ever since the Norman influx into the south-east in the early 1070s, south-west Wales had been open to a direct Anglo-Norman land threat. In addition to this, the south-west suffered the same strategic weakness as much of the rest of Wales in that its extensive coastline left it open to sea raiders and to the establishment on the coast of alien fortifications that could be supplied from the sea. While much of the interior was wild, wooded and difficult of access, south-west Wales lacked the mountain massif of Gwynedd meaning that, although subjugation of the area was difficult, a determined invader could soon grind down resistance. While native Welsh control persisted in many of the upland and heavily wooded regions of the south-west – notably Ystrad Tywi (the Tywi valley) and parts of Ceredigion – the richest, most attractive lowlands were conquered, colonised and planted with strong castles in the first century after the Norman conquest. Nowhere was this more evident than in south-western Carmarthenshire and southern Pembrokeshire, 'little England beyond Wales'. In the early years of conquest these lands often attracted men of obscure origin and uncertain future; younger sons, household knights and other landless men seeking a rich future for themselves and their family. As well as Normans, settlers came from Flanders, Brittany, Maine and other parts of France, while large numbers arrived from the south-west of England.[4] By the thirteenth century, the roots laid down by such families ran deep and they would not be easily removed by any native Welsh rising.[5] Such colonisation of Welsh land that would ultimately fall under the domain of the English king is indicative of the point made by Professor Rees Davies: 'Englishness – be it settlers, laws, or institutions – was an exportable commodity within the British Isles. That is not true elsewhere within the Angevin empire. The zone of Anglicisation was the British Isles; that served to demarcate it from the rest of the lands of the Angevin rulers.'[6]

The changing environment

If it can be taken as a general military truth that difficult, mountainous, wooded and marshy terrain worked to the benefit of the native Welsh, it can be seen that marcher lords and English kings made deliberate attempts to alter the natural environment to their advantage. This was perhaps most commonly seen in attempts to widen roads and clear surrounding woodland; for example, Henry III's August 1228 expedition to the middle march largely revolved around such activity:

> The knights and soldiers of the garrison of Montgomery ... sallied forth with the inhabitants of the district, to widen and render more safe a road near the castle, on account of the Welsh bandits who robbed and murdered travellers there. They therefore marched to the place with swords, axes, staves, and other weapons, and commenced cutting down the trees, hedges and shrubs, to render the road wider for travellers. This

circumstance having reached the ears of the Welsh, they came in great force and attacked them, forcing them to retreat into the castle, though not without some slaughter on both sides. [This prompted the arrival of Henry, who raised the siege then] marched with a large body of soldiers to the above-mentioned wood, which as was said was very large, extending for about five leagues; but although it was large and very difficult to destroy on account of the thick growth of the trees, it was after much difficulty cut down and burnt.[7]

In addition to the environment, the seasons and the weather would prove changeable factors that impacted significantly on the fluctuating military fortunes of Welsh and English. The former found particular success when conducting winter campaigns, English kings proving slow or reluctant to mobilise in force outside the regular summer fighting season. Henry III was particularly loath to endure the Welsh cold, and his decision to pull back from the Conwy at the beginning of September 1257 was said to be because he feared the winter snows! By contrast, his successes in 1241 were helped by 'the heat, which had continued intense for four months, had dried up all the lakes and marshy places of Wales'.[8] It was a very different story in the winter of 1256, the remarkably successful Welsh campaign said to have been helped by the fact that 'the whole of that year was so wet and stormy that the entire country of Wales, which was without roads, and of a marshy nature, was utterly inaccessible to the English'.[9]

The resources of war

It has been stressed that the history of clashes between the peoples east and west of the Severn and Dee can never be seen in simple 'England *v* Wales' terms, but if we were to look at the resources available to these peoples it is clear that it was always something of an uneven contest. At the most basic of levels, it has been estimated that *c.*1300 the population of Wales was around 300,000, while that of England was between 4 million and 6 million.[10]

Pre-1066, the Anglo-Saxons controlled the richest lands in the island of Britain, while large tracts of the territory ruled by the Welsh was mountainous, wooded and inhospitable; what is more, over time the limited territory ruled by the Welsh was impinged upon from the east, reducing their resources even further. Wider events after the Norman Conquest of England increased the disparity of resource; the Norman and Angevin kings controlled major swathes of valuable territory on the continent, although the distractions of ruling such diverse lands also kept Wales from the full weight of their military attention. Within Wales itself, the years after 1066 led to an increase in the rate of loss of native land to political masters from the east. The lands targeted for takeover and control by the marchers and by kings of England were, again, the richest and most valuable lowlands. In a general description looking at the period between the arrival of the Normans and the Edwardian conquest, Professor Rees Davies estimated that the fluctuating territory of native Wales was 'well over half of the surface area of Wales, though in terms of population and wealth the proportion was very much smaller'.[11]

Historically, the military potential of Ireland and the wider Hiberno-Scandinavian world had served as something of a counter-weight to the power of the Anglo-Saxon and Anglo-Norman kings in Wales. Some native Welsh rulers made use of this military resource, while others suffered under its weight. This changed in the 1170s with the Anglo-Norman (perhaps more accurately described as the Cambro-Norman) conquest of Ireland. From then on, much of Ireland was controlled by great marcher families who also ruled territory in Wales and/or England. This left Ireland as another potential resource to be tapped by an English king planning a campaign in Wales, and his near-total control of the Irish Sea would further tighten the strategic noose around the neck of any Welsh leader seeking to take an independent line.

For all that, the resources of the thirteenth-century princes of Gwynedd were considerable. Much of the economy was based on mountains and upland moors, but there are also large areas of lowland in the region, and even the uplands have long, fertile valleys. Post-conquest records indicate the relatively high density of population in upland areas such as Penllyn and Edeirnion: an indication of population pressure that drove people to marginal lands, but also of the viability of living and working on such territory. In the war of 1282–3, royal officers were astounded by the number of animals and the amount of corn that the Welsh resistance had been able to stockpile in this area.[12] Gwynedd rulers could rely on the produce of rich lowlands such as Llŷn and – when they controlled this part of the country – Tegeingl, but their crown jewel was Anglesey. According to Gerald of Wales:

> [Anglesey] produces far more grain than any other part of Wales. In the Welsh language it has always been called 'Môn mam Cymru', which means 'Mona the Mother of Wales'. When crops have failed in all other regions, this island from the richness of its soil and its abundant produce, has been able to supply all Wales ... Just as Anglesey can supply all the inhabitants of Wales with corn, so, if all the herds were gathered together, Snowdon could afford sufficient pasture.[13]

There is a need for caution when discussing agricultural and pastoral zones, though, as the economies of most areas, Anglesey included, promoted a healthy mixture of both. The inhabitants of Wales were well used to making the most of the resources available, practising transhumance to make best use of the uplands in the summer and the lowlands in the winter. Such ready, rehearsed movement of people and chattels was, of course, an invaluable skill in a military situation, when facing an invading force looking to plunder and to follow the typical medieval strategy of slash, burn and steal. For example, John's first expedition to Wales in 1211 was thwarted by Llywelyn ap Iorwerth in the following manner:

> Llywelyn removed both his people of Perfeddwlad and their chattels to the mountains of Eryri [Snowdonia], and the people of Anglesey and their chattels likewise. And then the king and his host went [from Chester] to the castle of Deganwy. And there the host suffered such lack of food that an egg was sold for a penny-halfpenny; and it was a luxurious feast for them to have the flesh of horses. And because of that the king returned to England about Whitsun with his mission unfulfilled, having ignominiously lost many of his men and of his chattels.[14]

Welsh leaders and their followers would tour their courts (*llysoedd*), staying at their main residences (*maerdrefi*). Under powerful leaders like the thirteenth-century princes of Gwynedd, the demesne lands alone would be insufficient to support the entire court or the leader's other expansionist ambitions, meaning that other sources of revenue would be exploited. The princes took from their territories traditional dues from the population in the form of food renders, labour duties and military service; increasingly in the thirteenth century, many of these rights were being commuted into cash. In addition there were the profits of justice and the booty gained from successful war in the form of pillage, ransoms and, on occasions, conquered land. According to Professor Rees Davies:

> Money circulated freely if not abundantly in the country ... one major incentive to the increased circulation and usage of coins in native society was the growing fiscal demands of princely government. Until the end of the twelfth century, the occasional tributes rendered by Welsh princes to English kings had normally been paid in animals; from the early thirteenth century they were increasingly proffered and paid in cash ... The demands of justice also habituated the inhabitants of native Wales to the use of money; the records preserved in the Red Book of St Asaph (*Llyfr Coch Asaph*) indicate that, from at least the mid-thirteenth century, fines and amercements were a major source of revenue and were calculated exclusively in cash, at least in north-east Wales ... Most of the renders in Anglesey and northern Arfon seem to have been almost totally commuted before 1282; but in Nantconwy, Ardudwy and Eifionydd the

process was still in its early stages and it was still uncollected in Merionethshire in the fifteenth century. There is also some evidence to suggest that in north Wales at least the pace of commutation was brisker among free tenants than among bondmen.[15]

It has been estimated that, at the height of Llywelyn ap Gruffudd's power in the 1260s, his annual income may have reached £6,000. According to Professor Huw Pryce, Llywelyn's annual ordinary income was in the region of £3,500, a figure that could compare reasonably well against the greatest English lords:

> Earl Gilbert the Red drew only about £1,200 from his lordship of Glamorgan, out of a total of £4,500–5,000 yielded by his estates throughout England, Wales and Ireland. [Llywelyn ap Gruffudd] with his stone castles ... his nascent urban centres at Nefyn on the Llŷn peninsula and Llanfaes on Anglesey, his university-trained clerks capable of undertaking diplomatic negotiations as well as drafting letters and accounts, a supportive network of Cistercian abbeys and his French wife, Eleanor de Montfort ... had much in common with other European potentates of his age.[16]

Professor Beverley Smith also estimates the prince's annual finances at around £3,000–3,500, but notes that this figure must be cut in the period 1267–74 – perhaps by as much as £1,000 – in order to allow for the lands where Llywelyn's brother Dafydd had been given lordship.[17]

Llywelyn's resources were far from negligible, and in the thirteenth century he would gear his small domain for war. The demands he made enter the historical light through a series of post-conquest extents and records, and through the complaints of the communities he ruled. The bishops of Bangor and St Asaph had their run-ins with the prince's administration, but the most famous criticisms were raised at Nancall in the summer of 1283, the so-called *gravamina* (grievances) of the community of Gwynedd against its former prince. Amongst other things, the people were angered by the 'harshness and exactitude of officers and their increased numbers'; increased taxes, especially an unprecedented 'income tax' based on head of cattle; exacting levels of military service; increased demand on those not serving to give supplies for soldiers and horses; the seizure of land for agriculture and vaccaries; the exercise of wardship over heirs during minorities; rigorous exploitation of regal rights, including justice and shipwreck; and the blurring of the distinction between free and unfree people.

If such sources suggest the harsh rule of an unpopular lord, the context of the complaints must be remembered; those raising the issues were tenants seeking to obtain more favourable terms from their new lords. However, some such grievances can be substantiated from known cases, and it is clear that Llywelyn used methods that could squeeze his subjects and create resentment. Even so, however much he squeezed, it was obvious that he could never compete with the mobilized resources of the king of England. As one simple example, the customs duties owed to Llywelyn brought him something like £17 a year; in contrast, Edward's customs duties brought him around £10,000 from just his lands in England.[18]

England's resources were far from unlimited; it has been estimated that the total amount of money in circulation was relatively small, perhaps in the region of £1m.[19] Poor administration and the misuse of limited funds were the cause of many of the problems endured by Henry III, but Edward I was determined to learn by his father's mistakes. As described below, at the outset of his reign the new king was able to raise around £80,000 from a one-off general tax and to arrange access to almost unlimited credit from the wider European financial world thanks to his relationship with Italian bankers, in particular those known as the Riccardi of Lucca. The disparity in resource was such that the ultimate result of any war between the king of England and the prince of Wales could never be in doubt; the best the prince could hope for was to survive.

Religious resources

All medieval rulers relied heavily on their intimate relationship with the clerics of their land, in both a spiritual and practical capacity. The landed wealth of the church was not immune from the king's tax, while the military service of tenants from church land was required. Clerics were important agents in the soft power of medieval lordship, offering moral, religious and propaganda support. Educated churchmen were used by lay rulers for clerical work, administration and diplomatic missions, while stone abbeys and churches were important centres for the safe storage of documents and wealth.

All of these factors applied to the princes of Gwynedd, who forged a particularly close connection with the monks of Aberconwy and Cymer, and with the other Cistercian houses throughout Wales. However, Llywelyn ap Gruffudd would have problems with the two bishoprics of Gwynedd – Bangor and St Asaph – which were indicative of the fact that churchmen in Wales were beholden to more than one master.[20] By the thirteenth century the bishops were subject to the primacy of the archbishop of Canterbury and, despite regular run-ins with lay power, the archbishop would almost invariably side with the king of England over a ruler of Gwynedd. This would be evident at the height of the war of 1282–3, when Archbishop John Pecham attempted to mediate between the two sides. Although he had more than his share of arguments with Edward I, Pecham was well known for his disparaging views of Welsh culture, society and behaviour; while he seems to have made a genuine attempt at mediation, his ultimate judgement would be far from impartial. Llywelyn would be excommunicated in both the wars of 1277 and 1282–3.

The other call on the loyalty of the clergy was, of course, the Pope in Rome, and at times the Welsh attempted to use appeals to the papal court to help in their struggles with the English king. This occasionally yielded positive results, as in 1244 when Dafydd ap Llywelyn asked the Pope to intervene in his dispute with Henry III.[21] Innocent IV's response was initially welcoming, but when the king made a number of concessions to Rome the final papal ruling came back in the English favour, stating clearly that 'the prince of Wales is a minor vassal of the king of England'. The king's pockets were deep and the papacy would always prove keen to avoid the ultimate alienation of one of the great monarchs of western Europe. This was made clear by Pecham in his failed attempt at mediation in 1282; urging the beleaguered Welsh to accept his intercession as their only hope, he noted that England enjoyed the special protection of the Pope and that the papal court would not tolerate anything that would prove damaging to the status of the kingdom of England.[22]

Military organisation and conduct

Any analysis of the military styles, strengths and weaknesses of the English and Welsh needs first to acknowledge the disparity in the resources of the two sides that has been highlighted, and the fact that it was not a clash of nations. A failure to grasp these essential points would lead the observer into crude national stereotyping and cliché. Much of the blame for such an ethnographic approach to military history must sit with Gerald of Wales, whose very popular works included easily grasped and quotable descriptions of the Welsh at war:

> In war the Welsh are very ferocious when battle is first joined. They shout, glower fiercely at the enemy, and fill the air with fearsome clamour, making a high-pitched screech with their long trumpets. From their first fierce and headlong assault, and the shower of javelins which they hurl, they seem most formidable opponents. If the enemy resists manfully and they are repulsed, they are immediately thrown into confusion. With further resistance they turn their backs, making no attempt at a counter-attack, but seeking safety in flight. As the poet knew only too well, this is disastrous on the battlefield ... Their sole idea of tactics is

either to pursue their opponents, or else to run away from them. They are lightly armed and they rely more on their agility than on brute strength. It follows that they cannot meet the enemy on equal terms, or fight violently for very long, or strive hand-to-hand for victory ... Although beaten today and shamefully put to flight with much slaughter, tomorrow they march out again, no whit dejected by their defeat and their losses. They may not shine in open combat and in fixed formation, but they harass their enemy by their ambushes and their night attacks. In a single battle they are easily beaten, but they are difficult to conquer in a long war, for they are not troubled by hunger or cold, fighting does not seem to tire them, they do not lose heart when things go wrong, and after one defeat they are ready to fight again and to face once more the hazards of war.[23]

This passage comes from the second section of Gerald's *Description of Wales*, a book written to enhance his own literary fame and that repeatedly uses the thesis/anti-thesis technique of presenting praiseworthy characteristics followed by flaws. The work revived the classical tradition of ethnographical writing undertaken by authors such as Tacitus and was used by Gerald to present the little-known Welsh to the Anglo-Norman audience. Gerald and his family were men of the Anglo-Norman march in Wales, and an additional reason for this presentation of the Welsh was to stress that only his people knew how to handle them; in other words, the interfering Angevin kings should keep this strange land at arm's length. Gerald's family were also at the heart of the Cambro-Norman conquest of Ireland, and the following passage from the *Description of Wales* is an almost word-for-word copy of his treatment of the Irish in his earlier work, the *Conquest of Ireland*:

They [the 'French'] are used to fighting on the level, whereas here the terrain is rough; their battles take place in the open fields, but here the country is heavily wooded; with them the army is an honourable profession but with us it is a matter of dire necessity; their victories are won by stubborn resistance, ours by constant movement; they take prisoners, we cut off their heads; they ransom their captives but we massacre them. When troops fight in flat open country, heavy complicated armour, made partly out of cloth and partly out of iron, offers good protection and certainly looks smart; but in a marshy or thickly-wooded terrain, where footsoldiers have the advantage over cavalry, light armour is far better. Against men who wear no armour at all and where the battle is almost always won or lost at the first onslaught, light protection is much more suitable. When the enemy is retreating at full speed through narrow defiles and up mountain-sides, the pursuers must be able to move quickly:

they need to be protected, but their armour should be very light. If they have high curved saddles and wear heavy complicated equipment, mounting their horses and dismounting will be a great problem, and they will never be able to advance on foot. Against men who are heavily armed, fighting in the flat where victory is won by main force, and relying upon brute strength and the sheer mass of iron which they wear, I have no doubt at all that you must pit armour against armour and weight against weight ... Against an army so mobile and lightly armed as the Welsh, who always prefer to do battle on rough terrain, you need troops with little equipment and who are used to the same sort of warfare.[24]

Again this passage provides an easily understandable picture of warfare in Wales, but much of it falls into the domain of simple common sense that would have been understood by any semi-competent general on the ground. This section is part of the book's 'anti-thesis' that presents the unworthy aspects of the Welsh character and the artificial construct is highlighted later; having stated that the 'French' need to fight like the Welsh in order to master the country, he then criticises the Welsh for failing to adopt the 'French' methods of warfare that would best allow them to defend themselves.[25]

The truth of the matter was that the basic structure of the English and Welsh military hierarchy was much more similar than Gerald cared to admit. It suited his argument to portray the Welsh as a people amongst whom 'not only the leaders but the entire nation are trained for war. Sound the trumpet for battle and the peasant will rush from his plough to pick up his weapons as quickly as the courtier from the court.'[26] In fact, the Welsh military elite was as structured and proudly protective of its status as the ruling, martial classes in England and the rest of western Europe.

Welsh military service

At the heart of a Welsh leader's rule – and almost always at his side – was the martial element of his household that formed a permanent military force and was known as the *teulu*. This was typically composed of relatives and other noblemen, including young nobles forging their careers and earning their military stripes; some of these men may eventually have gone on to become leading noblemen in their own right and to have a *teulu* of their own. While membership of the *teulu* would have been denied to the unfree bondmen of Welsh society, it would have included freemen of lesser means, men who had perhaps earned their place by their military skill and who would look to win favour, booty and, ultimately, land through their service to their leader.

The *teulu* was a mounted force that was fully capable of fighting from horseback but, as would be expected from military professionals, was also more than ready to dismount and fight on foot. We have evidence that such forces were effective in siege operations, and also of them engaging in what may be termed 'special forces operations'. Tactics were flexible and tailored to the weather, topography and the size and nature of opposing forces. Leadership of the *teulu* was sometimes deputised by the king or prince to a key officer known as the *penteulu* ('leader of the household'), a man who was often a close relative of the leader. In thirteenth-century Gwynedd there is evidence of another administrative officer known as the *distain* ('steward' or 'seneschal', a Welsh ruler's leading lay adviser) performing a very similar role to the *penteulu*. It is possible that this was because the princes were keen to take military power from the hands of their close kin (and potential rivals), but I favour the interpretation that the increased military demands the princes faced led to the need to create more subordinate military officers. Dr David Stephenson says that military leadership was not a formal duty of the office of *distain* and it did not supplant the *penteulu*, but that military leadership was 'the sort of duty which might follow simply from prominence in the prince's service and from personal aptitude in military matters'.[27]

When larger forces were gathered, members of the *teulu* would play a key role in the muster, and would then employ their experience in a leadership role to give organisation and direction to less experienced troops. The numbers in a *teulu* are impossible to define, one reason being that there would never have been a standard size; it would depend on individual circumstances, but as the roughest of benchmarks we may picture a force of around 50 men. Numbers in the *teulu* of more powerful leaders like Gruffudd ap Llywelyn (d. 1063) were significantly higher than that, though, and this was also the case with Llywelyn ap Gruffudd in the thirteenth century. We have a reference to him taking provender for 500 men from the lands of Basingwerk Abbey when he went to Penllyn to hunt each year, but this was for his entire court, not just the *teulu*.[28]

There were often times when a Welsh leader required military force in greater numbers than could be supplied by his regular *teulu*, and such a larger army was often referred to as a *llu* ('army'). In the early middle ages, the *llu* was made up of the combined *teuluoedd* of numerous leaders, each of whom may have referred to himself as a 'king'; military organisation was personal rather than territorialised. Over time, though, the smaller kingdoms lost their royal nomenclature as they were subsumed by larger over-kingdoms, which gradually acquired territorial definition. In such circumstances – which can also be observed in England, France and other parts of post-Roman western Europe – rulers needed to find new ways to ensure military service as they lost personal contact with more distant parts of their expanded domains. This led to the territorialisation of military service, something which can be seen in

Welsh law, the codification of which is traditionally attributed to Hywel Dda (d. 950). Care needs to be taken, though, as surviving copies of law codes are from much later dates and they were subject to numerous changes over the centuries, notably by the thirteenth-century princes. The laws outline duties to attend royal musters, all freemen over the age of 14 owing – at their own expense – indefinite service within the bounds of the kingdom and six weeks' service a year outside those bounds. There are examples where this theoretical service is reflected in thirteenth-century reality, while surviving evidence from the fourteenth century suggests that the periods of service could be extended by negotiated agreements, with the prince meeting the cost of service outside the kingdom for longer than six weeks.[29] According to Stephenson: 'There is nothing to suggest that the purchase of voluntary extended service was not the usual method by which the thirteenth-century princes raised forces for long campaigns. In the majority of cases, the wage-bargaining might begin after forty days' service; in others (where individuals benefited from a grant of privileges which included immunity from military obligations), it would precede the start of service.'[30]

Such service was the most important duty imposed on freemen by the laws, which also stress the military duties owed by unfree bondmen. The laws required each bond township to supply to the leader's host a pack horse along with a man and an axe to make camps for the army; in the thirteenth century the princes would turn such labour duties to use for the construction of their castles. According to the legal texts, the ruler was to pay the costs of this labour service, but in the fourteenth century some bond communities took on these costs and it may be that much of the labour service had been commuted to cash, even in the thirteenth century.[31] Other fourteenth-century evidence suggests that bondmen could be subject to the same six-week service demands as freemen, meaning a blurring of the distinction between freemen and bondmen and leading Stephenson to conclude: 'It would seem that at some time in the pre-conquest period the villeins of some, but by no means all, parts of Gwynedd had become liable for military service of the same kind as that performed by freemen.'[32]

Despite these attempts at legal control of the land, the key to military power was still securing the loyalty and service of nobles at a local level: the powermongers on the ground who could ensure the practical delivery of military might. In Wales these noblemen were known as *uchelwyr* and they were, in very many cases, descendants of the petty kings who, in an earlier age, would have led their own *teulu* into battle as part of the over-king's *llu*. Such proud, headstrong men needed careful handling; get it wrong and a Welsh prince would soon find that his position was built on sand. One element in this handling of the prince's leading men that became particularly important in the course of the thirteenth century was the granting of lands on privileged terms, free of military service and other dues. As best as surviving evidence allows us to judge, this does not seem to have been a feature of rule under Owain Gwynedd in the twelfth century, but to have begun in the early-to-middle years of the reign of Llywelyn ap Iorwerth and to have continued – to an extent – under Llywelyn ap Gruffudd in the later thirteenth century. Important nobles can be seen to have been given such privileged land grants in a number of instances, but with a notable focus in the Gwynedd heartlands of Anglesey and Arfon. This was not typically close to the major landholdings of the families of these nobles, one of the motivations for the grants being to increase the territorial cohesion of the realm, giving the leading men an interest in the integrity of Gwynedd that went above and beyond their local inclinations. While this policy may have had its advantages, it also increased the problems for the Gwynedd dynasty at times when the loyalty of its leading men was called into question.[33]

Even when the loyalty of the *uchelwyr* was won and a large *llu* was gathered, all of our evidence points to the fact that the army was a select levy, not the 'entire nation trained in war' that Gerald of Wales purports to describe. There are a handful of references, mostly in literature, that suggest the military gathering of all the people of the land, demands that were typically in response to an enemy invasion when the options were to fight or be slaughtered. In almost all such examples, the untrained forces of the universal levy were notably ineffective, highlighting the importance and value of experienced, professional soldiers. One of the grievances laid against Llywelyn ap Gruffudd by his people was attempts he was said to have made to get military service from boys under the age of 14. If this could be interpreted as an attempt to simply increase numbers at a time of urgent military need, it seems that what Llywelyn was actually seeking was fines for the non-attendance at muster of these boys, not the questionable value of their presence in the field; the community accepted that fines were due from old men who were no longer suitable for military service, but denied that those under 14 should also pay.[34] No Welsh leader would have seen value in placing an inexperienced rabble in the military theatre, an ineffective force that would have required precious logistical resource to support. The key deficiency faced by any Welsh leader engaged in conflict with the English state was not simply numbers of able-bodied men; it was in numbers of well armed, trained men, and in the whole logistical machine required to put such military professionals in the field, then keep them there.

If this outlines the way a Welsh leader would go about organising the military resources of his land, it would only apply to his own lordship. The princes of Gwynedd also held the allegiances of various other Welsh lords –

from Powys, Deheubarth and elsewhere – and each leader was responsible for the gathering of his own forces; the prince had no right to levy tax from their territory, to undertake a due-collecting *cylch*, nor to levy military service from there directly. Some such allied lords joined the princes in Snowdonia because they had been disinherited from their own lands, and these leaders are likely to have arrived with part of a *teulu* and no more. But more formal treaties of alliance were also made with ruling Welsh lords, whose military organisation resembled that within Gwynedd itself. An example of such a formal treaty can be seen in the agreement made in 1261 between Llywelyn ap Gruffudd and one of the leading lords of Deheubarth, Maredudd ap Rhys Gryg.[35] Maredudd was bound to provide military service to Llywelyn to withstand his enemies in Deheubarth, and under the terms he was pledged to come in person 'with his whole strength'. Outside Deheubarth, Maredudd was again bound to come 'with his whole strength', and to campaign with any or all the other lords of Wales, according to need. A singular exception was placed on this, with qualifying conditions regarding Maredudd's particular dynastic rival and enemy, Rhys Fychan. The military obligations also worked in reverse, with Llywelyn taking on duties with regard to defence, support and the sharing of spoil with Maredudd; this can also be seen in a treaty made by Llywelyn with another Welsh ruler, Gruffudd ap Gwenwynwyn of southern Powys.

Estimating the numbers of medieval armies is notoriously difficult – and when such estimates are made they are notoriously unreliable. Even so, the numbers of troops that could be gathered by these methods of Welsh recruitment appear impressive. In the Treaty of Woodstock of 1247, England was able to impose military service on the princes of Wales. The Welsh leaders – Owain and Llywelyn, the sons of Gruffudd – were, at the time, only ruling Gwynedd west of the Conwy, but they were expected to supply twenty-four knights and 1,000 footsoldiers to serve the king in Wales and the march, at the expense of the princes and under their leadership. If service was required in England, they were to provide 500 footsoldiers and ten knights under their leadership.[36] This is unlikely to have been the full military capability of western Gwynedd and – in the years that followed – Llywelyn would establish his rule over far more extensive territories, but such numbers were significant. In 1257 Matthew Paris said that the prince's army of '500 knights, well-armed, and mounted on iron-clad horses', plus 30,000 infantry (surely an enormous over-estimation), was so large that it needed to be split in two 'that they might thus the more easily procure provisions'.[37] When Llywelyn was close to the peak of his power in 1262, terrified English accounts suggest that he led in Maelienydd 300 cavalry and 30,000 infantry.[38] Early the next year, his troops were active in the Usk valley, supported by the native Welsh of

calculated that the feudal summons provided approximately 123 knights and 190 sergeants for forty days' service;[44] such numbers were largely irrelevant within the overall scale of the conflict. The thirteenth century, and especially the reign of Henry III, had seen major cuts in the levels of feudal service demanded, a fact that can be attributed to the rising sophistication and cost of arms and armour. This meant that, by the time of Edward, great magnates such as the earl of Gloucester, Gilbert de Clare, owed just ten knights to the muster. In reality, a lord such as de Clare would feel impelled on account of his status and reputation to attend the host with a far larger contingent of followers, and would serve beyond the forty-day period at his own expense. The matter of paid service would become a major bone of contention between Edward and his leading nobles, the latter group feeling that accepting such money diminished their dignity and would lead to further royal demands; in 1282–3, none of the English earls took pay, although the Scot Robert Bruce, earl of Carrick, did.[45]

Extreme examples of the problems caused by the arcane nature of some elements of feudal service are not hard to find. One such reference records a man who was required to join the host with adequate provisions; he arrived with a side of bacon, ate it, then departed. Another man, Hugo fitz Heyr, was obliged by the terms of his tenure to serve with a bow and arrow; he turned up for the 1300 Scottish campaign and – at the first sight of the enemy – fired a single arrow before quickly turning around and heading for home. In the light of such obvious problems, older studies of the military organisation of Edward's reign saw it as the triumph of paid retinues over feudal forces, the rise of so-called 'bastard feudalism' where the personal retaining of men in return for money, office and influence replaced old tenurial ties to the lord of the manor. But Prestwich, while highlighting the importance of retained households, points out that household troops had been vital to both previous and future kings of England, and that a hybrid recruitment of feudal and non-feudal forces would be a feature of all Edward's campaigns. 'It was not the case, as has sometimes been suggested, that this period saw the transformation of an old-fashioned feudal host into a more modern paid army, but the manner in which Edward was able to deploy the resources of the whole country in support of his military efforts was something new.'[46]

Feudal summonses continued to be issued throughout Edward's reign, and the king met opposition both when he tried to issue non-feudal calls and when he made attempts to introduce military service qualification by wealth rather than knighthood.[47] In February 1296, for example, inquests were ordered to find out who held land worth more than £40 a year; those who fell into this category were to be ready to serve, armed and mounted, at three weeks' notice in return for royal wages.[48] Previously, such wealth classification had been used to force men to take up knighthood, a process known as distraint of knighthood; if they refused, they would pay a fine, giving the king the resources to meet his military commitments by other means. In this instance, though, the whole issue of knighthood was ignored, meaning that if a man was rich enough to have the appropriate military equipment, he needed to provide service at the king's command and expense. In 1296 recruitment on these terms was successful, but by the end of Edward's reign political opposition forced the king to drop attempts at such innovation, which it was felt would lead to the crown demanding additional services. The final baronial victory on this matter came in the period 1301–3.[49]

When mounted forces did receive wages, the actual rates remained constant throughout Edward's reign: earls received 8 shillings a day, bannerets 4 shillings, knights 2 shillings and men-at-arms, or sergeants, 1 shilling.[50] Such forces were often contracted for forty days at a time, either to supplement the feudal levy, or as a familiar period of service used to extend the length of feudal service – and, hence, the campaign – for as many forty-day periods as proved necessary.

Beyond these issues over the service of knights and mounted sergeants, Edward imposed significant demands on England in terms of infantry recruitment. While the supply of defined numbers of suitably armed men was a requirement of the community, the wages of the infantry would then be paid by the king.[51] Requests for infantry were generally for 'footsoldiers skilled in arms', rather than for particular types of arms; often the troops are generically referred to as 'archers' and the bow and arrow was probably the most prevalent weapon, but others would carry pikes and lances, while the use of knives was universal. Despite the references to 'archers', we do not see records of the comprehensive and systematic supply of ammunition to these men that would be characteristic of the Hundred Years War in the fourteenth century; infantry would rely on the weapons supplied by their locality, and archers would carry perhaps one quiver of twenty-four arrows. There are references to infantry hurling stones in battle, a possible indication of the under-armament of archers. Crossbowmen were a more specialised, expensive sort of professional soldier who were comparatively few in number – and all the more valuable for it. They were able to make themselves available for campaign at short notice, suggesting that they were either already serving as garrison troops in the king's castles, or ready to act as what the historian John Morris called 'first-class reservists'.[52] The same crossbowmen were called up for repeated campaigns, as in the case of the Welsh wars of 1277 and 1282–3 when they served to the end of the action, before being pressed into garrison service. Edward would go to lengths to increase the numbers of such men in his armies by securing the service of experienced Gascon crossbowmen in Wales, including large numbers of elite mounted crossbowmen.

To gather the regular infantry muster, commissions of array were sent to chosen counties with orders to recruit a defined number of infantry. The commissioners were chosen according to expediency, with the aim of using their knowledge to help recruit the right, professional, military men; in 1277 sheriffs acted as commissioners, in 1282 the task was assigned to household knights and in 1294–5 the local knowledge of councillors and justices was employed. Often these commissioners would delegate the task of selecting the individuals who would actually serve to the hundred and village communities, which sometimes also named their own army commanders.[53]

Although this system was capable of delivering large numbers of troops, it also proved open to corruption, with officers taking bribes to excuse people from service. At a more local level, people were able to hire substitutes to take their place in the ranks, something that could happen on an individual or a community basis. But this led to the rise of individuals touring local communities, taking fees from multiple men to act as their substitute, or promising to hire a military contingent, then disappearing with the cash. The difficulties of recruitment led to the increasing use of alternative methods of finding infantry, such as pardoning felons; the practice became much more prevalent later in Edward's reign during the Scottish wars and would eventually lead to major law and order problems in England.

Even when infantry made it to the muster, desertion would prove a major problem and many ordinances were enacted to try to combat this. After the conquest of Wales, the Welsh infantry serving in Edward's armies proved less ready to desert than English footsoldiers, arguably as a result of the poverty they were facing at home and their desperate need for the king's wages.[54] The king's infantry was grouped into units of twenty, a standard footsoldier receiving 2 pence a day while the unit's leader – known as the vintenar – received 4 pence (the same as a crossbowman). Five of these twenty-man units were put under the leadership of a centenary, a fully equipped cavalryman on an armoured horse. Infantry forces could be grouped by county, or even by estate; the nature of pre-industrial warfare meant that the social cohesion of such a group could be valuable, without them typically being subject to the major psychological traumas that came with the high percentage of fatalities suffered by 'Pals' battalions in the First World War. Such units and groupings would, of course, be subject to reorganisation in the course of the campaign as losses and desertions began to bite.

The burden of recruitment did not fall evenly on all English counties and tended to weigh most heavily on the regions closest to the war zone. During Edward's Welsh wars, this meant that a particular reliance was placed on

Herefordshire, Gloucestershire, Shropshire, Lancashire, Staffordshire and Cheshire, although they were all outnumbered by the very large numbers of Welsh troops that fought on Edward's side; these troops were drawn from both the march and from the lands of native Welsh leaders who were loyal to the king. When the king's attention turned to Scotland later in the reign, the Welsh again formed a large proportion of his footsoldiers, while the counties of northern England took a heavy burden of recruitment. Other counties such as Derbyshire and Nottinghamshire faced heavy demands for infantry during both the Welsh and Scottish conflicts, perhaps because their experienced troops were highly valued. South-east England was comparatively untouched by the infantry calls, although the wealth of this region would have helped supply the king's war chest.

Despite the onerous demands on certain regions, the problems of recruitment, the corruption and desertions, it does not seem that there was opposition to the king's right to make such calls for the military service of his people. When hostility did surface, it was more related to the supply needs of his army and, in particular, to the practice known as prise, the compulsory purchase of goods at a set price. According to Prestwich: 'There was little surplus wealth in the economy which could be diverted to pay for war, and the yields of the harvests were needed to feed the population, much of which existed at subsistence level.'[55] The armies gathered by Edward were too large to live off the land, especially when they entered challenging, upland terrain in Wales and Scotland, and supplying them would prove to be Edward's greatest challenge. Even if the land could support the army, should the king allow his forces to engage in unrestrained plundering he would alienate the communities he was trying to win dominion over, increasing resistance and the possibility that they would renew opposition the moment the royal army moved on. Edward tried to delegate some of the burdens of supply onto his magnates and also went to lengths to arrange for markets to be held close to campaign centres, thereby encouraging merchants and private enterprise.

While the calls on private enterprise may appear enlightened, Professor Bernard Bachrach has shown how they caused problems with the increasing scale and duration of Edward's campaigns.[56] Whenever possible, supplies would be carried by water; it has been estimated that land transportation costs were twice those of goods delivered by river, and eight times that of chattels delivered by sea. Even so, carts, wagons and horses were needed to transport supplies to and from ports of embarkation, and in the Welsh wars of conquest merchants carrying royal letters of protection worked in competition for such crucial means of transport with the government's sheriffs. Problems were exacerbated by the fact that the huge numbers of horses and vehicles available from ecclesiastical institutions were exempt from requisitioning for much of the king's reign. The relatively small scale of the war of 1277 limited these problems, but matters worsened in 1282–3, leading both to the compulsory requisitioning of ecclesiastical means of transport later in the reign, and to the shifting of the burden of responsibility for supply away from private hands and onto the sheriffs. Through his officers, Edward thus increasingly extended the use of compulsory purchase to supply the entire army, a mechanism that had traditionally only been used to support the royal household. In 1277 prise was used on a small scale, but its use increased in 1282–3 and then expanded enormously in the 1290s when it became unacceptable to the community of the realm.

English naval forces

Just like the land armies, Edward's naval forces were built up from a hybrid mix of feudal obligation and paid service. The fourteen days' service owed by the ships of the Cinque Ports was repeatedly utilised and – after the fortnight was over – Edward would readily pay for the extended use of these valuable boats; the sailors took the wages in return for their time, although there are suggestions that the disruption caused to trade was resented. The Cinque Port vessels were usually supplemented with a fully paid fleet, the king seeking suitable ships from Ireland and the continent, with boats coming from as far south as Gascony.

The ships used by Edward came in a wide variety of classes and sizes, meaning that the number and type of sailors required to man them also varied considerably. John Morris contended that the standard organisation on board would see the employment of a sailing master at 6 pence a day, plus a leader of the fighting men on the same wage.[57] There would be about nineteen sailors employed at 3 pence a day, with on-board soldiers (crossbowmen and other infantry) supplied from the main land army at 3 pence a day. Numbers would vary according to need and the size of the individual ship; around ten soldiers per ship was the average, although this could rise to about forty on larger ships. A total of 114 such marines can be traced from the records of 1277 and 350 in 1282, all paid at 3 pence a day.

Military strategy and tactics in Wales

Gerald of Wales' comments on the nature of Welsh warfare have led to a widespread misunderstanding of the nature of military affairs in the country in the middle ages, a misunderstanding that has been fuelled by the perspectives and biases contained in our source material. Warfare in Wales was a professional affair, characterised by the careful preservation of forces as they manoeuvred for control of resources and key strategical points. Welsh tactics have regularly been denigrated as mere 'cattle raiding', but the targeting of an enemy's chattels was characteristic of warfare throughout medieval Europe; a leader who could not defend his territory, its people and their property would no longer merit his position of authority, and would lose his conflict with his opponent. The work of the Roman military writer Vegetius was valued throughout the middle ages; for example, when on crusade, Edward I was presented with a copy of the work by his wife.[58] Vegetius wrote that 'the main and principal point in war is to secure plenty of provision and to destroy the enemy by famine'.[59] To defend a position against an opposing force and prevent scavenging for supplies, a military leader would typically shadow the enemy's movements, engaging in skirmishes and seeking any opportunity for ambush on favourable terms. Full-scale battles were the exception rather than the rule; they were too dangerous and unpredictable, and results were rarely as decisive as we may envisage. Again according to Vegetius:

> It is much better to overcome the enemy by famine, surprise or terror than by general action, for in the latter instance fortune has often a greater share than valour ... Good officers never engage in general actions unless induced by opportunity or obliged by necessity.[60]

All of these general military rules also applied in Wales, where the topography and climate naturally leant themselves to skirmishing tactics. While it is incorrect to imagine that warfare in the country could ever be described in nationalistic 'Wales *v* England' terms, the mismatch of resources that occurred whenever a king of England directed his forces into the region would further strengthen the resolve of the opposing Welsh to avoid battle and engage in guerrilla warfare.

If one side was engaging in tactics that were out of the ordinary when it came to medieval warfare, it could be said to be the 'English'. That term itself needs further qualification, starting with the fact that the word 'English' should, perhaps, be 'Anglo-French', with a healthy mixture of Flemings, Irish, Welsh and many others in the mix! In this context, I am thinking of 'English' as the forces marshalled by the king of England for what was, almost always, a time-restricted campaign in Wales, where he hoped to overcome his enemies before his resources ran out, or an emergency drew him to another part of his far-flung dominions. Given this context, a typical campaign by such an English king in Wales would see him engaged in an unusual, aggressive, battle-seeking strategy, hoping to force his opponents out into the open where they could be crushed. Welsh leaders were too canny to be drawn into such engagements; this was something every English king must surely have expected, meaning that campaigns tended to be a tactical game based on supply lines and resources. The more powerful English forces would edge forward, employing detachments as a screen to protect the main column where workers would clear difficult terrain as the juggernaut ground remorselessly on towards a chosen strategic point. A scorched earth would be left in the trail of the advancing army, highlighting the value of Welsh transhumance: their ability to transport vulnerable people and property out of the way. The opposing Welsh could not stop the main English force but would seek to outmanoeuvre it and harry its flanks; if successful, they could delay the column for long enough to thwart the king, or even leave it so dangerously exposed that it would be forced to turn back from its main target in order to protect its supply lines. The culmination of such campaigns was almost always a negotiated settlement, the terms of which would depend on the success achieved by whichever side. Such a royal campaign typically differed from the regular, localised warfare seen between Welsh leaders and marcher lords; in these clashes no side would necessarily have enjoyed an overwhelming superiority in resources and, if they did, the balance of power may have been in favour of the Welsh. Battle was still comparatively rare, but it was a viable tactical option for both sides, rather than just for one.

When tactics and strategy are considered in this context – with position and supplies the key to success – it can be seen that the importance placed on the equipment and technology used by the opposing forces can be downplayed. This impacts on the widespread belief that the gradual conquest of Wales in the period 1066–1283 was facilitated by the impact of superior military technology, notably the castle (discussed below), the mounted knight and the archer. Professor Rees Davies, for example, contended that: 'There can be little doubt that the initial overwhelming impact of Anglo-Norman invaders in Wales and Ireland represented the victory of superior military technology and tactics – notably, of course, heavily armed cavalry, carefully deployed bands of archers, and the rapidly built castle.'[61] In reality, both the 'English' and the 'Welsh' used castles and employed mounted, armoured soldiers, who could fight from horseback or dismount to stiffen the lines when required.

The main weapons used by both sides were the spear, sword and bow, with axes, crossbows and daggers also common, and the employment of mixed forces of cavalry, infantry and archers was the typical (and sensible) arrangement. There is little evidence to suggest that the Welsh employed the tactic of the massed charge of heavy cavalry with couched lances, but also no evidence of such a tactic ever being used by the English in Wales in this period. While this may be partly explained by the unsuitable topography in certain parts of Wales, the importance of the heavy cavalry charge in the rest of medieval Europe has been significantly over-emphasised in historiography and a variety of modern studies have corrected this view, stressing the importance and prevalence of mixed forces. The one area where the English did have a significant advantage was in the quality and abundance of their equipment, a reflection of the superiority of their resources on the wider scale of manpower, transport and supplies. Professor John France considers that, in the period 1000–1300, the amount of metal in military equipment tended to grow in line with the social and economic growth of western Europe:

> By the time of Edward I's Assize of Winchester in 1285, the regulations demand even more metal weapons. Those with land to the value of £15 and with 40 marks per year must have a full hauberk, helm, sword, knife and horse: lesser men with land worth £10 and incomes of 20 marks can make do with a short-sleeved hauberk, but must have helmet, sword and knife. The 100 shilling freeholder must provide a padded surcoat, iron cap, sword and knife, and a sword is expected even of a 40 shilling freeholder, along with a knife, bow and arrows. Even the 20 shilling man must produce a spear, scythe and knife, and only the poorest are limited to bows and arrows.[62]

In the field, the superiority of English equipment over Welsh is likely to have been most apparent when it came to armour. However, heavy plate armour would not always have been appropriate to the guerrilla warfare that characterised the Welsh campaigns, and the infrequency of pitched battles has already been stressed.

Castle strategy

All of these factors play into the much-misunderstood area of fortification strategy. Castles played a key part in the conquest of Wales, but that was not because the Welsh were ignorant of their use or their means of construction. Relying on a fortification strategy for defence would tie a Welsh leader to a fixed point upon which an enemy with superior resources could concentrate his attack, and in this period it was customary that a garrison could honourably surrender to a besieging army if it saw no hope of relief; fortifications which surrendered on terms could expect those conditions to be honoured, but those taken against resistance lost all rights.[63] Such military codes of conduct applied equally in Wales;[64] as just one example, in 1210 a combined Anglo-Welsh force laid siege to the Welsh-held castle of Llandovery: 'And the garrison surrendered the castle, after they had despaired of any kind of support, upon their being given their lives and their safety and what was theirs and all their chattels free and sixteen steeds.'[65]

The Welsh did rely on castles in warfare against their native rivals and against marcher lords, where the fortifications were used to secure and define borders, controlling territory against local raids and infringements. But they never made serious attempts to defend such structures when faced with the expedition of an English king.[66] As noted, Glanville Jones contended that the thirteenth-century princes of Gwynedd attempted to bolster their realm's natural defences with strategically placed stone castles, thus blocking the entrance points to, and navigation through, three distinct barrier zones. The first, and much the strongest, of these zones was the inner citadel defined by the river Conwy and the mountains of Snowdonia. The next region started east of the Conwy in the rolling uplands of Hiraethog, curving south to take in the Migneint range, and stretching into Meirionydd and the summits of Ardudwy. Finally, the 'outer barrier' was made up of the Clwydian, Berwyn and Cader Idris mountain ranges. Llywelyn ap Iorwerth was responsible for the construction of the stone castles of Dolwyddelan, Dolbadarn, Cricieth, Castell y Bere, Ewloe and, possibly, Carndochan. His grandson, Llywelyn ap Gruffudd, undertook additional building work on these fortresses and built new castles at the extreme edge of his lands, most notably at Dolforwyn.[67] The fact that castles such as Dolwyddelan and Dolbadarn were built away from traditional sites associated with the rulers of the land (*maerdrefi*) and that resources in the surrounding area were limited supports Jones' overall contention that they were positioned for military purposes, not administrative or economic ones. However, Jones himself stressed the importance of military mobility to the Gwynedd princes, as highlighted by their establishment of vaccaries (cattle farms) at strategic points in the pastoral uplands; this gave their forces a source of supplies as they engaged in guerrilla activities from the wild lands.[68] A limited reliance on the defensive strength of Welsh castles helps explain some of the idiosyncrasies that are obvious in their design; for example, obsolete square towers were regularly inter-mixed with round and apsidal ones, Ewloe is all but indefensible as it is overlooked by higher ground, entrance points into Welsh castles are typically weakly defended and even the state-of-the-art twin gatehouses at Cricieth do not make effective use of arrow slits to cover the approaches. The princes were well aware of some of the latest and most elaborate fortifications in England and the march, but impregnable defence was never their overriding concern when it came to castle design.

For invaders of Wales, though, a defensible castle was a formidably effective instrument of conquest, which allowed the planting of small military enclaves deep within hostile territory. Such fortifications formed connected chains throughout Wales that could support one another and that could, in many cases, be supplied by sea. In the face of Welsh uprisings and aggression, these castles could often stand secure as they awaited ultimate relief when the huge resources of the mighty English military machine were mustered. There has been an understandable focus placed on the imposing stone castles built by Edward in north Wales to secure his conquest of the region, but in many ways this has distracted attention from the extensive castle building that preceded these works and that, in many ways, prepared the way for the conquest. The marcher lords constructed fortifications on a huge scale, as perhaps most strikingly seen in the case of Caerphilly Castle (discussed below). Henry III also built major new castles at Montgomery in 1223 and Painscastle in 1231 following the royal expeditions of those years and these fortifications, situated at strategically vital points, would play important roles in the conflicts that followed.

Siege warfare

The points made about castle strategy are, of course, closely related to siege warfare, where English resources and technology would appear to give them a huge and obvious advantage over native Welsh leaders. However, the Welsh would rarely sit in their fortifications and await the arrival of the English king's engineers and their formidable array of siege equipment. Even when these mighty engines of war were deployed in medieval conflicts, they were not always successful, and few new techniques emerged in siege warfare between the fall of Rome and the end of the middle ages. The human element – surprise, cunning and political machinations – proved the most efficient way to overcome a fortification; such techniques are reflected in practice and are emphasised in military manuals. Direct assault could be costly and success was far from assured due to the physical advantages gained by the defender of even the most modest fortification, but when attempted the simplest techniques were often the best; fire, scaling ladders, rams and bores were far more prominent than anything more sophisticated. In the Welsh prose tale *Breuddwyd Macsen Wledig* (*The Dream of Macsen Wledig*), the elaborate assaults made by the emperor Macsen's army on Rome over the period of a year are described, but success was only achieved when his British troops tried a more cunning approach, by making one wooden ladder for every four of their men and scaling the walls whilst the enemy was at lunch.[69]

In Wales, the professional troops of the *teulu* were often associated with successful sieges, their triumphs based on cunning stratagems and military acumen.[70] Above and beyond this, though, native leaders were more than capable of conducting lengthy, elaborate and successful siege operations against even the most sophisticated fortifications, providing they enjoyed control of the military theatre and did not fear the arrival of a powerful English relief force; this fact was illustrated with the destruction of the royal castle of Deganwy in 1263, as discussed below.

Conduct of warfare in Wales

It can be seen, then, that Welsh military organisation, strategy, tactics and equipment were closer to the norm seen in England and on the continent than has generally been acknowledged. What, though, of the conduct of war in Wales which – as part of the so-called 'Celtic fringe' – has tended to be seen as more brutal and with a greater capacity for atrocities than warfare elsewhere. If the non-combatant population could expect little mercy in war in the middle ages, it is generally agreed that certain unwritten conventions were followed by the military elite in most of western Europe which went some way towards limiting the brutality of warfare. These conventions only applied to the nobility and even then they were subject to qualifications and were often flouted, but it is held that they marked a delineation between warfare in the heart of Europe and that on the periphery.[71] In general terms, Wales tended to be seen by observers as a part of the 'Celtic fringe' where the usual rules of war went out of the window, but complaints over Welsh conduct in this area are not as common as for, say, the Scots. This was because the settled lowlands of England tended to be beyond the reach of Welsh military aggression and controversial incidents typically occurred in Wales itself.

When atrocities were perceived in warfare, they particularly related to a refusal to accept the immunity of the church from military campaigns; indiscriminate killing; and the mistreatment of noble prisoners. To deal firstly with conduct towards the church in war, it is quite clear that native Welsh leaders respected the attitudes towards church immunity that governed contemporary behaviour elsewhere in western Europe.[72] As just one example, a document detailing issues of contention between the bishop of Bangor and Llywelyn ap Gruffudd dealt with the case of a man the prince was said to have seized when he was in the refuge of the church; the facts of the case were to be judged and, if the prisoner had been illegally seized, Llywelyn agreed to make amends for his action.[73] Whether in Wales or elsewhere, the demands and furies of war meant that codes of conduct with regard to the church were frequently flouted, with observers able to define different degrees of acceptability. It might be suggested that the seizure of church goods and provisions by armies on campaign was common behaviour and that, if suitable reparation was made by the lay lord after the conflict, clerical outrage and punishment were kept to a minimum. By contrast, the killing of clergy was more unusual, serious and morally unacceptable; such behaviour was typically subject to major clerical censure, or would require a serious act of reparation from the lay lord. In the wars of 1277 and 1282–3, it will be seen that the vast majority of complaints about the abuse of church rights came from the Welsh and were directed against the armies of Edward; this, of course, may be expected given the fact that the king's armies were on the offensive, operating in hostile territory.

With regard to instances of indiscriminate killing and the mistreatment of noble prisoners by the Welsh, Gerald of Wales claimed that 'they [the English and French] take prisoners, we [the marchers and Welsh] cut off their heads; they ransom their captives but we massacre them'. It should be stressed that only noblemen and women typically 'counted' when such areas were discussed; the civilian population of the land was seen as fair game and just another of the resources of the land that could be targeted. In Wales and the march, the fact that atrocities on both sides led to increased brutality can be seen as a recurring theme, notably in a number of passages from the chronicler Matthew Paris that are considered below. Even in such examples, the anticipated conduct of warfare in Wales conformed to the standard elsewhere in Europe, but racial, social and cultural differences between Welsh and English – allied to the experience of bitter, frontier warfare – meant that mistrust continued to exist between the two sides and they never enjoyed the mutual respect seen amongst the military elite in the Anglo-French world. The complexities and contradictions of the issue are revealed in Matthew Paris's account of the death of an English noble, Herbert fitz Matthew, in Wales in 1245. Paris initially says that Herbert was killed in an accident when he was struck by a rock; such a death would be acceptable, a hazard of war. However, he continues:

> Other persons state that the said Herbert fitz Matthew fell from his horse, and whilst still alive the Welsh came up and contended with one another as to whose captive he ought to be, for the sake of the ransom, and one of them, wishing to put an end to the strife, ran Herbert through his body from behind, saying, 'Now whoever chooses may take him'. On the morrow he was found with his body pierced through, and with his hand placed on the wound, and, being naked, was only recognized amongst the other dead by an emerald ring.[74]

The initial Welsh response was to capture and ransom the noble; the numerous 'other dead' were of no significance. However, Paris and his audience believed that the Welsh were capable of slaying their helpless noble victims. Similar incidents undoubtedly occurred in the wider Anglo-French world, but when allied to the social and cultural differences in Wales they played a part in alienating the native nobility from the chivalric world of their neighbours.

If there is a need to search for examples of such behaviour, it should also be noted that in thirteenth-century Wales we have plentiful evidence of conduct in war that would be recognised and respected as chivalric if found in conflict in lands such as England, France or Germany. As just one example, succession disputes in Gwynedd were bitter, with fundamental questions of rule at stake, but there was a marked reluctance from men such as Dafydd ap Llywelyn and Llywelyn ap Gruffudd to kill or maim their dynastic opponents; imprisonment tended to be the main recourse when more conciliatory methods had failed, and even such action led to criticism from the wider Gwynedd community for its harsh nature. The later Welsh prose romances also reflect the chivalric attitudes to honour, the notion of a brotherhood in arms and the ideals of correct noble behaviour seen in literature throughout Europe.[75]

The issue of atrocities will be considered in the course of the following chapters, but it should be noted that the bias of our sources plays a major part in our view of this area, and also that atrocities could be committed by both sides; if a more brutal form of warfare was undertaken in Wales, the question of 'who started it' obviously becomes a pertinent one. The outrage felt by Llywelyn ap Gruffudd at the lack of acceptance he and his countrymen received within the wider chivalric community of medieval Europe would prove a major stumbling block in relations between Wales and England; this would be a contributory factor in the outbreak of war, and in its severity. At the height of the war of 1282–3, Llywelyn would write to the archbishop of Canterbury that: 'Who truly delights in the shedding of blood is clear from the facts: for the English have spared neither sex nor age nor feebleness and have shown no regard for any church or sacred place; the Welsh have not done such things.'[76] At the end of the war, the treatment that would ultimately be meted out to the prince, his brother and their offspring would suggest that Llywelyn had reason to feel uneasy about what he perceived as the lack of acceptance for the Welsh nobility into the chivalric world.

Chapter 3

The Rise of a Prince

Before his death in 1240, Llywelyn ap Iorwerth attempted to add permanence to his achievements in a variety of ways, including in the titles he used. He is never known to have called himself 'Prince of Wales', instead trying a variety of epithets that included Prince of Aberffraw, Lord of Snowdon and *Dominus Wallie* ('Lord of Wales'); the Aberffraw title was boosted by the promotion of mythology claiming that Aberffraw (on Anglesey) was superior to the other chief courts of Wales in Powys and Deheubarth.[1] But Llywelyn's most testing challenge was to try to ensure that his dominion was passed on to a single heir. According to Gerald of Wales, amongst the things causing the 'ruin of the Welsh people' were:

> All their sons, both legitimate and illegitimate, insist upon taking equal shares in their patrimony ... through their natural pride and obstinacy, they will not order themselves as other nations do so successfully, but refuse to accept the rule and dominion of one single king.[2]

Gerald's statement is misleading; partible inheritance between brothers applied to the lands of freemen, but it did not apply to the succession to rule of a Welsh 'kingdom'. The Welsh laws make provision for the designation of a single heir by a ruling king, the heir known as the *edling*.[3] Confusion and problems could be caused by the fact that multiple members of the royal line were eligible to become the *edling*; the primacy of legitimate over illegitimate children was not an established principle, nor was the concept of primogeniture (the succession of the eldest son).

When the *edling* succeeded to become the new king, other family members were only given a landed estate; their noble status then depended on the land they held, not on their membership of the royal kindred. This system of succession can be observed in late twelfth-century Gwynedd, Powys and Deheubarth; but so can the problems that were caused by the interference of external political powers with an interest in keeping the Welsh domains weak and divided. Owain Gwynedd (d. 1170), Madog ap Maredudd of Powys (d. 1160) and the Lord Rhys of Deheubarth (d. 1197) all arranged for the succession of a single heir, with landed estates created for other potentially eligible candidates. These estates, though, served as powerbases from which other members of the royal dynasty could mount military challenges for the kingship. This meant that rule in each of the regions of Gwynedd, Powys and Deheubarth was fragmented after the deaths of Owain, Madog and Rhys. Professor Beverley Smith says that this was 'the result of a compromise made when the king's designation was frustrated, the heir designate's position challenged, and a contest waged in which no-one among the contenders was able to secure an ascendancy'.[4]

The eldest of Llywelyn ap Iorwerth's known sons was Gruffudd, the product of a liaison with a woman named Tangwystl that pre-dated his marriage to King John's daughter, Joan. While the view from England was that Gruffudd was illegitimate, this is unlikely to have been the way his position was seen in Wales. But even before the birth of Llywelyn and Joan's son Dafydd, the prince had ruled out the possibility that Gruffudd would be his successor. When Llywelyn submitted to John in 1211, he agreed that – should he die without an heir to his body by his wife – then Gwynedd would pass to the king and Gruffudd would get only what John chose to provide for him. Gruffudd was taken as a hostage by the king and would not be released for four years. Even when he was freed and John was dead, it was clear that Llywelyn's eldest son would not be his chosen successor. Professor Beverley Smith contends that the prince introduced the notion that illegitimate children would not be considered for inheritance on terms of parity with legitimate sons.[5]

In 1220 Henry III's government acknowledged Dafydd as Llywelyn's successor, and in 1222 this was confirmed by the Pope, rejecting the claims of the illegitimate Gruffudd. In 1226 the Pope offered further support by declaring Joan legitimate, and in the same year the leading men of Wales were required to swear an oath of fealty to Dafydd. In 1229 the English government took Dafydd's homage for his lands and rights, acknowledging him as Llywelyn's successor, and in the same year he moved closer to one of the most important marcher families by marrying Isabella de Braose. In 1238 Llywelyn summoned all the native Welsh lords to the abbey of Strata Florida in order for them to swear allegiance to Dafydd as his heir, and this resulted in the prince handing over effective power to his son for the last two years of his life.

Gruffudd was by no means cast aside, being given a substantial provision of land away from the true Gwynedd heartland of Snowdonia. The apanage was created in contentious areas where rival dynastic claims existed, such as Llŷn, Ardudwy, Meirionydd and southern Powys (Powys Wenwynwyn).[6] But for all Llywelyn's attempts to secure his legacy, the question of whether it would prove more than a personal achievement remained. Gruffudd did not take the favour shown to his younger brother in good part and his children – Owain, Llywelyn, Dafydd, Rhodri, Gwladus and Margaret – would have grown up sharing that feeling of rejection. The prince had to expel his eldest son from his lands in 1221, he imprisoned him for six years from 1228 and in 1237 there was again open rivalry between the two. Gruffudd's unresolved ambition would prove fertile ground to be ploughed by rivals and enemies of Dafydd after Llywelyn's death in 1240.

The reign of Dafydd ap Llywelyn

Up to the point of Llywelyn's death, the historian Dr Richard Walker contended that Henry III's activity in Wales – including major expeditions in 1223, 1228 and 1231 – was aimed at 'defence and recovery'.[7] That quickly changed in 1240, when Dafydd immediately felt compelled to make a humiliating submission to the king at Gloucester. He did homage for his right to north Wales in a manner suggesting that both his personal and territorial status were dependent on the king of England. The reasons for the vulnerable position he found himself in were closely connected to the succession question, with the new prince having to secure his position in his Gwynedd heartland in the face of the counter-claims of Gruffudd. Meanwhile, the rulers of outlying Welsh territories such as Powys and Deheubarth were eager to throw off any dominion claimed by Gwynedd, and Dafydd was in no position to press his claims over them.

His prospects were somewhat improved by the autumn of 1240, when Dafydd had both Gruffudd and his eldest son, Owain, imprisoned in the castle of Cricieth; the Welsh chronicle says that, in seizing his brother, Dafydd 'broke his oath to Gruffudd', while Matthew Paris also indicates that treachery played a part in the imprisonment of the prince's dynastic rivals. Almost immediately, Dafydd proved more ready to stand up against the king's will, and he was soon offering military help to Welsh lords of the middle march who were resisting the ambitions of Ralph Mortimer. It is in this troubled landscape that we get the first glimpse of the man who would dominate the native Welsh political scene for the remainder of its independent existence: Llywelyn, the second son of Gruffudd and the grandson of Llywelyn ap Iorwerth.

Llywelyn ap Gruffudd

Henry III was already planning an expedition in 1241 to bring Dafydd to heel when Gruffudd's wife, Senana, arrived in his court to plea for help in releasing her husband and eldest son, Owain. As part of the negotiations, she offered the king custody of her two infant sons, Dafydd and Rhodri, but made no mention of Gruffudd's second son, Llywelyn.[8] This suggests that Llywelyn was already his own, independent man and not a pawn to be played from the hand of his mother, or his uncle. Both Owain and Llywelyn are thought to have been born in the 1220s, and by 1241 Llywelyn was exercising dominion in Dyffryn Clwyd, one of the four *cantrefi* of the Perfeddwlad.[9] His uncle, Dafydd, was ruling the other *cantrefi* of Rhos, Rhufoniog and Tegeingl, meaning Llywelyn had intruded himself into the Perfeddwlad in opposition to Dafydd and with the unofficial backing of Henry, who saw him as a useful check on the Gwynedd prince. Backing the youngster was the marcher lord Ralph Mortimer, a bitter enemy of Dafydd who was married to Gruffudd's sister, Gwladus. Mortimer had just secured hold over the long-contested territories of Gwerthrynion and Maelienydd, and a 1241 charter preserved from his family's cartulary indicates that he was prepared to support Llywelyn in return for the Welshman's assurance that he and all his heirs in perpetuity would surrender all claims to the two lordships.[10]

The recognition of Llywelyn as an important player on the political scene – a leader who was likely to be in place for some time – is clear, and it is also possible to trace in the youngster's following prominent men from the leading ministerial families of Gwynedd. Many of these men would remain at his side, a sign that a brotherhood of arms had been forged, but there are also indications of the splits caused by the fact that such men and their dynasties – who dominated the administrative, political and religious affairs of Gwynedd, east and west of the Conwy – had to choose between the overlordship of Llywelyn, Dafydd and the king of England. A charter of Llywelyn's from 1243 recognises that certain land belonging to Einion ap Maredudd was to be held free of military service, a clear concession to one such leading man. Llywelyn would face problems securing the loyalty of members of Einion's dynasty in years to come, while two of the names witnessing the 1243 charter – Cynfrig Sais and Gruffudd Gryg – would be found as loyal servants of the crown in the Perfeddwlad in 1245, acting in opposition to Llywelyn.[11]

The expedition of 1241

Senana's appeal for Henry's intercession led to the king's pronouncement that he would make judgement 'according to Welsh law' regarding Gruffudd's release and the securing for him of a portion of his father's patrimony, that he would then hold as a tenant-in-chief of the king. As far as we know from surviving evidence, this was the first time that an English king had stated his desire to divide the patrimony of Gwynedd into two parts, thereby using his interpretation of the so-called 'customs of Wales' to weaken and divide a potentially dangerous opposing polity. The decision carried implications for all native Welsh lords, and in the years to come the principle would be applied in Powys and other Welsh lands. In future disputes, both Welsh leaders and English kings would use a veil of tradition to justify novel, opportunistic and self-interested moves, but the repeated division of Welsh patrimonies would prove the most enduring and effective of all such tactics.

Henry set out from Chester in the summer, his rapid advance aided by 'the heat, which had continued intense for four months, had dried up all the lakes and marshy places of Wales'.[12] After just a week, his progress was such as to force Dafydd's total submission; the king was praised for a victory 'without bloodshed and without having to tempt the doubtful chances of war'.[13] Gruffudd and Owain were released from Cricieth, only to be handed straight into Henry's captivity in the Tower of London; this was far from the result that Senana had intended when she had made her appeal to the king. A junior branch of the Gwynedd dynasty was imposed in Meirionydd to cause further headaches for Dafydd and, perhaps most ominously of all, it was spelt out that if the prince breached his fealty his land would be forfeit to the English king in perpetuity; the same would apply if Dafydd was to die without an heir.

In addition to these humiliations, major territorial losses were imposed on the Welsh leader. He had to hand over Tegeingl to the king, who looked to secure his hold on the eastern side of the Clwyd with the construction of a major new royal castle at Diserth. This was an ancient fortified site on a formidable hill, 2½ miles east of the old castle at Twthill, Rhuddlan. Although only ruins now remain, the formidable strength of the rock on which the castle was situated is suggestive of the power of this stone fortification. However, the decision to build it away from any sea or river supply points would prove to be a major strategic weakness. A town was established around the castle, with burgages offered to those willing to settle there.

The building of Diserth was just part of the king's plans for control of north Wales. Although Dafydd had retained Rhos and Rhufoniog, a significant clause in the terms of surrender carved out a portion of the former for the king, the prince acknowledging that: 'The castle and lands of Deganwy will remain forever with the king and his heirs for the expenses of the royal expedition to Rhuddlan.'[14] Deganwy is another imposing, elevated site, perched on two hills above the eastern bank of the Conwy estuary. It had been a fortified site associated with the leaders of Wales since the early middle ages, although after 1066 there were long spells when the region was under Anglo-Norman control. Dafydd held a castle there in 1241, but as Henry advanced he abandoned and destroyed it. The king appears to have done little with the site between 1241 and 1245, concentrating initially on Diserth, but he would eventually construct an elaborate stone castle that enclosed the two hills, a hugely expensive project that would cost over £2,200.[15] This would prove a key location in the coming years, the only English castle between the Clwyd and Conwy. Again, though, there were strategic problems with the site, which was easily isolated from the sea and river. It was also poorly placed to serve as an administrative centre, and the free borough that was developed under the castle walls failed to flourish. In 1251 burgage lands were laid out with privileges modelled on those of Chester, but by 1253 all the townsmen who had been attracted to Deganwy had left.

Rebellion and submission

Following Henry's success in 1241, the threat to divide the patrimony of Gwynedd remained in place, but there was a tacit understanding between king and prince that this would not be done so long as Dafydd obediently toed the royal line. He was forced to do this while seeing the gradual encroachment of English administration and justice into Wales, something that was made far more difficult to bear by the harsh exactions of English officers on the ground. A tinderbox was created throughout the lands of native Wales, and news from London in 1244 provided the spark to set it alight. In the weeks preceding St David's Day in 1244, English records make a number of references to the government's most illustrious Welsh captive, Gruffudd ap Llywelyn; his custodians were replaced because they had 'proved worthless' and there are details of orders for bedclothes for the incarcerated noble. Gruffudd was said to be 'deeply affected by the tedious and unaccustomed long imprisonment' and so, on 1 March:

> Having deceived his jailers and made a cord out of his sheets, tapestries and table-cloths, he let himself down perpendicularly by means of the same rope from the top of the Tower. And when he had thus descended some distance, from the weight of his body, the cord snapped, and he fell from a great height; for he was a big man, and very corpulent; and in this way he broke his neck, and died; and his pitiable body was found in the morning near the wall of the Tower, and afforded a lamentable spectacle to all who saw it, as his head, together with his neck, was almost buried in his breast between the shoulders.[16]

The Welsh chronicles describe the incident as an accident, but the possibility of a more sinister plot is left open by the poet Dafydd Benfras, who refers to a 'killing'. Matthew Paris says that the king was angry at the incident, scolding the guards and ordering that Gruffudd's son Owain – who had been imprisoned with his father – should be more closely guarded.

The death of his brother and dynastic rival made things much simpler for Dafydd ap Llywelyn in Gwynedd, enabling him to tap into the discontent that existed throughout Wales and assume the leadership of a popular rising. Disinherited Welsh lords of Deheubarth and Glamorgan hastened to join him in Gwynedd, but the most significant recruit to his cause was his nephew, Llywelyn. The reasons for the latter's decision to abandon his lands in

Dyffryn Clwyd and join his uncle in Snowdonia cannot be fully known; it may have been the impression made by English officers in his lands, a sense of Welsh patriotism, or the knowledge that Dafydd was not a well man and that he had a chance to position himself as the heir to Gwynedd.

While the union of the main leaders of Gwynedd offered significant strength, the rulers of Powys were firmly under Henry's control. Setting out from Chester, the king made it as far as Deganwy and his forces took Anglesey where they wrought much destruction. The royal army made its base on the east bank of the Conwy as the king put into practice his ambitious plans for the new stone castle. Matthew Paris preserves a lengthy letter from a noble in the royal army at this time that is worth repeating in full; it illustrates the difficulties of the Conwy crossing, the nature of Anglo-Welsh warfare in the day, the atrocity stories alleged by each side and the supply issues that would ultimately define any conflict:

> His majesty the king is staying with his army at [Deganwy], for the purpose of fortifying a castle which is now built in a most strong position there; and we are dwelling round it in tents, employed in watchings, fastings, and prayers, and amidst cold and nakedness. In watchings, through fear of the Welsh suddenly attacking us by night; in fastings, on account of a deficiency of provisions, for a farthing loaf now costs 5 pence; in prayers that we may soon return home safe and uninjured; and we are oppressed by cold and nakedness, because our houses are of canvas, and we are without winter clothing. There is a small arm of the sea which flows and ebbs under the aforesaid castle, where we are staying, and forming a sort of harbour, into which, during our stay here, ships have often come from Ireland and from Chester, bringing provisions. The arm of the sea lies between us and Snowdon, where the Welsh quarter themselves and is, at high tide, about a crossbow shot wide . . . a ship from Ireland, bringing provisions to us for sale, was coming up towards the entrance to the harbour, but being incautiously steered, as the sea receded, it remained aground under our aforesaid castle, but on the opposite bank towards the Welsh who immediately rushed down and made an attack on it as it lay on dry ground. We therefore, seeing this proceeding from the bank on this side, sent 300 Welsh, our borderers from Cheshire and Shropshire, across the water in boats, together with some crossbowmen, to defend the said ship; on seeing which, the Welsh hurriedly retreated to their accustomed and well-known hiding places in the mountains and woods. Our knights, attended by their followers, pursued them for a distance of two leagues and, although they were on foot (for they had not brought their horses across the water with them),

they wounded and slew many of the Welsh. Our people then returned, after defeating their enemies and, like greedy and needy men, indulged in plunder and spread fire and rapine through the country on the other side of the water, and, amongst other profane proceedings, they irreverently pillaged a convent of the Cistercians called Aberconwy, of all its property, and even of the chalices and books, and burnt the buildings belonging to it. The Welsh, in the meantime, having assembled a large host of their countrymen, suddenly rushed with noisy shouts on our men, who were laden with booty acquired by the most wicked means, and impeded by their sins, and put them to flight, wounding and slaying many as they retreated towards the ship; some of our people choosing rather to trust to the billows, and to perish by drowning, than to be slain at will by their enemies, threw themselves of their own accord into the waves, there to perish. Some of our knights they took alive, to imprison them; but hearing that we had slain some of their nobles, and above all Naveth, son of Odo, a handsome and brave youth, they also hung these knights of ours, afterwards decapitating and mangling them dreadfully: finally they tore their miserable corpses limb from limb, and threw them into the water, in detestation of their wicked greediness in not sparing the church, especially one belonging to religious men.

There fell in this conflict on our side some knights of the retinue of Richard, earl of Cornwall; namely, Alan Buscel, Adam de Moia, Lord Geoffrey Sturmy and a fourth, Raymond, a Gascon crossbowman, of whom the king used to make sport; and about 100 retainers were killed, besides those drowned and the same number of Welsh, or more. In the meantime, Walter Bissett, who was on board the ship with his followers, bravely defended it, and was engaged until about midnight in continued fight with the Welsh, who fiercely attacked him on all sides, and if our men had not had the sides of the ship for a wall, they would have altogether fallen into the hands of the enemy. At length, as the sea rose, the ship began to roll and, it being now inaccessible, the Welsh withdrew, lamenting that our people had been snatched out of their hands. On board this ship were sixty casks of wine, besides other much desired and seasonable provisions of which we were at the time destitute. When morning came and the tide receded, the Welsh returned with alacrity, thinking to seize on our people in the vessel, but by God's providence they had, during the night when the tide was high, made their escape to us by means of our boats, before the arrival of the Welsh, leaving only the ship; the Welsh, however, approached, carried off nearly all the wine and the other things on board and, leaving it as the tide rose, set fire to the ship, a portion of which was consumed; the other part, however, was saved, in which were seven casks, which we dragged to the near shore.

Whilst we have continued here with the army, being in need of many things, we have often sallied forth armed, and exposed ourselves to many and great dangers, in order to procure necessaries, encountering many and various ambuscades and attacks from the Welsh, suffering much and often, by the fortuitous chances of war, doing damage to them. After one conflict, we brought back in triumph to our camp the heads of nearly 100 decapitated Welsh. At that time there was such a scarcity of all provisions and such want of all necessaries that we incurred an irremediable loss both of men and horses. There was a time, indeed, when there was no wine in the king's house and, indeed, not amongst the whole army, except one cask only; a measure of corn cost 20 shillings, a pasture ox 3 or 4 marks, and a hen was sold for 8 pence. Men and horses consequently pined away and numbers perished from want.[17]

Accounts of Henry's campaign in 1245 tend to be unfavourable, his eventual retreat back to England said by Matthew Paris to be because he was 'unwilling and unable to stay any longer' through 'the want of provisions and the near approach of winter'. The Welsh chronicles say that '[the king] left many corpses of his men dead in Gwynedd buried, some in the sea, others on land'.[18] But he also left behind him a formidable fortification: '[Deganwy], well-supplied with men, provisions, engines of war, and arms, was, as it were, a thorn in the eye of the wretched, yea, most wretched Welsh; and they could not, by any means, pass into England without being intercepted by the castellans.'[19] On his return march the king

cruelly put to the sword and reduced to ashes everybody and everything that remained there; so much so that the whole country seemed reduced to one vast and uncultivated desert solitude ... The unhappy Welsh, therefore, as the inclemencies of winter set in on them, were oppressed by want in all shapes, homeless and destitute of all kinds of provisions, nor were they buoyed up by any hopes of an amelioration in their condition, as all their lands were lying uncultivated and rotted of their own accord, and thus, overcome with hunger and cold, as well as by mental and bodily despair, they pined away and died.[20]

The English strategic advantage improved further in February 1246 with the news that the sickly Dafydd had passed away. The leadership of the Welsh resistance passed to the sons of Gruffudd, Llywelyn having been joined in Snowdonia by his elder brother. Owain had been sent to Chester by Henry as early as November 1244, but he did little until after Dafydd's death, on receiving the news of which: '[Owain] at once left the king of England and took sudden flight, like a hare, to the lurking places of the Welsh, although the said king had received him in the bosom of his compassion, had honourably brought him up for a length of time past and raised him to rank.'[21] The difficulties facing the brothers were increased by the highly effective progress made by the southern commander of the English forces, Nicholas de Molis. Having quelled the resistance in Deheubarth, he moved north, breaching the southern defences of Gwynedd and arriving at Deganwy by the summer of 1246.

Henry now chose to reverse his previous ruling regarding the right of Gruffudd to a share of the patrimony of Gwynedd, by stating that the latter's sons – Llywelyn and Owain – had no right to inherit the land. Ecclesiastical backing was won for this decision from Richard, bishop of Bangor – previously a supporter of both Gruffudd and Llywelyn – while the king increased the pressure by supporting the claims of other, junior branches of the Gwynedd dynasty. Owain and Llywelyn were forced to come to terms and the Treaty of Woodstock of 30 April 1247 would prove to be one of the most imposing ever dictated by the English in Wales. The terms saw the Perfeddwlad pass to English royal rule, it was stated that the Welsh leaders only held Gwynedd west of the Conwy by royal grant and military service to England was imposed on this territory. Furthermore, it was made clear that the homage and service of all barons and nobles in Wales was owed directly to the king, shattering the pretensions of any potential 'prince of Wales'. In Meirionydd, Llywelyn ap Maredudd – a direct descendant of Owain Gwynedd through Owain's son Cynan – was granted rule as a tenant-in-chief of Henry. The division of Gwynedd west of the Conwy between Owain and Llywelyn had also opened the way for further division of the patrimony when their younger brothers, Dafydd and Rhodri, came of age.

Outside Gwynedd, the imposition of English royal rule on Welsh lands went even further, as most clearly symbolised by extensive rebuilding at Montgomery, Builth, Carmarthen and Cardigan castles, the latter also getting new town walls. Amongst the complaints that would arise from the native Welsh in succeeding years would be the payment of reliefs required by heirs entering into their lordship and the increasing encroachments being made by English justice. This applied on both Welsh and marcher territories; although often couched in terms of the judgment being made according to Welsh or marcher law, the ultimate source of arbitration was the officers of the English king. It was this state of affairs that Edward I would look to recreate when, thirty years later, he turned his full attention on Wales. But, for all the success achieved by Henry, he had not been able to lead his forces west of the Conwy and the surrender made by the leaders of Gwynedd was not unconditional. As discussed below, the king would face growing problems in England and on the continent in the period 1247–55, and in this time developments in Gwynedd would be dramatic.

Gwynedd under divided rule

The division of Gwynedd west of the Conwy between Llywelyn and his brother Owain was roughly done with a split between north and east (Llywelyn) against south and west (Owain), something that applied both on the island of Anglesey and on the mainland.[22] Our limited evidence for the period suggests that both men proved respected and capable rulers, either one of whom could have won the loyalty of the community of Gwynedd, although Llywelyn was perhaps the more proactive and dynamic. In many ways the division of land between the brothers was equitable; Owain got the chief court of Aberffraw while Llywelyn got the more extensive lands, and the economic potential of each portion was roughly equal. But what Llywelyn was able to secure was the military heartland of Snowdonia, the mountain citadel and its stone castles of Dolwyddelan and Dolbadarn. Beverley Smith believes that this was due to Llywelyn's decision to join the rising of Dafydd ap Llywelyn west of the Conwy in 1245, while Owain remained at Chester; 'Llywelyn established himself in the fastnesses of Snowdonia and no-one would ever remove him.'[23]

Upheaval arrived with the coming of age of a man whose vaulting ambition and mercurial character would make him, for the rest of his life, the catalyst for many of the major changes that occurred in native Wales. If the motives that drove Dafydd ap Gruffudd, the younger brother of Owain and Llywelyn, are frequently difficult to fathom, he was a man whose ability was always recognised by his peers, but of a character that left those same peers wary of the purpose he would turn his talent to. Historians have been rather scathing in their judgement, Professor Rees Davies speaking of Dafydd's 'record of defection and treachery' and Sir John Edward Lloyd portraying a 'restless, discontented, shifty schemer, true neither to the Welsh nor to the English side'.[24] In 1247 he appears as a witness to one of Llywelyn's charters, perhaps having arrived back in Gwynedd with his brother Owain. Dafydd served as the leader of his eldest brother's military household (he was Owain's *penteulu*), and conspicuous military ability is a recurring theme in his career. In 1258 the Welsh chronicle described Dafydd as 'a young man splendid in arms and powerful in cavalry', and his love of hunting was well known, while the poet Bleddyn Fardd remembered him thus:

Tristan's his manner of shearing shields ...
Blood-spilling spear of Beli's lineage,

Steel-speared, like Arthur, at Caer Fenlli,
Dead lord's splendid assault, reddened gold sword,
When Gwynedd's troops went to Teifi's lands.[25]

By 1252 Dafydd was ruling Cymydmaen on the westerly tip of the Llŷn peninsula; this indicates that Owain had made territorial provision for him. Llywelyn, though, made no territorial concessions to Dafydd from his share of the patrimony, and this would prove the spur that led to civil war in Gwynedd.

In 1253 Dafydd's desire for a greater share of the land led him to the king's court in London; Henry was absent in Gascony, but the young Welshman swore fealty to the king and built alliances with his officials. Henry's council warmed to him and the disruption he could brew in Gwynedd, citing the so-called 'customs of Wales' in advising both Owain and Llywelyn to give their brother 'the portion due to him'. A commission was ordered to look into the matter, indicating that further division of the patrimony was likely to follow;[26] it was a fateful decision that would derail the entire settlement that Henry had imposed on Wales in 1247.

The battle of Bryn Derwin

Before the king's commission could deliver its verdict, the divided brothers of Gwynedd had determined to find their own conclusion, with the allies Owain and Dafydd taking the lead. In mid-June 1255 the two advanced from Llŷn, while Llywelyn blocked the way into Snowdonia, meeting them close to the mountain pass known as Bwlch Dau Fynydd, between Arfon and Eifionydd. The battle of Bryn Derwin was recorded in the Welsh chronicle thus:

> Strife arose between the sons of Gruffudd ap Llywelyn, Owain Goch and Dafydd, his brother, on the one side, and Llywelyn on the other side. And Llywelyn, trusting in God, fearlessly awaited the coming of his brothers against him, and with them a mighty host. And unperturbed in the fighting, in the space of an hour he captured his brothers and imprisoned them, after many of their men had been slain and others put to flight. And he gained possession of all their lands without any opposition to him.[27]

The conflict was also well remembered by the poets, including Llygad Gŵr:

> Bryn Derwin! He [Llywelyn] was the stay of a celebrated army!
> There were no regrets the day he withstood
> The shameless attack of his own stock;
> He who saw Llywelyn, the jubilation of warriors,
> On the borders of Arfon and Eifionydd,

Would see a lord over men in hosts
Like a man dispelling honour.
It was not easy, a lion in a host and fearsome in combat,
To vanquish him by Drws Daufynydd.[28]

After his victory, Llywelyn was able to capture and imprison Owain and
Dafydd, an indication of a controlled form of warfare in Wales that may have
been described as chivalric if practised elsewhere in Europe. There is no
suggestion that Llywelyn saw the killing of his dangerous dynastic rivals as an
acceptable option, and even his long incarceration of Owain was the cause of
considerable tension within the community of Gwynedd, as made clear by the
poet Hywel Foel ap Griffri:

A warrior [Owain] made captive by the lord of Eryri [Llywelyn],
A warrior, were he free, like Rhun fab Beli,
A warrior who would not allow England to burn his borders.
A warrior of the lineage of Merfyn, magnanimous like Beli,
A warrior of hosts, warrior of splendid armour,
A warrior protecting his people, ordering his army,
A steadfast warrior ruling his forces,
A warrior of battle, he maintained his generosity ...
A warrior no more lacking than Elfri.[29]

Despite such concerns, Llywelyn was now the undoubted master of the land
west of the Conwy and in a position to unite the wider community of
Gwynedd – and native Wales generally – behind his banner. The English
plan to back Dafydd with a view to the further fragmentation of Welsh power
had backfired spectacularly.

Chapter 4

The Young Panther

If the reign of Henry III was troubled, his family life was a happy and loving one, and one of the most joyous times was in June 1239 when Queen Eleanor gave birth to their first son at the Palace of Westminster.[1] There may have been some surprise throughout the kingdom when the new heir was given the strange, archaic name Edward. But those closer to Henry would have been well aware of his fascination with the penultimate Anglo-Saxon king of England, Edward the Confessor. The Confessor's saintly reputation, established in the decades after his death, was seen by Henry as part of a golden age to hark back to, allowing him to forget the indignities of the final years of the reign of his father, John, and the problems of his own minority that followed. The Palace of Westminster had been established by the Confessor when he rebuilt the nearby abbey, and Henry would devote huge resources to again rebuilding Westminster Abbey, producing the building that is so familiar today.

The king's love of art and luxury was also reflected in his home life, and the young Edward was brought up in style in the lavishly redecorated Windsor Castle. His education would have included readings of the most popular romances in Europe, the stories of King Arthur and the knights of the Round Table. The tales had undergone momentous transformations since the transmission from their original British/Welsh authors, Geoffrey of Monmouth having played the main part in this as the stories became a keystone of mainstream European culture. Edward was close to his uncle, Henry's brother Richard of Cornwall, who would have filled the youngster with stories of his exploits on crusade, perhaps instilling a yearning for the glamour and glory that such martial endeavours could bring. Within the kingdom, a more controversial influence on the young prince would have been Peter of Savoy and his other five great-uncles on his mother's side, described by Dr Marc Morris as 'clever and ambitious, these men, who hailed from the Alpine province of Savoy, saw in their niece's marriage the opportunity for self-advancement, and she in turn looked to them for help and advice'.[2]

Edward made his first impact on the political stage in 1252 when – following a crisis in Henry's territory of Gascony caused by the high-handed rule of the royal lieutenant, Simon de Montfort – the young prince was asked to take the loyalty of the independent-minded Gascon lords. Gascony (also referred to as Aquitaine) was the last remaining continental territory of the English king following the huge territorial losses in John's reign, and its wine and other trade made it an extremely valuable resource. King Alfonso X of Castile also had an interest in the region, something that forced Henry to make an expedition there in 1254. The campaign ended with an agreement that Edward would marry Alfonso's half-sister, Eleanor. The deal had far-reaching implications that would stretch into Wales, as Alfonso insisted that Edward was endowed with lands worth £10,000 a year. It is likely that this is more than Henry would have been inclined to give away, but he had little choice and he proceeded with the deal that made his son the second wealthiest man in the realm, behind only the king himself. Henry was careful, though, to ensure that the grant was composed of land on the outer edges of his dominions, being made up of Gascony, the vacant earldom of Chester, the castle of Bristol, various manors in the English midlands, and the royal lands in Ireland and Wales. The Welsh territory was composed of the Perfeddwlad, Montgomery, Builth, northern Ceredigion, Cardigan, Carmarthen and the 'Three Castles' in Monmouthshire, Skenfrith, Grosmont and White Castle.

Edward travelled to Gascony and then on to Burgos, where he was knighted by Alfonso. By now he would have been approaching the maturity that would see him develop to a physically imposing 6ft 2ins, a height that would earn him the nickname 'Longshanks'. He was reportedly blond, broad chested, strong and handsome, with the same drooping left eyelid that was characteristic of his father. His character, though, was not beyond reproach; in the eyes of the hostile author of the *Song of Lewes*, when in his twenties Edward was:

> A lion by pride and fierceness, he is by inconstancy and changeableness a panther, changing his word and promise, cloaking himself in pleasant speech. When he is in a tight spot he promises whatever you wish, but as soon as he has escaped, his promise is forgotten.[3]

His character did not necessarily change as he matured; according to his biographer Michael Prestwich: 'He was capable of deviousness, and the great legislator could take a surprisingly cavalier attitude towards the law.'[4]

The adolescent Edward may have returned from Spain ready to be a lord, but when he arrived in Gascony he found problems aplenty. The finances of the duchy were in pieces, and any demands for more taxes would most likely lead to rebellion amongst the hard-headed nobility of the region. Perhaps an even greater source of frustration to the youngster was the attitude of his father; although Henry had handed over major territories to his son, he proved reluctant to let go of the levers of power.

The king was enduring problems of his own back home, his continental expeditions a major cause of his financial woes. In response, Henry called parliaments to raise money ... only to find that the assemblies were nowhere near as compliant as he had hoped and that his problems had multiplied. Henry had increased the discontent by welcoming to the kingdom his relatives from Poitou, a group collectively known as the Lusignans. These were the descendants of Henry's mother, Isabella of Angoulême, through her second marriage, to Hugh X of Lusignan. Most prominent amongst the group were Aymer and William de Valence, plus Guy and Geoffrey de Lusignan; these men had a violent reputation and would prove implacable rivals of the Savoyards in the quest for power and patronage.

Edward returned to a troubled England for Christmas in 1255, when he had his first recorded argument with his father, the dispute arising over the management of Gascony. The prince's wife brought with her an entourage of Spaniards to a country where xenophobia was already piqued by the influence of foreigners, and further consternation was caused as Edward surrounded himself with a lavish, alien household of 200 horsemen, restless, unpredictable souls who seemed to pander to the vanity of the young prince as they engaged in obnoxious and excessive behaviour.[5] According to Matthew Paris: 'Edward's retainers and followers disturbed the peace of the inhabitants of the country through which they passed, by plundering their possessions as well as abusing their persons.'[6] The chronicler related one notorious incident when Edward was staying as a guest in Wallingford Castle:

> His retainers forced their way into the priory adjacent to the castle, rudely and by force, and not asking hospitality as was the custom; then, irreverently pushing the monks aside, they seized on all that was necessary for supplying their table, fuel and fodder for their horses, broke the doors, windows and seats; insulted, abused and beat the servants of the monks, as though they had been slaves, or convicted thieves, and drove them from the place ... those greedy freebooters were never equalled.[7]

Complaints about the prince were not restricted to the character and activities of his followers, Matthew Paris again the source of this famous account of the young Edward:

> As he was passing through a peaceful part of the country at a time of peace, a young man met him and Edward – without any pretext for killing or maiming the young man being given him – ordered one of his ears to be cut off and one of his eyes to be pulled out, which was done, though contrary to every rule of justice. Men who saw this, and still more who recalled to memory an enormous and sanguinary injury he

had done to a certain noble when younger than he now was, began to despair of him, remarking: 'If this occurs when the tree is green, what is to be hoped for when it is old and dry?'[8]

In June 1256 we hear of Edward competing in his first tournament, before he headed to Whithorn in Scotland for a more genteel activity: a family pilgrimage. In July he returned south to visit some of his new lordships for the first time, starting with Chester. Friendship and alliance with the earl of Chester had been a key plank in the policy of Llywelyn ap Iorwerth, but when Earl John the Scot died without heirs in 1237 his land had passed to the crown. Professor David Carpenter calls the retention of Chester 'perhaps the best move of [Henry III's] career', and it would prove a base that was key to all future royal expeditions into north Wales.[9] Edward moved on from the port city for a brief visit into the Perfeddwlad. By August he was back in Chester then soon on to London, but if his Welsh excursion was short, it had huge repercussions. Tensions caused by English rule in the Perfeddwlad were already at snapping point and the visit of Edward and his extravagant, unsympathetic household may have been the final straw.

Trouble in the Perfeddwlad

Edward's tour was certainly a factor in the drama that followed, but longer-term issues were also at stake. Complaints about the rule of the Perfeddwlad from Chester had been making their way to Henry since the appointment of the justice Alan Zouche in 1251 and, although the king was prepared to listen to the grievances, he had done nothing to settle the underlying problems. When Edward took the lordship a new steward was appointed, Geoffrey de Langley, whose rule was even more harsh and uncompromising; according to Professor Michael Prestwich: 'The evidence of the substantial landed estate that Geoffrey built up for himself, largely at the expense of impoverished knightly families, strongly suggests that he was a corrupt and unscrupulous man.'[10] It should be remembered, though, that Geoffrey was not the appointment of the young and inexperienced Edward, but of Queen Eleanor and the royal council.

Edward, Henry, Eleanor, the royal advisers and the officers in Chester all deserve a share of blame for the problems in the Perfeddwlad, but it was perhaps the nature of Edward's succession to rule there that really made war inevitable. In the build-up to the battle of Bryn Derwin, the royal council's promotion of Dafydd's right to land west of the Conwy had upset the peace in Gwynedd. Llywelyn, while refusing to give up a piece of his patrimony, had instead propounded the idea that provision should be made for Dafydd from the royal land holdings in the Perfeddwlad, something that would have accorded with his interpretation of 'Welsh custom', if not with Henry's.[11] The king had firstly refused to take account of this proposed solution, then granted the Perfeddwlad in its entirety to his son Edward. These decisions were accompanied by harsh English rule, increasing the likelihood that, after Llywelyn's victory at Bryn Derwin, the put-upon Welsh of the four *cantrefi* would turn to him for help. According to the Welsh chronicle:

> Edward, son of king Henry, he then being earl of Chester, came to survey his lands and his castles in Gwynedd round about August. And after his return to England the gentlefolk of Wales, despoiled of their liberty and their rights, came to Llywelyn ap Gruffudd and revealed to him with tears their grievous bondage to the English; and they made known to him that they preferred to be slain in war for their liberty than to suffer themselves to be unrighteously trampled upon by foreigners.[12]

In late 1256 Llywelyn released his younger brother from captivity and, in the campaigns that followed, Dafydd may have served as the leader of the prince's warband (*penteulu*). In November the brothers crossed the Conwy to enter the Perfeddwlad, where the Welsh community rose in open revolt to join them. A campaign outside the usual summer fighting season was always a sign of a leader's resolve, the problems of supply and the practical difficulties of keeping troops healthy and warm creating major difficulties for all forces involved. It also limited the response that an English king could make, effectively ruling out a campaign from the full feudal muster until the following summer. Within days of Llywelyn's advance, all that was left of English rule in the Perfeddwlad was the besieged castles of Deganwy and Diserth.

Llywelyn pressed the king to recognise what was now a *fait accompli*, Dafydd's establishment in the Perfeddwlad, and Henry's initial reaction to the Welsh rising was to seek a negotiated settlement. But Edward was said to be 'not a little ashamed and injured by the rebellion of the Welsh as well as by their bravery for he was called the lord of the Welsh, and yet could not check their rebellious proceedings'.[13] His humiliation and, arguably, his inexperience meant he was out for revenge, but he lacked resources and also the full support of the marchers, who were alienated by the presence of foreigners in his household. Our fullest account of the conflict is provided by Matthew Paris and it comes from a unique perspective; the St Albans chronicler reflected the criticisms prevalent in England of Henry III and his foreign advisers, and the author who, in 1245, had spoken of the 'wretched, yea, most wretched Welsh' now showed a remarkable sympathy for their cause. Theirs was, he said, 'a confederacy on the gospels boldly and faithfully to fight to the death for the liberty of their country and the laws of their ancestors, declaring that they would rather die with honour than drag on an unhappy life in disgrace. This manly and brave determination might justly shame the English, who lazily bent their necks to foreigners, and to everyone who trampled on them, like vile and timid rabble, the scum of the human race.'[14] The initial phase of the war is described thus:

> The Welsh, who had been oppressed in manifold ways, and often sold to the highest bidder, were at last so immeasurably and tyrannically oppressed by the king's agent, Geoffrey de Langley, that they roused themselves for the defence of their country and the observance of their laws. Entering into a confederacy, they invaded the provinces of England adjoining Wales, and attacked the subjects of Edward, their lord, whom, however, they did not then acknowledge as such; and they succeeded so well in their warlike expedition that it was believed that they met with the goodwill of the neighbouring people. On hearing of this, Edward flew to the bosom of his uncle Richard, and as the king was become inglorious and poor, borrowed [£2,666] from him, being determined to check the impetuous rashness of the Welsh, to punish their presumption, and to wage war against them to their extermination. But the whole of that year was so wet and stormy that the entire country of Wales, which was without roads, and of a marshy nature, was utterly inaccessible to the English, and thus Edward's labour and expenditure of money were fruitless and of no avail. The aforesaid Geoffrey then repented, but too late, of having provoked a war, and of his cruelty in plundering the Welsh, as he had some few years before done to the people in the north of England. There were some that said that Geoffrey, either willingly or unwillingly, would make good the losses of Edward as far as he was able.[15]

Llywelyn moves south

If the loss of the Perfeddwlad was bad enough for Henry and Edward, it soon became clear that – despite the difficulties of winter campaigning – Llywelyn had even more ambitious targets in his sights as he sought the position of dominance within Wales that had been enjoyed by his grandfather, Llywelyn ap Iorwerth. Before the year's end he had already turned south into Meirionydd, driving out his distant cousin Llywelyn ap Maredudd, who fled to the English court that had granted him the lordship in 1247. With a greater Gwynedd now under his rule, Llywelyn ap Gruffudd would soon cross the Dyfi into Deheubarth to take more of Edward's lands and reap the benefits of the alliance he had forged with the native lords of the region.

Since the death of the Lord Rhys in 1197, the fracturing of the royal line of Deheubarth caused by disputes over the patrimony had been even more intense than anything seen in Gwynedd. In the dynasty's heartland of Ystrad

Tywi, the main rivals at this time were Maredudd ap Rhys Gryg and his nephew, Rhys Fychan. In September 1256 Rhys had sought help from Stephen Bauzan, Edward's officer in south-west Wales. A combined English–Welsh force had driven Maredudd to seek shelter under Llywelyn's wing in Snowdonia, and he had joined the prince for the attack on the Perfeddwlad; now, Llywelyn would repay the favour with an expedition south in support of his ally.

Their forces first took control of royal land around Llanbadarn Fawr (Aberystwyth), a move that led the influential Maredudd ab Owain to submit to Llywelyn, giving the allies effective control of much of Ceredigion. Moving south-east into Ystrad Tywi, Maredudd ap Rhys Gryg was restored to his land and also given control of Rhys Fychan's territory, meaning that he was ruling his ancestral homeland from its chief court of Dinefwr. The Welsh chronicle praised Llywelyn for his generosity and for 'keeping naught for himself, but only fame and honour'.[16]

Soon after the successes in the Perfeddwlad, Llywelyn's forces had also driven into Powys, Gruffudd ap Madog – the ruler of northern Powys – fleeing to England and leaving his territory under Gwynedd's control. Early in 1257 attention was turned to southern Powys, the lordship of Gruffudd ap Gwenwynwyn. Both Maredudd ap Rhys Gryg and Maredudd ab Owain were with Llywelyn for an attack that burnt Gruffudd's main castle at Welshpool; Gruffudd was able to recover the fortification with royal help from Montgomery, but much of his lordship was lost to Llywelyn. Still the road south beckoned, leading Llywelyn to ignore his 1241 deal with the Mortimers and take Gwerthrynion, then secure much of the lordship of Builth for Maredudd ab Owain. Before the end of February, the Gwynedd leader was campaigning deep in the marcher territories of south Wales, reaching as far as Gower and burning the castle of Swansea.

The battle of Cymerau

A lack of resources stymied Edward's chances of making an effective response; the loan from his uncle was long gone, while arguments between the prince and his father damaged his chances of help from that quarter. The king was, in any case, focused on raising funds for a hugely unpopular plan for a crusade to Sicily, and when Edward did eventually approach him for financial aid in Wales he was met by the response: 'What is it to me? The land is yours by my gift. Exert your powers for the first time, and arouse fame in your youth, that your enemies may fear you for the future; as for me, I am occupied with other business.'[17]

Edward began tapping his lands in Ireland for resources, stockpiling men and goods from there in Cardigan. Matthew Paris says that the Welsh resisted, the only known example of an attempt by them to challenge English control of the Irish Sea in the thirteenth century: 'As Edward threatened, with the help of the Irish, whom he had called upon to aid him, to crush them like a potter's vessel, the Welsh took precautions and provided some galleys well-manned and armed and supplied with a good stock of provisions, and put to sea with the intention of giving battle to the Irish there.'[18]

Edward's efforts were helped by the marchers, who were alarmed by the deep inroads into their territory that had been made by Llywelyn. They chose to target the Gwynedd leader's key ally in the south, Maredudd ap Rhys Gryg; Bauzan planned to restore Rhys Fychan in the latter's place, and so led an army from Carmarthen into Ystrad Tywi on 31 May 1257. A day's march brought them to Llandeilo Fawr and the shadows of Dinefwr, but during the night they were surrounded by the forces of Maredudd ap Rhys Gryg and Maredudd ab Owain. A dawn attack put the Anglo-Welsh forces in severe difficulty and this prompted the defection of Rhys Fychan, something that would have made questionable the loyalties of the large numbers of Welsh-men in the invading force. After suffering through a second day of attacks, Bauzan's men were forced to admit that they had no chance of reaching Dinefwr and chose to set out for Cardigan. The march through difficult terrain was doomed from the outset, and at Coed Llathen most of the army's supplies were lost. The main force laboured on to Cymerau where their enemies finally chose to engage them in a battle made famous by the scale of the losses, with 3,000 said to have been killed from the invading force.[19]

The great Welsh victory did have one major downside; if the tactical posi-tion for Llywelyn's allies on the ground had been helped by Rhys Fychan's defection before the battle, it had now created a serious political problem for the Gwynedd leader. Llywelyn came to Deheubarth soon after the victory at Cymerau and made a fateful decision in choosing to provide for Rhys in Ystrad Tywi. Soon afterwards, Llywelyn took Maredudd ap Rhys Gryg's son hostage in order to ensure the good behaviour of his father. A rift had been driven between the Gwynedd leader and the most important of his southern Welsh allies, and it would never truly be sealed.

The English response

A disaster on the scale of Cymerau forced Henry to act, and a muster was called for 8 August at Chester. While this main force targeted the Perfeddwlad and Anglesey, help was also sent to the beleaguered middle march, while 100 knights from the feudal host were sent to south Wales. There, they would be led by the highly capable Richard de Clare, Earl of Gloucester, with experienced help from the recalled Nicholas de Molis. It was this southern force that was able to secure the most success, largely thanks to their winning of the allegiance of Maredudd ap Rhys Gryg. In the north, though, it was a very different story, and the account of Matthew Paris reveals that the Welsh may have had considerable sympathy from Henry's subjects:

> The Welsh, learning that the king intended to take the field against them with his army, prudently sent away their wives, children, and flocks into the interior of the country, about Snowdon and other mountainous places inaccessible to the English, ploughed up their fields, destroyed the mills in the road which the English would take, carried away all kinds of provisions, broke down the bridges, and rendered the fords impassable by digging holes in order that, if the enemy attempted to cross, they might be drowned. Fortune favoured them in this war, for their cause appeared, even to their enemies, to be just; what chiefly supported and encouraged them was the thought that, like the Trojans (from whom they are descended), they were struggling with a firmness worthy of their descent, for their ancestral laws and liberties. Woe to the wretched English who, trodden underfoot by every foreigner, allowed the ancient liberties of their kingdom to be extinguished, and were not put to shame by the example of the Welsh. Far from showing obedience to the king's son Edward, they only ridiculed and heaped insults and derision upon him, and he, in consequence, conceived the idea of giving up Wales and the Welsh as untameable.[20]

The story of the 1257 royal campaign in the north was one of mismanagement and inertia. After tarrying at Chester, the king was able to quickly advance to relieve the besieged castles of Diserth and then Deganwy by 25 August. A planned attack on Anglesey was cancelled when the fleet from Ireland and England failed to arrive, something that contributed to the army's supply problems. In the first week of September, Henry ordered the retreat back from Deganwy to England, noting the dangers of the approaching winter; the invaders were harried all the way back to Chester by their Welsh enemies.

Prince of Wales

By October 1257 Henry was back in Westminster and Llywelyn had re-established the sieges of Deganwy and Diserth. He had also won over another important native Welsh ally, Gruffudd ap Madog of northern Powys leaving the king's protection to pledge himself to Llywelyn. With England riven by its own internal disputes (see below), on 26 April 1258 Maredudd ap Rhys Gryg also offered his homage to Llywelyn. The Gwynedd leader made some notable concessions to Maredudd, promising never to take his son hostage again, never to imprison Maredudd or his son, and never to take possession of his castles. Even so, it seems that Maredudd's move was only calculated to secure the release of his son Rhys, and by the summer of 1258 it was well known that his true loyalties lay with Henry. Maredudd could also count on strong marcher support, and on two occasions in 1258 Llywelyn's forces, in alliance with the other lords of Deheubarth, campaigned against him. Both expeditions were successful, the first led by Llywelyn himself, the second by his brother Dafydd.

The second expedition was the occasion of a notorious incident at Newcastle Emlyn, where Maredudd and Patrick de Chaworth, the king's seneschal of Carmarthen, arranged a parley with Dafydd and the men of Gwynedd. The former thought that they were stronger and more numerous and so treacherously turned on Dafydd, but he distinguished himself in the subsequent clash, which resulted in the death of de Chaworth and many of his followers. The deceased's breach of the truce and of expected noble conduct was condemned by English and Welsh sources, and the incident is most probably that sung about in the poet Bleddyn Fardd's celebration of Dafydd's military prowess 'when Gwynedd's troops went to Teifi's land', as quoted above.[21]

It was in this period of spectacular and sustained Welsh military success – with most of the other native lords bound to Llywelyn by homage and fealty – that the Gwynedd leader began to officially use the title Prince of Wales (*Princeps Wallie*). This is first seen in an agreement of March 1258, made between Llywelyn and his allies and a number of disaffected Scottish nobles, a deal that envisaged their mutual support against English ambitions. The initiative for this came from Wales, revealing the confidence of the native lords. The prince also enjoyed significant church support at the time, while the political situation facing Henry in England was steadily deteriorating. Even so, Llywelyn's use of the Prince of Wales title at the time was limited, probably due to a wariness of upsetting his Welsh allies as much as his English enemies. It was less than 100 years since each of Deheubarth and Powys had enjoyed periods as the most dominant of the native Welsh polities, and the thirteenth-century rulers of these regions may well have felt that – if there was to be a Prince of Wales – their dynasties had better claims than that of Gwynedd. The rulers of both southern and northern Powys could claim direct male descent from the important eleventh-century leader Bleddyn ap Cynfyn, the acknowledged successor of the only king of all Wales, Gruffudd ap Llywelyn (d. 1063). The rulers of Deheubarth boasted direct descent from another important late eleventh-century leader, Rhys ap Tewdwr, and hence connection to a royal line that had never been prepared to accept the rule of Gruffudd ap Llywelyn. The dynasties of Gwynedd, Powys and Deheubarth all had links back to the key figure of Merfyn Frych (d. 844), although the Powys connection was through the female line.

The bards of Gwynedd may have struggled to convince other Welsh genealogists of the supremacy of their claim to rule all of Wales, but *force majeure* meant that by the 1250s Llywelyn was the only realistic option amongst the native nobility, and his propaganda would work to reinforce this. He was in a strong position, but Llywelyn would have been aware that a similarly favourable situation in Wales had been won by his grandfather forty years earlier, at the time of Magna Carta. Keen to avoid a repeat of the problems that had then followed for the dynasty of Gwynedd, Llywelyn was determined to secure his achievement and legacy by means of a formal treaty with the king of England. The situation was imaginatively outlined by Matthew Paris:

> The Welsh, notwithstanding frequent victories over their opponents, prudently began to weigh future events in their minds, and taking counsel amongst themselves, said: 'We know that the kingdom is in a very disturbed state, but when peace is established – a result the nobles of the country are trying to bring about – we shall not be able to resist them, as they will all unite in falling upon us. Let us consider, above all, that Llywelyn's brother, the eldest son of our lord Gruffudd who died in prison at London, is detained a prisoner, and if he is released he will be provoked to take vengeance; and that his other brothers will also incline the same way, and we shall be divided and desolate. In this helpless state, if the English attack us, they will demand an account at our hands of the blood of their brethren, and will blot us out from the face of the earth, and crush us irreparably, like a clay pitcher.'[22]

To bring about peace, Llywelyn was said to have offered Henry £3,000, with a further £200 promised to Edward and £166 to the queen. 'The king, on hearing this proposition, trusting to evil counsel, replied with anger: "What means this? One good man is of more value than the amount they offer for the required peace".'[23] If this was one of Llywelyn's earliest recorded attempts at bartering for peace, it would not be his last, and – despite continued Welsh military success – the price he would be required to pay for a treaty would only continue to rise.

Chapter 5

The Road to Montgomery

While political instability in England had undoubtedly helped Llywelyn's rise to supremacy, the same chaos at the heart of the English realm proved fatally damaging to the Welsh leader's hopes of gaining a workable and lasting treaty that would secure the future of his fledgling principality. Henry and Edward were not necessarily opposed to granting such a treaty in the years after 1258, but many of their most important nobles – including both royalists and members of the baronial opposition – were hostile to Llywelyn and his ambitions. The expansion of Gwynedd had been at the expense of a host of powerful marcher lords and, in the succeeding years, there would be almost constant border warfare involving countless breaches of truces. Both the delays in agreeing a formal treaty and the military successes that Llywelyn enjoyed led him to build a principality that was enlarged beyond anything he had originally planned, and beyond anything he could realistically hope to defend in the long term.

Turmoil in England

The loss of many of his Welsh lands had left Edward feeling he had been let down by his closest advisers, his mother's Savoyard relatives. This pushed him closer to Llywelyn's marcher enemies, and in 1258–9 he would build a faction of like-minded men around himself, including marchers like Roger Clifford and Hamo Lestrange. To the horror of the Savoyards, another marcher to move closer to Edward was one of the leaders of the Lusignan faction, William de Valence, the earl of Pembroke. At a parliament in April 1258 aimed at addressing the crisis in Wales, the Lusignans accused various English lords of colluding with the Welsh. But they were caught cold by a Savoyard-led alliance that included Roger Bigod (earl of Norfolk), Richard de Clare (earl of Gloucester) and Simon de Montfort (earl of Leicester). This party moved against both the Lusignans and the king, promoting a reform agenda that the Savoyards had little invested in morally or intellectually, but that they found preferable to the dominance of the Lusignans.

In the Oxford parliament of June 1258 the desire of the country to reform Henry's regime could not be contained, resulting in the revolutionary Provisions of Oxford. The king was forced to accept a new form of government which would be shaped by a council of twenty-four men, twelve of whom were selected by the crown, and twelve by the barons. The performance of the system would be monitored by parliament, which would meet three times a year, and the arrangements were set down in a form that has been called England's first written constitution. An attempt was also made to regulate the conflict with Llywelyn, the following truce sealed at Oxford on 17 June:

> Roads and passes shall not be obstructed with woods or other means ...
> The king and his men will be allowed access to his castles of Diserth and
> Deganwy and supply them as necessary; if such supplies cannot easily be
> transported because of a storm or other impediments at sea, Llywelyn
> shall, at the summons of the justice of Chester, conduct the supplies
> safely by land together with their guards ... If any of the garrison or
> servants of the said castle become ill, the king may send others in their
> place without any hindrance from Llywelyn.[1]

In the aftermath of the Oxford parliament, the Lusignans were banished from the realm, while major restrictions were placed on the independence of Henry and Edward. The alliances between the various factions were in a constant state of flux, though, with the so-called baronial party far from united and facing multiple problems. In 1259 the interests of de Montfort and his nephew Edward came together, meaning that a compact was formed between the two. But the return of Henry from peace talks in France put the entire reform party position in doubt and in early 1260 de Montfort was put on trial. This trial was derailed by the latest news of English disaster in Wales.

The fall of Builth

In early 1257 Llywelyn had conquered much of the lordship of Builth and handed it to his ally, Maredudd ab Owain, but Edward's royal castle of Builth was still held by Roger Mortimer, who continued to challenge Maredudd for possession of the rest of the territory. Builth was a key strategic point in the battle for control of the middle march; for the Mortimers, the loss of Gwerthrynion had left Maelienydd badly exposed, and if Builth was to fall the road further south towards Brecon would lie open to Llywelyn. Early in 1260 Llywelyn moved his forces to the area, determined to support Maredudd and, probably more significantly, to win royal attention for his calls for a formal peace treaty. The traditional six-week service of Welsh freemen outside their native kingdom seems to have started from their arrival at the siege camp outside Builth, but Llywelyn was determined to force the issue and his troops would continue the siege for six months.[2] Siege engines were brought in to batter the castle walls, although we have no way of knowing whether these were the most elaborate and formidable type of weapon, known as the trebuchet.

Llywelyn himself pressed on for a campaign in Deheubarth, but by midsummer was back at Builth and on 17 July the fortification at last fell into his hands. The ease with which the castle was finally taken is noted by our sources, the poet Dafydd Benfras seeing this as a factor that redounded to Llywelyn's credit: '... unimpeded brought to him Builth/Without damage, with his flaming straw he sets fire'.[3] Mortimer would successfully defend himself against accusations of collusion with Llywelyn; the Welsh chronicle accounts indicate that the besiegers had won over a small number of the garrison by bribery and that it was these men who then betrayed the castle:

As men from the castle were opening the gates for others who were without, behold Llywelyn's men leaping in by night and taking the castle. And so it was taken without so much as an arrow-shot, and such men and horses and arms and equipment as were in it; and it was destroyed to the ground. And then Owain ap Maredudd of Elfael came to Llywelyn's peace.[4]

Had the garrison as a whole agreed to surrender then their persons and possessions would not have been forfeit, and there would have been no need for Llywelyn's forces to 'leap in by night'. One supposition could be that the garrison included men loyal to Owain ap Maredudd of Elfael, and that they were responsible for surreptitiously opening the gates as part of a deal that their lord had made with Llywelyn.

News of the loss and destruction of Builth caused huge consternation in England, most notably to Edward who was furious at such a loss which he had been left powerless to prevent. Edward headed to Chester to prepare for an attack on Llywelyn and it seemed for a while that the nobles of England would put their own differences aside in order to meet the Welsh challenge. But others called for peace negotiations with Llywelyn, a move favoured by the king, and shortly before the muster was due at Chester a new, two-year truce was arranged. This largely repeated the terms of the 1258 truce, a significant addition demanding that 'roads and passes shall not be obstructed, nor woods folded back, other than they were at the time of the Oxford truce'.[5] The order not to cut back woods would seem to be a concession to Llywelyn and the Welsh, but even so the truce fell far short of the formal peace treaty that the prince desired.

In the aftermath of these events, de Montfort and Edward formed an unlikely alliance with Richard de Clare to control the government. Edward, after knighting de Montfort's sons Simon and Henry, returned to Gascony where – to the fury of his mother – he re-established links with the Lusignans.

In February 1261 Henry, Eleanor and the Savoyards turned on de Montfort and de Clare, prompting Edward to rush back to England with the Lusignans at his side. On arrival, William de Valence immediately went over to Henry, and he was soon followed by Edward, whose finances were in a parlous state. To complete the isolation of de Montfort, Henry obtained a letter from the Pope absolving the king of the oath he had taken to uphold the Provisions of Oxford, while de Clare joined the royal party. De Montfort beat a hasty retreat to France and was soon joined on the continent by the heir to the throne. This appears to have been a rather listless period for Edward, and he headed for Gascony in a move that his biographer Dr Marc Morris suggests may have been prompted by his father's duplicitous rejection of the entire reform agenda.

Open war resumes in Wales

Throughout the period 1258–62 regular conflict continued throughout the march, justifying Llywelyn's dissatisfaction with the temporary truces that had been made. Richard de Clare died in July 1262 (to be succeeded by his son Gilbert), and it was about this time that erroneous news reached Henry in France that Llywelyn had also passed away. The king's immediate response was to issue orders to seize any opportunities to restore the royal position in Wales and to stop Dafydd from assuming the native leadership. Should the very-much-alive Llywelyn have heard of this reaction, it can only have increased his resentment of the truce and raised his awareness of the long-term vulnerability of the position he had built. In autumn 1262 the Welsh leader concluded that the time was right to once again turn to the field of battle to pursue his ambitions, a decision that would take him far deeper into conflict with the powerful marcher lords of mid- and south Wales. The opening shots were fired on familiar territory and against a well known foe: Roger Mortimer in Maelienydd. This was a calculated move, as Llywelyn targeted the man he saw as the main obstacle to a permanent treaty with the king; what the Welsh prince did not engage in at this time was a wider attack on all of his marcher rivals and enemies.

The first attack fell on Mortimer's castle of Cefnllys in south-west Maelienydd, a hill-top site 3 miles east of Llandrindod Wells. The castle was built by Roger Mortimer between 1240 and 1245 at a time when the family's winning of Maelienydd, Gwerthrynion and Radnor made it a prominent fortification and a symbol of their rule at the heart of their newly secured territories. But Llywelyn's conquests in the period since 1258 now left the castle in a vulnerable position on the border of Mortimer lands, part of the undermining of the family's power that now left its heartlands under threat.

The conflict at Cefnllys was well recorded in both English and Welsh sources, all substantially agreeing with the following Welsh chronicle account:

> Certain men by counsel of the men of Maelienydd, came to the new castle which Roger Mortimer had in Maelienydd. And after they had come inside by treachery they slew the gate-keepers and seized Hywel ap Meurig, who was constable there, and his wife and his sons and his daughters. And they made that known to the seneschal and the constable of the Lord Llywelyn. And those hastened thither to burn the castle. And when the said Roger heard that, he came, and a mighty force along with him to help him, to the site of the said castle. And he encamped within the walls for a few days. And when Llywelyn learned that, he gathered a host and came to Maelienydd and he received the homage of the men of Maelienydd. And after two other castles had been won he gave Roger Mortimer leave to return. But he himself, at the request of the men of Brycheiniog, went to Brycheiniog. And after receiving the homage of the land he returned to Gwynedd.[6]

Terrified English reports speak of Llywelyn's forces in the area numbering 300 cavalry and 30,000 infantry.[7] That Mortimer's army was left at the prince's mercy but was spared by Llywelyn is a further indication of Welsh chivalric behaviour in war that goes against Gerald of Wales' comment that Welsh and marcher troops routinely slaughtered their helpless enemies; a report sent to Henry is clear that 'Llywelyn allowed them to retreat, although he could easily have forced them to surrender in a short time because of the shortage of provisions and the difficulty of escape'.[8] The assault on Mortimer territory continued with the destruction of Bleddfa castle, followed by the capture of Knucklas, Knighton and Presteigne, moves that put Wigmore itself in danger. A suggestion of the bitterness of the war is contained in a Westminster chronicle, which states that Mortimer 'attacked [the Welsh] in frequent sallies, slaying sometimes 300 men, sometimes 400, sometimes 500, and even more, until they amounted to an incalculable number; and thus, with his victorious army, he inflicted miserable slaughter on them; but once, of the infantry who entered the marches, he lost about 300 men himself, who were treacherously slain by that people'.[9]

The conflict widens

King Henry had been in France and only heard of Llywelyn's successes on his return to England, shortly before Christmas, the news prompting him to send a scathing letter to his son asking why he tarried abroad while his lands in Wales burnt.[10] Edward made it back to the country in February 1263 and marcher lords such as Roger Clifford and Roger Leybourne hoped that this would allow them to make common cause with the king's heir. While there was certainly understanding and mutual interest, the possibility of an accord was damaged by the extensive household of knights that Edward had brought from the continent, men who would be seen as yet another source of foreign influence and as rivals for power and patronage. The country was already seething with resentment against Henry and the Savoyards who had rolled back the reform agenda, and in April de Montfort returned to England to lead the opposition party.

In the meantime, Llywelyn's failure to make any progress with his demand for a formal treaty drew him even deeper into conflict in south Wales, the prince emerging as a leader prepared to stand by all men regarding them-selves as Welsh by language and custom. In March 1263 – again away from the usual summer campaign season – his forces pushed into the Usk valley towards Abergavenny, their arrival in this area at the invitation of the native Welsh of Brycheiniog, who supplied significant numbers of troops. Also present were the native lords of Deheubarth, the army – estimated by horri-fied English observers at 180 armoured cavalry, an untold number of un-armoured horses and 10,000 infantry – under the overall leadership of Llywelyn's *distain*, Goronwy ab Ednyfed. The opposition forces outside Abergavenny were well led by Mortimer and John de Grey, who managed to outflank Goronwy. After suffering heavy losses, the Welsh force fled onto the Blorenge mountain for safety; the immediate Welsh threat was ended, but the English in the region remained wary of Llywelyn's power and ambition. Although he had failed to take the castles of Brycheiniog, much of the lord-ship was effectively under the prince's control.

The defection of Dafydd

For the moment, though, Llywelyn was distracted by the wavering loyalties of his brother Dafydd. He may have been acting as *penteulu* for Llywelyn since 1256, a position he had formerly filled for Owain, but Goronwy ab Ednyfed's leadership of the army outside Abergavenny in March 1263 suggests that the prince was already unsure of Dafydd's allegiance.[11] In April he defected to the king, a move that came soon after an accord was arranged between Edward and Mortimer. Once again, Dafydd's motivations are hard to work out, especially as he was Llywelyn's heir; one version of the Welsh chronicle says that the decision was made 'at the instigation of the devil'.[12] Dafydd was promised land in the Perfeddwlad and that Henry and Edward would press his claims in Snowdonia, but Llywelyn was at the height of his power and the king was in no position to enforce the promises.

According to the Welsh chronicle, Edward was active in campaigning in the march and in 'burning townships in Gwynedd'; this is suggestive of some success, although the Westminster chronicle also records the familiar problems faced on a Welsh campaign:

> Advancing towards Snowdon, he marched on a mighty expedition against the Welsh; but as they retreated, and as our soldiers, by reason of the inequalities of the ground, the thickness of the woods, and the darkness of the deep morasses, could not venture to pursue them so closely as to bring them to battle, we must suppose that their rebellion was assisted, and the valour of Edward and his comrades hindered by this circumstance. At length, having strengthened the fortresses in those parts with abundant supplies of provisions and a powerful garrison of armed men, he was recalled by his father, and returned to England.[13]

Civil war in England

By this point in time, Llywelyn's forces were also acting in support of de Montfort in the march; relations between the prince and earl were distant and wary, making it unrealistic to talk of an alliance, but they were capable of working together when they had a mutual interest. Edward's strategy in Wales was prematurely curtailed in June when open warfare broke out in England between the royalist party and the baronial opposition. The power of London was firmly behind the latter party, and Henry and Eleanor were forced to shelter from the hostile population of their capital, holing up in the Tower. Edward hastened back from Wales to help, but despite his strenuous efforts the royal party was forced to submit. The extent of the humiliation was exemplified by an incident at London Bridge in the course of the conflict; Queen Eleanor, attempting to make her way down the Thames from her Tower imprisonment to her son at Windsor, was pelted and humiliated by the townspeople and – with her life believed to be in danger – made to turn back. Although Eleanor's relationship with her son had been a strained one, Dr Marc Morris says that this incident had 'a profound effect on Edward, he would never forgive those responsible'.[14]

As the crisis developed in England, the remaining royal presence in north Wales was snuffed out, the long-beleaguered castles of Deganwy and Diserth finally falling to Llywelyn's power. The siege of Diserth began on 1 July and it was taken on 4 August, the fortifications being utterly (and finally) destroyed. On 28 September Deganwy was surrendered to the Welsh and was then subjected to the same treatment. The fact that Deganwy's gates were opened to the Welsh could suggest treachery, that the garrison troops were starved out, or that they had despaired of relief, but archaeology has uncovered the most probable reason. Professor Leslie Alcock's excavation of the enormous fortification revealed that:

> The bailey defences had been savagely destroyed by mining, under-pinning with timber, and then firing the props ... Not less than 1,500 linear feet of walling was systematically thrown down, implying the labour of a large force of miners, as well as the provision of an untold quantity of props. All this is striking testimony to the authority, power and malice of Llywelyn ap Gruffudd.[15]

Amongst those Edward held responsible for this series of disasters, de Montfort was high up on the list; until now, the relationship between uncle and nephew was ambiguous, but from this point on the hostility between them is clear. Although de Montfort and his supporters had triumphed in England in the short term, the problems facing him were numerous and growing. Just one was the fact that the peace deal's stipulation that Edward's household knights return to the continent had removed the barrier preventing the prince's reconciliation with Clifford and Leybourne, while it was another marcher lord, Mortimer, who was at the forefront of the royalist recovery when it came in October 1263. The king had granted him three manors in Herefordshire which had previously been ceded to de Montfort, and conflict over this territory set off warfare throughout the march that soon spread throughout the country.

Much of the conflict went in favour of the royalist party, but Llywelyn found significant success; this was alongside de Montfort and against the earl's enemies, but the prince was acting in his own interests. He secured a notable coup in December 1263 when his long-time rival, Gruffudd ap Gwenwynwyn of southern Powys, came over to Llywelyn's allegiance. It is not possible to see an allegiance to any imagined 'Welsh cause' in Gruffudd's actions, and his move was more related to the fluctuating ambitions and allegiances of his marcher neighbours in the ongoing conflicts in England. In 1264 Gruffudd's forces united with those of Llywelyn to target Mortimer, and the Welsh were joined by de Montfort's men for an attack on Radnor.

The battle of Lewes

Despite such successes, baronial losses elsewhere meant that by May 1264 de Montfort's position was desperate. It was this that led him to make an aggressive march out of London towards Henry and Edward, who were with their army at Lewes. The earl was following a highly unusual, highly danger-ous, battle-seeking strategy, and the royalists may have been well advised to adopt the usual, cautious tactic of avoiding such a showdown. But the earl's reportedly tiny army encouraged the royalists to meet their enemy in the field on 14 May, Edward bullish in promoting this decision. The prince matched his words with bravery on the battlefield, leading a cavalry charge in an assault that routed the forces opposing him. However, he also pushed the pursuit too far, a rash decision that cost his father the battle by exposing the rest of the army; by the time Edward made it back to the field, the fight was lost.

De Montfort was triumphant, but the terms of the subsequent royalist submission included the free release of Henry's marcher allies. Oaths were taken and hostages given to ensure their good behaviour, and the most prominent of the prisoners were Henry and Edward. But there were soon problems in the west, and in July Llywelyn joined de Montfort for an expedition through Hereford, Hay, Ludlow and Richard's Castle, devastating Mortimer territory on their way to Montgomery, where de Montfort accepted the submission of his enemies. Even so, a second expedition was required to bring the same men to heel, again with Llywelyn in alliance. The marchers were again defeated and made to promise to depart for Ireland, but little was done to enforce this exile and de Montfort's failure to drive home his advantage – especially against Mortimer – led to Llywelyn losing all faith in his ally.

The crucial factor in breaking de Montfort's power was the alienation of his chief supporter at Lewes, the new earl of Gloucester, Gilbert de Clare (also known as Gilbert 'the Red'). In the aftermath of the battle, he was both resentful at the influence exercised by de Montfort's family and concerned over Edward's incarceration, his anxiety no doubt fed on the likelihood that the imprisoned prince would one day be his king. There were suggestions that de Montfort intended to take things further and attempt to disinherit Edward, and it was in this atmosphere in early 1265 that de Clare broke from court and headed for his estates in Wales. De Montfort followed him (with Henry and Edward in forced accompaniment), apparently in hope of a reconciliation. But when news came that a major royalist landing under William de Valence had been made in de Clare's lordship of Pembrokeshire, it became obvious that he had switched allegiance.

De Montfort based himself in Hereford and still, it seems, held out naïve hope of a friendly reconciliation with his enemies. Edward's captivity was relaxed and comfortable, and the prince was allowed visits from his marcher friends. He was also allowed leisure time, and during a ride on 28 May he was able to enact a carefully prepared escape plan, galloping away from his guards who had been left on ridden-out horses, before meeting up with the waiting Mortimer. They moved to join de Clare in Ludlow before seizing control of the crossings of the Severn to thwart de Montfort's desperate desire to flee to the east.

The agreement of Pipton

Despite his association with Llywelyn, up until this point there had been no suggestion that de Montfort had any real empathy with the Welsh prince and his ambitions, nor that he would advance Llywelyn's aims of a formal treaty with the English government. But, in the critical situation that now faced the earl, talks with the Welsh were rapidly progressed, de Montfort desperate to secure the military aid that might help him make his escape across the Severn to his remaining supporters. Llywelyn engaged with the earl at a distance, apparently aware that de Montfort would soon lack the ability to enforce any treaty that may be made, and wary of upsetting opinion in England by appearing to exploit the country's difficulties to extort an unfair deal.

Negotiations were conducted via letters patent issued by each side, and the agreement made is referred to as the Treaty of Pipton, named after the small Powys community where Llywelyn was based when he signed in June 1265. He agreed to pay £20,000 over ten years in return for official English acknowledgement of his title as Prince of Wales and of his consequent right to take the homage and fealty of all the native barons of Wales. The principality was to be ruled by Llywelyn and the heirs of his body; the latter clause suggests that a proposed marriage between the prince and de Montfort's daughter Eleanor was agreed at this time. Llywelyn's territorial conquests were recognised, and a promise secured from de Montfort that he would help the prince gain those lands he still claimed. Historians are reluctant to actually call this deal a treaty given the conditions it was created under, but it was granted in perpetuity, it carried the captive Henry's seal and it was an official English government document that recognised Llywelyn as Prince of Wales.[16]

The battle of Evesham

De Montfort's concessions failed to win him much real material help from Llywelyn. The earl had engaged in a wearying march through south-east Wales as he fruitlessly sought a way back across the Severn, but eventually ended up back where he started, in Hereford. His hope lay in joining up with a relief force from the north-east led by his son Simon, but Edward managed to ambush this army at Kenilworth, before turning and cornering de Montfort himself at Evesham. As battle was joined, the bitterness of the civil war meant that the expected chivalric rules of combat were abandoned. Hundreds of the baronial army were slaughtered, including many who had fled into the sanctuary of a church. A death squad was assigned to track down and slay de Montfort, although it was eventually his old enemy Mortimer who caught up with him and ran him through the neck with a lance. The earl's body was hacked to pieces, his genitals cut off and stuffed into his mouth, before his severed head was sent to Wigmore to be admired by Mortimer's wife, Maud. A heavily armoured Henry was himself lucky to escape death, the king able to announce himself to the victorious royalist army before they struck him down in the midst of the enemy force.

In the aftermath of the battle it was the king who was the chief driver of a policy of recrimination against the surviving rebels, insisting on their perpetual disinheritance. It was a decision that guaranteed further hostility with the surviving rebels and that led to two more years of war, characterised by bitter resistance and repeated outbreaks of guerrilla fighting. There was also a widespread belief that the royalist word could not be trusted, something that played a part in the decision of de Montfort's sons, Simon and Guy, to flee overseas. A measure of reconciliation was attempted with the October 1266 Dictum of Kenilworth, whereby huge fines were imposed on the rebels; if and when these were paid off, they would be allowed to reclaim their hereditary land. But in the midst of continued unrest, de Clare took the side of the rebels in early 1267 and he was able to seize London. This finally led to a workable peace in June, an amendment to the Dictum of Kenilworth allowing the old de Montfort supporters to immediately reclaim their land, although the requirement to pay off the fines remained.

The Treaty of Montgomery

The years of bitter warfare had exhausted England, fiscally and emotionally, and there was no desire for the renewal of conflict with the Welsh – at least not from the king and his eldest son. Edward's own landed interests in the country had been diminished when, in 1265, his territories in south Wales were ceded to his younger brother, Edmund. By 1267 Llywelyn was able to finally find from the government both the appetite for a lasting treaty, and the apparent authority and stability to be able to implement it. Lengthy negotiations began at Shrewsbury on 28 August with the papal legate Ottobuono – the future Pope Adrian V – heavily involved.

The talks concluded on 25 September, and four days later the key players were at Rhyd Chwima – an important ford of the Severn, close to the castle of Montgomery – to sign the treaty. The meeting at the border between England and Wales only emphasised what seemed to be the establishment of formal diplomatic relations between the two countries, with Henry prepared to travel west to meet Llywelyn and bringing along his sons, Edward and Edmund. This was probably Edward's first meeting with Llywelyn and personal relations appeared positive. Their accord was strengthened during a second meeting at Montgomery in 1269, Llywelyn afterwards writing to Henry to say he was 'delighted' with Edward's visit and, when the latter was away on crusade, Henry was able to describe his son as 'the friend of the prince' in a letter to the Welsh leader.

By the terms of the treaty signed near Montgomery on 29 September 1267, Llywelyn's title of Prince of Wales and Lord of Snowdonia was recognised for him and his heirs, and he was granted the homage and fealty of all Welsh barons with the single exception of Maredudd ap Rhys Gryg. Amongst the prince's acknowledged territorial gains were the Perfeddwlad, Gwerthrynion, Builth and Brycheiniog. The agreement was said to supersede any previous agreements between the English crown and the Welsh prince, including the position enforced by the crown at Woodstock in 1247. Neither king nor prince was to receive fugitives or enemies of the other within their lands, while Llywelyn was to make provision for Dafydd, a clause that seems to have been the cause of much of the wrangling in the talks at Shrewsbury.[17]

A heavy financial burden was placed on Llywelyn in return for the treaty; he was to pay Henry £16,666, plus a further £3,333 if the king ever chose to grant the prince the homage of Maredudd ap Rhys Gryg (something Llywelyn was desperately keen to secure). Llywelyn was to pay £666 immediately, to deliver another £2,666 by Christmas, and to then pay £2,000 annually. Such sums were vastly more than the £3,366 that Matthew Paris said Llywelyn had offered for peace in 1258; perhaps the humiliation he felt at the king's belittling rejection of this offer even played a part in the negotiations, the prince being determined not to lose face when such enormous sums were being discussed.

If the requirements placed upon Llywelyn for the treaty he had sought for so long were huge, perhaps more troubling were the matters that were left unresolved. In 1267 Llywelyn was holding a variety of territories that were disputed with the marchers and that received no mention at all in the treaty, while the deliberate fudging of decisions on other land ownership issues hinted at the problems that would soon arise. Perhaps most obviously, Llywelyn was in possession of Maelienydd, but Mortimer was acknowledged to have the right to refortify the castle of Cefnllys within the lordship's bounds. In other areas, notably Elfael, Cydewain and Ceri, there was land where possession was disputed between Llywelyn and the marcher lords, and the treaty left the way open for the issues to be decided by legal action, and even by private war.

If clashes over disputed territory would play a major part in undermining Llywelyn's achievements, arguably of even more significance was the prince's formal acceptance of the position of tenant-in-chief of the king of England, something that also carried the seal of papal approval. While Llywelyn hoped that this would bring him the king's protection, he struggled to come to terms with the nature of the corresponding responsibilities, and with Edward's interpretation of them. Above all else, it was clearly acknowledged that Llywelyn's land, authority and titles were given by the grant of the king of England, and were not acknowledged as being the prince's by right. Even so, at his moment of triumph Llywelyn had earned the praise of the bards, a contemporary poem by Llygad Gŵr lauding his qualities and achievements, while highlighting the authority he had won over the three chief courts of native Wales, Aberffraw, Dinefwr and Mathrafal (representing Gwynedd, Deheubarth and Powys):

> Roar of war's bold lion, fame-befriended,
> High tempest's howl above barren sea,
> Aberffraw's crowned, wealthy, well-spoken lord,
> Savage on raid, assault none withstands.
> Purposeful troop, deft with their high deeds,
> Famed, bold and fierce as a bonfire.
> Dinefwr's crowned, armed, belligerent lord,
> Leader's warband eager for plunder,
> Comely host, fine compatriots,
> Handsome, proud, notched sword trimmed with gold.
> Mathrafal's crowned lord, lengthy your border,
> Lord Llywelyn, four-languaged ruler.
> I stood in battle, no hidden speech,
> Before a foreign race, alien plaint;
> Let Heaven's King stand, rite of high rank,
> By the gold warlord who holds three crowns.[18]

Chapter 6

The Phoney War

That the potential territorial disputes left open by the Treaty of Montgomery were legion was highlighted by the fact that – when the agreement was signed – one such conflict was already in full swing. Upland Glamorgan was nominally under the control of the formidable Gilbert de Clare, earl of Gloucester, in his capacity as marcher lord of Glamorgan, but the region had been largely left to its own devices from the time when the Normans took over lowland Glamorgan at the end of the eleventh century. In the valleys running north from the coast, native lords from traditional Welsh dynasties still reigned. The marcher lords of the twelfth and early thirteenth centuries seemed happy with such an arrangement and reluctant to invest the men and resources that would be required to complete a colonial conquest of the economically under-developed uplands. By 1267, though, Llywelyn had intruded himself into the area, and the possibility that a powerful prince of Wales could become the new overlord of the region provoked a furious response from de Clare.

Carried along by the volition of his growing principality, the Gwynedd leader was claiming the leadership of all the native lords of Glamorgan, something that de Clare could not ignore. Conflict arose in Senghennydd, an upland lordship north of Cardiff; Llywelyn opportunistically entered the area in 1265–6, prompting a response in force from de Clare in early 1267, when the latter was able to capture and imprison the native lord of the area, Gruffudd ap Rhys, before beginning construction of a new castle at Caerphilly. The inability of the prince and marcher lord to resolve the dispute between themselves was the main reason for Edward's return to Montgomery in 1269; after arbitration, Edward ruled that one of Llywelyn's followers, Maredudd ap Gruffudd, should do homage to the prince for three upland lordships within de Clare's land in south-east Wales.[1]

The crusading years

This ruling reveals the strains that were repeatedly evident in the relationship between Edward and de Clare, who was predictably furious with the decision. It was also indicative of the good relations between Edward and Llywelyn, as further suggested by the former's successful 1270 appeal to his father Henry to allow Llywelyn to pay for the homage of Maredudd ap Rhys Gryg.[2] This was shortly before Edward was to embark on the expedition that was dominating his thoughts – a crusade to the Holy Land that would keep him away from Britain until 1274 – and may suggest that he was prepared to sacrifice a valuable pawn in Wales to secure desperately needed funds.

Given the fact that many of the problems of Henry III's reign had been caused by the king's shortage of cash, it is understandable that Edward had trouble finding the funds he needed. He turned to a number of external sources and to legislation against the Jews – the latter policy proving particularly popular in the country – and in the summer of 1270 he was able to set off. Edward's adventures took him to the Holy Land via Tunis and Sicily, a two-year odyssey that hugely increased his experience of military strategy, tactics and, perhaps above all else, organisation. He also brought back from the besieged crusader lands a knowledge of the most sophisticated fortification technology of the day; in 1275, for example, his extensive refortification of the Tower of London was overseen by 'Brother John of the Order of St Thomas of Acre'.[3] Edward's crusading exploits leant him a glamour and gave him respect throughout Europe but, perhaps most importantly, his greatest gain from the expensive expedition was the fellowship he formed with his leading magnates, including the marcher lords and even former supporters of de Montfort – the men who would shape Britain in the decades to come.

One man notably absent from this fellowship was de Clare; he had promised to join the crusade, but Edward's ruling in the Glamorgan dispute with Llywelyn meant he was more concerned with affairs closer to home. The need for his presence was made clear in October 1270 when Llywelyn fell on Caerphilly in force, razing the castle works to the ground in a campaign that won him the praise of Bleddyn Fardd:

> Ardent Llywelyn, noble in combat,
> Red-speared hawk in arms at Caerphilly.[4]

This brought Gwynedd's military threat to within touching distance of the earl's valuable Glamorgan lowlands and in 1271 de Clare mobilised his formidable resources to reply with a hammer blow. Moving into the uplands, he restarted the fortification work at Caerphilly on an enormous scale. Llywelyn swore to destroy the building, but by 1273 work on what was then the most formidable castle in Britain was nearly complete, leaving no doubt about who had won the fight for upland Glamorgan. The fortification occupies an enormous 30 acres, making it the second largest castle in Britain after Windsor. Extensive water defences surround the structure, which was the first castle in Britain to be entirely built in the modern, concentric style, meaning that the outer defences are overlooked and dominated by a higher, even more formidable defensive ring inside. Each wall section was treated as an individual defensive barrier that would need considerable effort to overcome, with mural towers projecting from the walls to give the defenders additional offensive options against an attacking force.

This defeat in Glamorgan was indicative of the problems that had faced Llywelyn since what was, for him, Edward's most unwelcome departure to the east. Henry's ineffectiveness as a leader had long been apparent, and Llywelyn's main marcher opponents – de Clare, Humphrey de Bohun and, above all, Roger Mortimer – were hugely influential voices at the heart of English government, with further restraints on them removed by the king's death in 1272. Llywelyn's defeat in Glamorgan was accompanied by losses to de Bohun in Brycheiniog;[5] the prince had been unable to win over the minor Anglo-Norman nobility of the region, and was also struggling to secure the loyalty of many of the native Welsh.[6] Llywelyn appealed to the English government for protection of his right to rule Brycheiniog, as outlined under the Treaty of Montgomery. Mortimer was a particularly influential and unsympathetic member of the regency government that heard the plea, which was then considered in more detail by the chief minister, Robert Burnell. He eventually agreed that the treaty was in favour of Llywelyn in this case, but added the rather perverse reasoning that the agreement made no mention of who owned the castles of the region. This meant that the government was free to support the defence of the castles of Brycheiniog against Llywelyn, and that it could punish the prince when he made war on these fortifications or held them himself.

It was against this background that Llywelyn made the fateful decision not to turn up at a requested meeting at Rhyd Chwima in early 1273, where he was to swear fealty to the absent Edward following Henry's death. Problems escalated in the summer of 1273, with Mortimer and Llywelyn engaged in what has been described as an arms race near Montgomery, repairing and building castles in the region. The regency government ordered the prince to stop work on his prized new castle at Dolforwyn, an elevated, hill-top site that lies just 6 miles west of Montgomery, its fortifications staring directly across the river Severn towards that castle. The strategic location protected access to the Berwyn range and the Severn valley, while guarding the hill routes through Ceri that were vital to Llywelyn's ambitions in the south.[7] In addition to the military value of the castle, the prince planned to foster the growth of a town and market around it, something likely to prove an economic threat to both Mortimer's interests and to Welshpool, the most important castle and borough of Llywelyn's ally, Gruffudd ap Gwenwynwyn.[8] The government's order to stop the building work prompted a withering letter from the prince to Edward, in which Llywelyn expressed his sure belief that the king could never have consented to the demand:

> Letter, acknowledging receipt of the king's letter dated at Westminster 20 June, ordering Llywelyn not to build a castle in his land near Abermiwl, nor to establish a town or market there to the harm of neighbouring lands or markets. Llywelyn is certain that the said letter has not had the king's consent and that, were the king present in his kingdom, such an order would not have been sent to him from his chancery. The king knows well that the rights of his principality are totally separate from the rights of his kingdom although Llywelyn holds his principality under his royal power, and he has heard and in part seen that Llywelyn and his predecessors have had the power to build castles, fortresses and markets within their borders without the favour of anyone or the announcement of new work. Llywelyn asks the king not to give heed to his enemies or to any others who have sought on account of the said occasion to turn the king against the prince.[9]

A further outraged missive was to follow regarding the extent of the building work that Mortimer was conducting at Cefnllys; the Treaty of Montgomery allowed for the castle's repair, but Llywelyn said that his rival was doing much more than that:

> Roger has, to Llywelyn's prejudice against the terms of the aforesaid agreement, built a new work in the disputed land, not only a fence, as has been suggested, but a deep and wide ditch, and stones and timber have been brought for the construction of a fortress unless it be prevented by the king or Llywelyn. The king should not be surprised if Llywelyn is irritated and seeks to prevent what he suspects would later harm him and his men and especially in a land in which he shall not desist from making a claim.[10]

Edward's return to Europe

Edward had returned from the east to Sicily in November 1272, and he was still there in January when news arrived from England that his father had died in November, and that he was now king. Although the news came as a shock, it had also been known that this was a possibility before Edward ever set out on crusade; the regency government had been set up to cope with such an eventuality, and this meant that there was no immediate urgency for Edward to return to England. Even so, it may be imagined that the new king would want to hurry back to his realm, but there were also plenty of pressing calls for his attention on the continent.

The first of these was the lingering spectre of the de Montfort family in the shape of his cousin, Simon de Montfort's son Guy. Both Guy and his brother Simon (who died in 1271) had fled to the continent after their father's death, and they had prospered in the service of Charles of Anjou, Guy earning the position of governor of Tuscany. When Edward was in Sicily in early 1271 preparing for his departure to the east, he was in need of Charles' support, and consequently sent his cousin, Henry of Almain (the son of Richard of Cornwall), to effect a reconciliation with the de Montforts. Henry made it to Viterbo, north of Rome, where he attended mass at the church of St Sylvester, but it was during the ceremony that Guy caught up with his cousin and stabbed him to death. Although Henry had not been at Evesham, Guy claimed that this was revenge for the death of his father and he dragged the body from the church to inflict upon it the same mutilations that had been performed on his father's corpse.

The murder scandalised Europe, even leading to a mention for Guy in Dante's *Divine Comedy*, and Edward was determined on revenge. But the killer was sheltered by his wife's wealthy family, meaning that the king had to leave for France with his rival still at large. His next destination was Paris, where he did homage to King Philip III for Gascony; the inconsistencies and uncertainties that were associated with one sovereign ruler taking the homage of another meant that the terms were kept deliberately vague. Edward then headed to the duchy, where he had to deal with the rebellion of some of its leading men, meaning that he did not return to England until August 1274.

The king's coronation

Preparations were already under way in London for the sumptuous coronation ceremony that would welcome the new king. In an event laden with pomp and circumstance, perhaps the most telling moment came after the gold crown was placed upon Edward's head. The king immediately removed it, saying 'he would never take it up again until he had recovered the lands given away by his father to the earls, barons and knights of England, and to aliens'.[11] The chronicler refers to 'lands', but this seems to have been a synonym for 'rights'. It was the rights of the crown that Edward was concerned had been alienated – a situation that had continued in the years of his absence on crusade – and he would spend much of his reign fighting to impose his interpretation of those rights.

Edward would carry this crusade into all aspects of his rule, including his relations with his English subjects. But it was the way he sought to impose his perceived rights on the rest of Britain that was arguably the most lasting legacy of his reign. According to Professor Rees Davies:

> [Edward] had no programme to redefine his position within the British Isles; but equally, as a monarch who was a stickler for his rights and the dignity of his crown in all spheres, it was unlikely that he would brook any perceived challenge to what he saw as his *superioritas*, nor would he pass by any opportunity to exploit his overlordship to the full.[12]

This allowed little leeway for the more relaxed interpretation of English dominion that had been imagined by the king of Scotland and by Llywelyn in Wales. Professor Rees Davies attempted to define what would have been their more traditional interpretation of the position they were in with regard to England:

> Overlordship or high kingship – it cannot be too strongly emphasised – is not the same as unitary, exclusive, direct kingship; it does not demand the sort of recurrent and intrusive power such as the king of England exercised within England itself; it even tolerated other sources of authority so long as they acknowledged their ultimate dependence on its overriding lordship.[13]

The full extent of the conflict that would be caused by differing interpretations of overlordship was not apparent at the coronation, a hopeful and joyful occasion. At the heart of the celebrations was King Alexander of Scotland, whose generous gift-giving helped define the carefree, party mood. But the Scottish king's presence may have only served to underline the absence of another of the greatest men in Britain: Llywelyn. The Welsh prince had been formally invited, and we have his letter of reply and polite refusal.[14] Given the problems he had experienced in 1270–4, it would seem that Edward's return can only have benefited Llywelyn and that the prince would have been well advised to perform homage and to re-establish cordial personal relationships with the king at the earliest possible opportunity. In 1273 he had refused to travel to the border to offer his fealty to the new king via messengers of the regency government, and his subsequent refusal to come to the coronation must be judged a tactical mistake, even though it can be plausibly suggested that Llywelyn's relations with his marcher rivals were now so bad that his life would have been in danger if he crossed the border.

A question of cash

In the months after the coronation, there are ambiguities in Edward's treatment of Llywelyn and, as discussed below, it is possible that he was aware of many of the weaknesses in the prince's position and sought ways to exploit them. However, he also repeatedly urged that the Treaty of Montgomery should be respected, and one reason for seeing this desire as genuine is the king's urgent need for cash. Despite the efforts of the hugely capable Burnell in the king's absence, Edward had returned from crusade with enormous debts, including an estimated £22,500 owed to the Italian bankers known as the Riccardi of Lucca. Llywelyn should have been paying the crown £2,000 a year, but he had problems finding the cash from as early as 1270, and payments stopped altogether in 1272. According to the prince, he was withholding payment because of breaches of the treaty and he had all he owed ready to be given to the crown when his grievances were addressed.

A generous assessment of Llywelyn's income at its absolute peak in the 1260s would be about £6,000 a year, but that level was unsustainable over the long term. Even if this income could be maintained, the Montgomery commitments would have taken a third of it, while Llywelyn was also required to outlay huge sums for his ongoing clashes with the marchers; in 1273–4 Dolforwyn alone required expenditure of £174, and there would be ongoing costs associated with garrisoning.[15] Given this, Dr Marc Morris says that Llywelyn's claim in 1274 that he was ready to clear the back-payments he owed the crown and meet future treaty commitments was 'ludicrous'.[16] David Stephenson, though, warns against the assumption that Llywelyn was not able to meet his fiscal obligations from Montgomery: 'In the five years after the Treaty of Montgomery, Llywelyn paid over [£10,000], or half of the total debt. When payments did cease, at the end of 1272, it is noteworthy that the prince showed few signs of financial exhaustion.'[17] In support of this, Stephenson cites Llywelyn's own statements and his promises of extra payment in return for peace, the rumours that he was planning another new castle near Clun, and the fact that after 1274 his territory and resources were significantly increased when he secured the lands of Dafydd and Gruffudd ap Gwenwynwyn (see below). The definitive analysis of Llywelyn's fiscal situation comes from Professor Beverley Smith;[18] the huge sum of £7,333 had been paid by the end of 1269, but the 1270 payment was first delayed, then made in instalments. The prince's situation was not helped by the poor harvests of 1270 and 1271, and the part-payments and excuses continued to late 1273, with no mention made of the king's failure to uphold the treaty; it was only in February 1274 that Llywelyn claimed his failure to pay was a matter of principle.

It was also in this period that Llywelyn's relationship with one of his most important churchmen, Bishop Anian of St Asaph, collapsed. He had been elected under Llywelyn's watch in 1268, but the bishop – who carried a lot of influence at Canterbury – felt so strongly about what he saw as harsh exactions from the prince that he wrote to Pope Gregory X with a list of serious complaints. The abbots of the Cistercian houses of Wales felt compelled to write their own joint letter to Gregory in defence of Llywelyn, but the complaints from the community of Gwynedd that would later be made against Llywelyn's exacting rule need also to be considered.[19] The fiscal demands made by the prince eroded the support base he enjoyed from even his heartlands and from the most trusted ministerial families in Gwynedd, suggesting that the financial promises he had made to the crown at Montgomery were unsustainable. As pointed out by Sir Goronwy Edwards, by both refusing to do homage to the king and failing to pay the money he owed him, Llywelyn had shattered the 'legal cornerstone' on which the entire Treaty of Montgomery was constructed.[20]

Edward's finances

While Edward was undoubtedly keen to secure the money owed by Llywelyn under his treaty obligations, he was also taking practical steps that offered a far more realistic chance of putting his finances on an even keel. He looked to build on his trusted relationship with the Riccardi of Lucca to establish a reliable source of credit, which was achieved by targeting the successful, booming wool trade. A customs duty worth an estimated £11,000 a year was imposed, but the real innovation came when the king handed control of the trade to the Riccardi. The agreement was that they would supply the king with a ready source of credit on demand, their security for the loans coming from the guaranteed income from the wool custom, from which they took a healthy profit.[21] According to Professor Michael Prestwich: 'Had Edward's credit with the Italian merchants in these years not been good, his success in Wales would have been impossible.'[22] The benefits the bankers would get from the relationship are far more questionable; in 1294 Edward's debt to them has been reckoned at £392,000, but their inability to retrieve £66,666 he had entrusted to their care led to their arrest.[23]

Even with this new, flexible system of finance in place, Edward needed a way to clear his huge existing debts, and the only way of achieving this was with a common tax. To secure permission for this, Edward would show the lessons he had learnt from the mistakes of his father's reign, and from the successes of his old rival, Simon de Montfort. The earl's baronial party had won widespread support from the knights of the shire, the very men whose votes were needed to secure a tax from parliament. On his return to England, Edward had almost immediately set in motion measures that harked back to the policies of de Montfort's day and that would be seen by the knights of the shire as reform. This helped to build popular support for the king, who also benefited from the lustre of crusading glory, but the crucial factor in securing the new tax was further anti-Jewish legislation that banned them from money lending. This played the key part in winning the support of the knights of the shire, who approved a new tax that raised £80,000 for the king's coffers: enough to clear his debts and to leave him comfortably in credit as he planned his next policies.

A failed assassination

Ongoing conflict with the marchers and fiscal demands were already major headaches for Llywelyn, but his problems were about to get a lot worse, and a lot closer to home. In April 1274 he had uncovered a plot against him involving Gruffudd ap Gwenwynwyn, the lord of southern Powys. The prince's response had been measured as he took land from Gruffudd and claimed his son Owain as a hostage, but things changed in November when Llywelyn began to learn from Owain the full extent of the conspiracy that had been made against him:

> Llywelyn ap Gruffudd sent messengers to Gruffudd ap Gwenwynwyn, to the castle of Welshpool. And he welcomed them, so it appeared, and invited them to their meat to the castle. And that night he had them served unstintingly with food and drink. And forthwith he went from the castle to Shrewsbury, and he bade the garrison imprison the prince's messengers. And when Llywelyn heard of that, he gathered the host of all Wales to lay siege to the castle. And he took the castle and released his messengers from the prison, and he burned the castle and subdued all the territory of Gruffudd ap Gwenwynwyn without opposition to him, and placed officers of his own in every place in the territory.[24]

Gruffudd had been aiming for the independence of Powys, a move that would have been facilitated by the assassination of Llywelyn. Even more seriously, the prince discovered that the real leader of the conspiracy was not Gruffudd but Llywelyn's brother and likely heir, Dafydd. Both conspirators fled to England to escape Llywelyn's wrath, the prince seizing their lands. They found shelter in Shropshire, from where they launched raids into southern Powys, selling their booty at the markets of Montgomery and Shrewsbury; as another letter of Llywelyn's to Edward makes clear, a further, serious barrier had been placed in the way of an agreement between prince and king:

> Letter, informing the king that, after the return of Llywelyn's messengers after the recent parliament in London ended, the men of Gruffudd ap Gwenwynwyn, who are maintained and harboured in the courts of Shropshire and whose trespasses are publicly defended, seized six lots of booty from Llywelyn's lands of Swydd Ystrad Marchell, Swydd Llanerch Hudol, Swydd Eginlle, Cydewain and Arwystli and sold one part of it in

broad daylight at Shrewsbury and Montgomery, and slaughtered and ate the other part, to the great damage and dishonour of Llywelyn and his men; another day they publicly decapitated one of his faithful men and took four horses from him to Montgomery. Since the piling of damages upon damages by such men is harmful to peace and the country, and the receiving of such men in the king's lands, though the king's men may in part be innocent, is in breach of the peace as much as if the king's men had committed such misdeeds. Llywelyn humbly asks the king to give consideration to this matter and write to the sheriff of Shropshire to arrest the said malefactors, whose names Llywelyn will supply, and compel them to make amends for their trespassers and to desist from any more in future, but the prince's men, who suffer daily injuries from them, suffer continuing trouble without amends. Asks the king to send his reply by the bearer of the present letter.[25]

Chances to perform homage

The coronation in August 1274 was far from the final opportunity that Llywelyn had to perform homage to Edward, but his apparent refusal to submit needs to be considered in the context of ongoing border conflict with the marchers, the plot to assassinate the prince and the king's awareness of the serious reversal of Llywelyn's fortunes.

The most opportune time for the prince to have submitted would appear to have been at Shrewsbury at the end of 1274, a convenient location for Llywelyn that lay close to his borders. However, Professor Beverley Smith points out that the invite to the prince was anything but straightforward.[26] The date was originally set for 2 December, with Llywelyn given just a month's notice, but the meeting was then brought forward to 25 November. The indications are that the prince planned to attend, but Edward's movements suggest nothing of the sort as he was heading away from Shrewsbury, moving from Northampton to Fotheringhay (18–21 November), then on to King's Cliffe. It was from there on 22 November that a letter was sent to Llywelyn to inform him that the king could not attend because he had suffered an abscess. Such a medical excuse cannot be proved or disproved, but there must be at least a possibility that Edward was keen to further exploit Llywelyn's discomfiture following the plot against his life.

The last realistic possibility that Llywelyn would submit to the king came in the summer of 1275; on 24 June Edward summoned the prince to Chester, where he was to perform his homage and fealty on 22 August. The king based himself at Chester until 11 September, with Llywelyn maintaining a correspondence with him from just 12 miles away at Treuddyn. Included in the prince's messages was the claim that it was unsafe for him to cross the border where his enemies were being sheltered, and that he feared for his life. Close by was the ford of Gresford, a traditional border crossing between England and Wales that could be compared to Rhyd Chwima and that would be a suitable location for a diplomatic meeting between the leaders of England and Wales. The Welsh chronicle suggests that the prince's refusal to go to Chester was made in consultation with his barons and leading men from all Wales but, with the benefit of hindsight, it must be judged to have been a major mistake. The chronicle's conclusion on the event is particularly ominous when read alongside its following entry: 'The king in rage returned back to England. And the prince came back. That year the earth quaked in Wales.'[27]

If Llywelyn felt that a border ford was a suitable meeting place for the leaders of England and Wales, Edward clearly believed that he had made more than enough of a concession in travelling to Chester. He wrote to the Pope that: 'In order to receive [Llywelyn's] homage and fealty we had so demeaned our royal dignity as to go to the confines of his land.'[28] The king ordered Llywelyn to appear at Westminster within the month, but he can have had little hope that the prince would show and any measure of personal understanding between the two was now at an end. No hope of reconciliation would have been found in the prince's reply, as reported by a Westminster chronicler: 'He would not come, saying he remembered the death of his father, Gruffudd, who fell from the Tower of London, and broke his neck, and died.'[29]

A provocative engagement

Edward was still writing to his officials in the march urging that they do their utmost to maintain the peace, but Llywelyn's next move raised the growing antagonism between the two men to new levels. Soon after the uncovering of the plot on his life, the prince had begun to put into place secret plans to marry Edward's cousin Eleanor, who was – more significantly – the daughter of the king's old enemy, Simon de Montfort. It is possible that this coupling had originally been planned a decade earlier, before the battle of Evesham. Reviving the marriage plans now could be seen as a deliberate, spiteful strike at the king, or as an attempt to revive any remaining de Montfort support base in England. Perhaps there was a measure of both of these things, but the overriding reason is likely to have been Llywelyn's dynastic position. The prince was a bachelor in his fifties and without any known children; this state of affairs may have even been deliberately agreed upon to ensure the support of Dafydd in return for the latter's recognition as heir to Gwynedd. But the discovery of Dafydd's treachery in late 1274 would have ended any such agreement and left Llywelyn in urgent need of a high-status bride, capable of providing him with a son.

Unsurprisingly, given his history with the de Montforts, Edward had ordered his intelligence network to keep a close eye on the family's activities on the continent. It seems certain that the king knew all about Llywelyn's plans to marry his cousin, something that can hardly have helped the already tense relationship between the two. Eleanor, accompanied by her clerical sibling Amaury, set out from France for Wales towards the end of 1275, but their ship was intercepted close to the Isles of Scilly by sailors from Bristol, and brother and sister were taken to be imprisoned in Windsor. Even before Eleanor's ship had sailed, though, solemn pledges between her and Llywelyn meant that their marriage already was, in the eyes of the church, signed and sealed; according to the Welsh chronicle, 'Eleanor the prince had married through words uttered by proxy'.[30] Added to the list of the prince's grievances against Edward was now the fact that the king was holding his wife captive.[31]

The descent into war

From this point on, any restraints Edward had placed on attacks along the borders were removed as from early 1276 he began furnishing material aid to Dafydd and Gruffudd, as well as encouraging marcher assaults on Llywelyn. Most activity again took place in the middle march, where the prince himself was active. Bogo de Knovill wrote to the king requesting help, indicating that Montgomery and the rest of the middle march was being harried 'night and day' by Welsh forces in great strength:

> If the king thinks to send certain crossbowmen or others, ten or twelve to Montgomery and as many to [Oswestry], and with [them] the neighbourhood will defend itself well until the king ordains otherwise, provided that the prince himself does not come with his power. Informs the king that … the king's people and his men cannot defend themselves at all … that there are sufficient good men if they had a little help from the mounted men.[32]

The local forces rallied from the campaign bases at the castles of Oswestry and Montgomery, the king's engineer Master Bertram having been sent to help improve the fortifications at the latter. On 5 February 1277 Edward would write to thank the local commanders for their 'spontaneous and gracious' service, an indication that their campaigns had not been paid for from the royal purse.[33]

Llywelyn, meanwhile, did not simply blunder over-confidently into a war he would have little chance of winning, but approached the Pope and the archbishop of Canterbury, Robert Kilwardby, to ask for intercession. He concentrated his arguments on the treacherous plot that had targeted his life, made concessions in his argument with Anian of St Asaph, showed himself willing to listen to the king's messengers in December, January and February, and suggested he was ready to make payments to the king in return for peace. But any overtures towards a peaceful settlement that were made by the prince were accompanied by the same earnest, naïve insistence on the redress of all his grievances – now including the release of his wife – before he would perform homage. In the words of the Welsh chronicle, 'Llywelyn frequently sent messengers to the king's court to seek to arrange peace between them, but he did not succeed at all.'[34]

The church's attempts to negotiate peace may have delayed the full English onslaught on Wales for as much as a year but on 12 November 1276 Llywelyn was declared 'a rebel and a disturber of the peace', and plans began to be set in motion for military action. In February the proud prince turned the archbishop's envoys away from his court, an act that led to his excommunication being pronounced by Bishop Anian of Bangor – a former supporter of Llywelyn, who immediately had to flee from Arfon into exile in England. By this point in time, the military forces moving against the prince were already well in motion.

Chapter 7

1277: The War of Domination

By the time of Llywelyn's excommunication, Edward had headed west to Worcester to orchestrate the first movements of the war, taking his extensive household with him. From the military element of the household, about forty knights and seventy esquires were immediately tasked with planning the initial stages of the campaign.[1] As well as these military professionals, the king put some of his closest associates to work. In the middle march, Roger Mortimer was placed in charge from Montgomery, where he would be assisted by his neighbour, Roger Clifford, the crusade veterans Otto de Grandson and John de Vescy, and the less experienced Henry de Lacy, earl of Lincoln. Another crusader, Payn de Chaworth, had been harassing the Welsh from Kidwelly since the spring of 1276 and he was now placed in charge of military operations in the south of the country. The northern theatre was entrusted to a royalist stalwart from the de Montfort wars, William de Beauchamp, earl of Warwick.

Brycheiniog and Ystrad Tywi

Before any serious effort was made against the heart of Llywelyn's power in Gwynedd, his authority was stripped away in all the outlying territories he counted as part of his principality. Between February and March household forces operating from Abergavenny in support of the local lords Humphrey de Bohun and John Giffard ended Llywelyn's rule in Brycheiniog. Towards the end of this operation they targeted a new stone castle that had been built by Llywelyn at Rhyd-y-briw, near Sennybridge.[2] This fortification appears designed to stop the movement of troops through the watershed uplands between the Usk and Tywi, the route between Brycheiniog and Ystrad Tywi.

Breaching these defences allowed the army from Brecon to link up with the successful advance that Payn de Chaworth had made from Carmarthen in the west, up the Tywi valley. This was the first major military activity that marcher troops had made in the area since their disaster at Cymerau in 1257, although in the meantime they had consolidated their positions, as most clearly seen with the construction work at the castles of Kidwelly, Llansteffan and Laugharne. Again household troops and other forces paid through the Wardrobe were crucial to the advance, the power of the invading army sufficient to protect the numerous Welsh lords willing to desert Llywelyn and take the king's side. Rhys ap Maredudd of Dryslwyn – the son of Maredudd ap Rhys Gryg – readily submitted in the middle of March, along with Gruffudd ap Maredudd of Ceredigion, the son of Llywelyn's old ally, Maredudd ab Owain. Rhys Wyndod, the lord of Dinefwr and son of Maredudd's old rival Rhys Fychan, proved somewhat more loyal to the prince, but his isolation also led to his submission and by 16 May most of Deheubarth was secured, although resistance continued in parts of Ceredigion. Five of the most important native Welsh lords of Deheubarth – Rhys ap Maredudd, Rhys Wyndod, Rhys Fychan ap Rhys ap Maelgwn, plus the brothers Gruffudd and Cynan ap Maredudd – travelled to the king's court and performed homage to Edward on 1 July.

The collapse of resistance in Ystrad Tywi allowed the release of the force from Brecon, which headed into Elfael; by 3 May the rebuilding of the castle at Builth was under way. This was the first new royal castle that Edward would build in Wales, the stone construction placed on top of the existing motte with its commanding views of the river Wye. It was, perhaps, the extent of the existing earthworks at the site that determined this castle would be a very traditional design, with its heart being a donjon atop an elevated mound; removing these earthworks to begin a new concentric fortification may have been prohibitively expensive. Government records over the next five years show expenditure of £1,650[3] – an impressive sum, but it would be dwarfed by the outlay on Edward's other castles. Nothing remains of the stone work, but at its heart was a great round keep, protected by a small chemise curtain wall, containing six towers. A twin-towered gatehouse guarded the entrance to the keep from the bailey, which was protected by its own curtain wall. After 1277 moves were also made to ensure the fortification was less isolated, with 120 axemen employed to cut roads in the woods between Builth and the Mortimer castle of Cefnllys. Edward's investment was well rewarded, as this key strategic fortification would never again fall to the Welsh.

The successful army from Brecon – which included many of the Welsh lords whose loyalty to Llywelyn had been in question in the early 1270s and whose sons the prince had taken as hostages – would continue its march north towards Dolforwyn, and would be in action in Gwynedd later in the year.

The middle march

The most intense fighting, and the area where Llywelyn had directed the bulk of his troops, was on the familiar battlegrounds of the middle march. The early commitment that Edward made to the conflicts in this area would prove crucial to the advance of his cause, with fifty cavalry arriving, including the highly capable captain Otto de Grandson. Roger Mortimer's command was further boosted by a hundred cavalry under Henry de Lacy, plus a large infantry force from Shropshire and Herefordshire. These troops were paid from the royal coffers, meaning that they would be available for as long as necessary; this would prove to be a period of four months.

The initial target was Llywelyn's prized new castle of Dolforwyn and it took several weeks of bitter slogging for Mortimer to advance the short distance from Montgomery to its perimeters. The fortification's main strength came from the fact that it was built on top of a steep, inaccessible hill-top, the approaches further impeded by (rather inadequate) rock-cut ditches at either end of the ridge. The castle itself was rather simple and, by the standards of contemporary defensive fortification, outdated, with long, rectangular curtain walls occupying the ridge line. A large, oblong keep stood at the front of the castle, with a round tower at the opposite end, and a solitary apsidal tower jutted out from the curtain wall. The gateways were rather weak and susceptible to undermining, the entire design reflecting the apparent recognition by the builder that he would never invest his hopes in a castle garrison being able to resist a lengthy siege.

Mortimer's forces came well prepared for a difficult siege, though, bringing with them the king's veteran engineer, Master Bertram.[4] Having served Edward in Gascony in the 1240s, he had earned his trust over a long career that may have included the crusade, and had been well rewarded in wages, robes and other signs of royal favour. Master Bertram had a particular expertise in siege engines, and in London in April 1276 he had set to work on the new weapons that would be put to use in the Welsh war. In early March 1277 he left the capital for the six-day journey to Montgomery, accompanied by the household officer Henry de Greneford, plus carpenters, crossbowmen and miners. At least three engines were brought to Dolforwyn, and a letter sent from de Lacy to the king on 3 April indicates that they did significant damage to Llywelyn's new castle in the course of a single day:

> The sender reports that they laid siege to the castle of Dolforwyn on the Wednesday in Easter week [31 March 1277]. Next day the garrison gave eight hostages, the best after the constable, as a guarantee that they will surrender the castle on the Thursday after the close of Easter [8 April 1277] unless they are relieved by Llywelyn, and if they are relieved, the hostages are to be returned to them. The writer has given a safe conduct to the garrison's messenger to Llywelyn, as he wishes Llywelyn to know that he is awaiting his coming. Informs the king that when his castle comes into his hands it will need much repair, wherefore there will be need of some man who will take these matters in hand, and will loyally employ the king's money. For if the sender details Master Bertram for

the work, he fears that Master Bertram will devise too many things, and perhaps the king's money will not be so well employed as it needs to be.[5]

A later letter from Mortimer to the king indicates that the agreement with the garrison was honoured, meaning that there had been just one day's fighting outside the castle walls; the real combat had taken place in the weeks of contested advance along the 6 miles from Montgomery as Dolforwyn was isolated:

> Announces that [on 8 April 1277] the castle of Dolforwyn was surrendered with all the goods of Llywelyn that were within it. Mortimer has put in occupation Gruffudd ap Gwenwynwyn, who has undertaken to guard it at his cost, except that Mortimer has placed there ten dismounted crossbowmen at the king's cost and a party of miners to dig out the rock and enlarge the fosses.[6]

Even in such triumphant missives, the awareness of the high fiscal cost of war rings out, Mortimer at pains to point out that it would have cost the king £666 a year to garrison Dolforwyn himself, and noting that he has left 'three good siege engines' outside the castle walls. In the bigger picture, the fall of Llywelyn's flagship castle was symbolic of the collapse of Welsh resistance in the middle march as a whole, and by the middle of May Mortimer was able to tell the king that the entire theatre was under his control.

Ceredigion

The campaigns in the south-west in early 1277 had done much to destroy the resistance of Deheubarth, but trouble continued in Ceredigion, something that may have played a large part in the decision to build a new royal castle at Aberystwyth.[7] When the main feudal muster of England was gathered at Worcester in early July, about 200 of the 1,000-strong cavalry force was split off and sent to Carmarthen under the leadership of the king's brother Edmund, the largest landholder in south Wales. He joined up with de Chaworth for an advance that left Carmarthen sometime after 10 July and reached Aberystwyth by 25 July, ready to start the building work.

We know of two earlier castles that were constructed in the vicinity, but a new sea-front location was chosen for the fortification, on a low headland protected by a sandbank to the north and a marsh to the east.[8] Much rebuilding work was needed after 1282, but this was laid out as a concentric fortification, built in an unusual diamond shape to suit the contours of the headland. Powerful gatehouses or towers were placed at each point on the diamond to offer formidable, projecting firepower, supported by the inner ring of defences. Of most importance was the castle's access to the Irish Sea, a fact that meant supplies could be delivered to a garrison even when it was closely besieged by land. Sea access was also of great help in the initial construction, with building supplies and manpower brought in from England's great south-western port, Bristol.

Through surrender and confiscation, royal control was secured over almost all of northern Ceredigion, from the river Aeron to the Dyfi. Such wholescale losses, secured by the new castle, caused further disquiet to the native Welsh of the region. The Ceredigion noble Rhys Fychan ap Rhys ap Maelgwn had done homage to the king on 1 July, but now chose to flee to join Llywelyn, along with the fighting men of the region of Genau'r Glyn (north of Aberystwyth). In Gwynedd he joined other noble exiles from Deheubarth, including Hywel ap Rhys Gryg and Rhys Wyndod's brother Llywelyn ap Rhys, but the overall picture in the south was one of submission to Edward.

Powys

Gruffudd ap Gwenwynwyn was able to reclaim most of his lordship of southern Powys (Powys Wenwynwyn) as part of Mortimer's successful campaign in the middle march, but the situation in northern Powys (Powys Fadog) was more complicated. This was a result of the death of Gruffudd ap Madog in 1269 and the subsequent rivalry between his four sons, Madog, Llywelyn, Owain and Gruffudd Fychan. Prince Llywelyn had helped Madog secure the main share of the patrimony, in line with his own interpretation of Welsh custom and the sole inheritance of leadership within a lordship, but the existence of rival claims would again prove fertile ground for Edward to exploit.

From his base in Chester, in the spring William de Beauchamp steadily built the pressure on Madog, and the earl of Warwick was soon joined by Dafydd and by a range of disaffected Powys nobles. These included one of the first Welsh lords to defect to the king, Llywelyn ap Gruffudd Fychan;[9] his switch of allegiance on 26 December 1276 had been conditional on Edward retaining his homage even if the king was later reconciled with Prince Llywelyn. Dafydd had command of his household troop (perhaps his traditional *teulu*) and 200 footsoldiers, all of whom were in the king's pay.[10] Perhaps predictably, Prince Llywelyn's brother was already bucking under the leadership of Edward's officers, refusing to hand them the king's share of the booty and insisting that his own regal rights meant he should keep it all. This was one of the issues outlined in a letter of 4 April 1277 sent by the royal clerk Ralph de Basages to Edward, although the main cause of Dafydd's discontent was wages:

> Dafydd ap Gruffudd demanded of the messenger, and still continues to demand, that payment of wages be made to his two horsemen and all his footmen, as to other knights and footmen. And the Earl of Warwick,

who was greatly disturbed on this account, fearing lest Dafydd might withdraw from the king's service with his men unless he was satisfied, ordered the writer to pay the men of the aforesaid Dafydd.[11]

Despite such problems in the king's ranks, in early April Madog ap Gruffudd chose to submit rather than be disinherited in favour of his brother Llywelyn; even so, his lordship was brutally partitioned and he lost his most important castle, Dinas Brân. Resistance continued from the lofty and impressive fortification above Llangollen, the castle most probably having been garrisoned by Prince Llywelyn's men from Gwynedd. Henry de Lacy moved up from the middle march to join the fray and on 10 May – as he prepared for an attack on Dinas Brân – the garrison set fire to the castle and departed.[12] The fortification would be repaired and retained for use by the king and, with the key to the remaining defence of northern Powys now lost, Gwynedd was left as the last bastion of Welsh resistance.

The advance on north Wales

With his outlying defences having evaporated, all that was left to Llywelyn was his Gwynedd heartland, and Edward had been preparing for the challenges of assaulting this natural citadel. The king had learnt from his father's botched expedition of 1257 and, after leaving Worcester at the beginning of the year, he had been busy organising supplies. The scale was enormous and the attention to detail intense, including the purchase of warhorses from France, the requisitioning of carts to transport the tents that would be used by his troops and the order of 200,000 crossbow bolts from the important production centre at St Briavel's Castle in the Forest of Dean. The significance of this work was emphasised by the historian Ifor Rowlands:

> [Success in Wales was won] not by brilliant feats of generalship or decisive battles but by the efficient garnering and intelligent deployment of resources. Welsh resistance was ground down by the patient amassing of men and material: in one sense, Welsh independence did not as much perish in a clash of arms as suffocate in a welter of parchment. The humdrum, unspectacular but vitally essential work was done as much by Edward's administrators as by his soldiers.[13]

On 3 July the king was back at Worcester to lead the military muster of his kingdom. The forty-day limit on feudal service would have been a factor in the delay in calling out the full muster until the summer campaign season, as well as the logistical planning that was needed to prepare for the management of a large force. As has been seen, the first half of 1277 had been used productively by Edward, his household and his marcher supporters, the victories in that period meaning that the best use could now be made of the feudal host during its compulsory six-week service. A cavalry force of about 1,000 men gathered at Worcester, from where 200 were directed to south Wales. The other 800 were sent to Chester, where they met the king on 15 July, arriving at about the same time as the fleet. This included eighteen ships from the Cinque Ports, there to perform their compulsory fourteen-day feudal service, plus other ships hired from as far away as Gascony; the fleet of thirty-five boats has been estimated to have been manned by around 700 sailors.[14] Already in the city was a force of 3,000 footsoldiers, including an elite force of 100 Macclesfield archers paid at an inflated 3 pence a day, plus 270 prized Gascon crossbowmen (twenty of them mounted) under Imbert de Monte Regali. The overall numbers were, though, somewhat short of what Edward desired, and the size of the infantry host would continue to grow.

If the infantry force was a disappointment to the king, he was more annoyed by the supply situation he found in the ancient port city. Officials in Cheshire had been commandeering corn since January and in February grain was ordered from Ireland, but now demands were sent out to nine English counties for more grain. This may have upset Edward's carefully laid plans for making the most of the compulsory feudal service period, but after a week at Chester the king was ready to begin his advance into north-east Wales.

As he prepared to counter this English juggernaut, Llywelyn is unlikely to have been able to call on more than about 500 troops that the English would identify as cavalry, and their equipment would have been generally inferior to that of their opponents. However, infantry numbers may have been significant and the distinction between 'mounted infantry' and cavalrymen unclear; in the difficult terrain, mobility and flexibility were more important than heavily armed knights. But the Welsh forces were massively outgunned and outnumbered, meaning that pitched battle was never an option and that Llywelyn would rely on hit-and-run, guerrilla tactics. In a war of manoeuvre, the prince was further handicapped by the fact that he had no fleet to challenge Edward's control of the north Wales coastline. He was, though, determined to make Edward's advance as problematic as possible, and along every invasion route the king would find broken bridges, ploughed-up fields and fords with dangerous holes dug in the middle of them.[15] Aware of such challenges from past, bitter experience, Edward would show himself at his cautious best as a commander.

The rock of Flint

Edward's cautious approach to war was revealed in the limited initial target he set for the campaign; moving from Chester, crossing the Dee and following the river to the north-west, the king had travelled barely 13 miles when he halted the army for a month at a spur of rock on the river estuary, the site of what would soon become Flint Castle. Since June the king had been recruiting huge numbers of carpenters, masons and labourers, and around 1,850 of them were set to work on the new fortification; over half the number were diggers, initially employed to make ditches and ramparts to protect the army. In the interest of speed, the initial construction was in wood and a huge naval operation from Chester provided the timber that was needed. But Edward was determined to secure the English hold on Tegeingl, and over time the timber would be replaced by a mighty stone castle. A powerful fortification with easy access to the sea and the nearby port of Chester, this would be a secure stepping-off point for any future English expedition into north Wales. The permanent nature of the plans may have caused further disquiet in the ranks from Edward's ally, Dafydd. Once again, Dafydd's motives are hard to work out, but it is possible that he was dissatisfied with the royal plans to retain the Perfeddwlad.

Edward's patience at this stage of the war is revealed by the fact that he left the front line for much of the first half of August, touring areas such as the Wirral and the Mersey estuary where his demands for supplies had been intense. By 8 August he was at Northwich in eastern Cheshire, where he chose to initiate a long-held ambition to found a new Cistercian abbey. The grandiose plans for Vale Royal – designed to be the largest abbey of its kind in Britain – were remarkable given the ongoing war, a sign of the king's confidence and trust in his resources and realm. There may have been a propaganda element, too, in indulging in a major act of religious patronage at the time of conflict; the fact that the Cistercian houses in Wales were such loyal supporters of the princes of Gwynedd may have added another dimension to the king's plans.

The month-long stay at Flint meant that the Cinque Port fleet now had to be paid, but Edward's finances were more than ready for this, the king also increasing the wages of the workmen and hiring increasing numbers to join their ranks. The sailors of the fleet had been authorised to plunder any Welsh who had not come into the king's peace, suggesting that the entire coastline of north Wales, and its river valleys, was open to surprise raids. In addition, Edward was already preparing for the next stage of his advance, which would mean penetrating the deep forests of Tegeingl, territory ripe with opportunity for Welsh ambushes. While the masons and carpenters continued their work at Flint, some of the labourers were detached under a protective shield of knights and crossbowmen to make a broad road along which the army could safely advance. The scale of this effort is suggested by evidence from later in Edward's reign in England where, in a response to law and order problems, the king would order road-widening schemes where he would insist that paths 400ft wide should be cleared; this is four times the width of a three-lane motorway.[16] After the 1283 campaign, a Welsh lord would be given the daunting order to cut passes 'a bowshot wide' all the way from Montgomery to Aberystwyth.[17] The scale of the challenge in 1277, and Edward's success in meeting it, was described by the chronicler Thomas Wykes:

> Between Chester and Llywelyn's country lay a forest of such denseness and extent that the royal army could by no means penetrate through without danger. A large part of this forest being cut down, the king opened out for himself a very broad road for advance into the prince's land, and having occupied it by strong attacks, he entered through it in triumph.[18]

The advance to Rhuddlan

On 23 August the army of the north began to move forward. This was on the same day that Edward had announced his campaign aims: to replace Llywelyn with his brothers Dafydd and Owain, who would be required to attend the king's court at Westminster, and who must be prepared to tolerate a major royal territorial presence in north Wales, a presence that would be anchored by the new castles and accompanying arms of administration. West of the Conwy, the king declared that he was weighing up two potential options: either to divide all the territory between himself, Owain and Dafydd, or else to retain Anglesey for himself while dividing Snowdonia between Owain and Dafydd. It is possible, though, that Edward's first-hand experience of the difficulties in handling Dafydd was the reason that the king would later alter his campaign aims.

While there are some suggestions of heavy fighting in the first week of the advance, the road-clearing work meant that, within a single day, the king's forces had made the twenty-mile journey across the breadth of Tegeingl to Rhuddlan, on the eastern bank of the Clwyd. Rhuddlan was chosen as the site of Edward's next new, formidable, concentric castle, an anchor point in western Tegeingl to complement Flint in the east, and a fortification that would serve as another secure stepping-off point for any future campaigns that may be needed beyond the Clwyd and deeper into north-west Wales. Again Edward was concerned that his new castle, positioned on the closest fordable spot to the sea on the marshy Clwyd estuary, should have easy access to the water, allowing supplies to be brought in should the walls ever come under siege from the Welsh; this was the reason why the site of Rhuddlan was chosen ahead of Henry III's old fortification at Diserth, which lay a little inland, 2½ miles to the east.

From the Clwyd to the Conwy

While major building work continued at Rhuddlan, Edward would not tarry here as he had at Flint; with his troop surge now bringing his infantry strength up to 15,640, the king had the numbers to spare to both protect his workers and drive across the Clwyd, while the strain on his finances would have encouraged positive action. The majority of these footsoldiers – an estimated 9,000 – were Welshmen, drawn both from marcher lands and territories that had recently been regarded as part of Llywelyn's principality.[19] One of the most prominent of the commanders of these Welsh troops was Hywel ap Meurig, a long-term adherent of Mortimer, who led large numbers of native infantry from the reconquered lands of Brycheiniog, Radnor, Builth, Elfael and Maelienydd.

The value Edward gained from these huge numbers of footsoldiers – recruited on a scale that was unprecedented in the history of warfare in medieval Britain – has been questioned by historians as eminent as Professor Michael Prestwich, who pointed to the logistical problems, the evidently poor quality of some of the troops and the belief that more value may have been gained by employing lightly armed cavalry, able to make swift, sweeping raids into Welsh territory.[20] But a small raiding party sent forward into unfamiliar, hostile ground would surely have played into Welsh hands, allowing them to fight in their territory, on their terms, against a force of manageable size. Edward clearly felt that the huge numbers of troops he employed were needed and their impact proved decisive, even if the campaign was unspectacular. By having an overwhelming number of boots on the ground, the king was able to make a comprehensive sweep of the hostile countryside, rooting out any Welsh hiding places and making small-scale resistance futile. At the same time he was able to protect the main body of his army and the ongoing work at his new castles, which would secure the land long after the mighty army had departed and dispersed. The effectiveness of overwhelming numbers of infantry could be questioned in later wars in Scotland and on the continent, but within the territorially restricted confines of Wales – and against an enemy who could never match such a mass of manpower – Edward's tactics proved irresistible.

Even so, an investment on such a scale would prove costly in both human and fiscal terms. From Rhuddlan, Edward despatched troops south towards Ruthin, his soldiers engaged in heavy and bitter fighting in the heart of the Perfeddwlad. Details of the conflict in this area are scarce, but Bishop Anian of St Asaph complained that Edward's forces desecrated churches and churchyards, committed rape and sacrilege, and damaged church property, including burning an episcopal manor.[21] Such behaviour resulted in a warning from Archbishop Kilwardby to the earl of Warwick that he should 'allow nothing that would not be seen in warfare in England'. At Ruthin, plans were put in place for another new royal castle; the decision not to continue with this fortification may have given Edward cause for regret five years later.[22]

While these forces campaigned south of Rhuddlan, Edward had moved west. By the end of August the king was at the ruins of Deganwy, where records indicate that the numbers of infantry in his army had dropped to around 7,500. A variety of reasons can be suggested for this, including campaign casualties, disease and desertion. All of these things are likely to have played a part, but Edward's supply lines and finances were being stretched, and he seems to have dismissed many of the infantry to relieve the burden on his resources and coffers. Certainly some of the cavalry were dismissed; they had now exceeded their forty days' feudal service and the assumption is that the king was unwilling to pay for extended service from them, or at least not for those he no longer wished to retain.[23] John Morris estimated that about 125 cavalry served for eighty days, taking them through to late October. Some of these men were paid for the second forty days of service, while others remained off the royal pay roll as they were household troops of the earls; included amongst the group claiming royal pay was a ninety-strong force under Reginald de Grey, who appear to have been paid for a contracted forty-two days dated from the end of the period of feudal service.[24]

If this was an indication of the challenges Edward was facing as he stared across the formidable barrier of the Conwy into deepest Gwynedd, it was also an indication of the limits he had set on the campaign. While the meticulous planning of the castles at Builth, Flint, Rhuddlan and Aberystwyth suggests the permanent nature of the king's intentions in these outlying domains, this was not a life or death struggle for the heartland of Gwynedd, and Edward would ultimately prove ready to consider a negotiated settlement that was comparable to the positions achieved in Wales by John (briefly) in 1211 and by Henry III in 1247. Moreover, Edward may by now have had serious doubts about the wisdom of replacing Llywelyn with Dafydd in the citadel of Snowdonia. But before any negotiations for peace took place, the king sought to strengthen his hand by plucking a ripe fruit that was easily within his grasp: the rich island of Anglesey.

The attack on Anglesey

If Edward had been reluctant to empty his coffers to pay to extend the service of his feudal cavalry host, he had no such reticence in paying to keep the fleet of the Cinque Ports for long beyond their obligatory fourteen-day period. In early September it was this fleet that was used to transport a force of

2,000 infantry and 200 cavalry, under the leadership of Otto de Grandson and John de Vescy, to Anglesey. There is no report of Welsh opposition, suggesting that Llywelyn was unable to resist a force of this size. This is despite the fact that the grievances of the community of Gwynedd produced in 1283 include the pressures of military demands in Dindaethwy, south-east Anglesey; Professor Beverley Smith says this may have resulted from the need to support a large garrison in this area in the wars of 1277 and 1282–3.[25] While the Welsh prince may have had the necessary troop numbers to challenge Edward's attack on the island, to expose such a major contingent of his forces on the open terrain of Anglesey would have invited an overwhelming military response from the king, a suicidal tactical option against an opponent with control of the sea. Llywelyn could do little more than watch from the mountains of Snowdonia as the English ships offloaded the army, followed by 360 men equipped with scythes, a workforce brought to the island to bring in the harvest; as winter approached, the produce of Anglesey – the 'mother of Wales' – would be denied to the prince's forces, and instead used to ease the supply problems facing the invading English army.

Defections in Gwynedd

Arguably even more troubling for Llywelyn than this crippling military blow was the defection of some of his key supporters from within the heartland of Gwynedd itself. The later complaints made by churchmen and by the community of the realm against the prince have been considered, but he was also losing support from the real props to his power, the great, landed ministerial families of Gwynedd. As discussed, such leading men had been receiving land grants on privileged terms since the time of Llywelyn ap Iorwerth. Llywelyn ap Gruffudd continued to give such grants, and his generosity as a ruler was praised by the poets; Llygad Gŵr described a 'man famed for honour, a man most free with wealth'.[26] But he could not maintain the level of land grants given by his grandfather, and over the decades the territories that had been received by the ministerial families were fragmented by the Welsh practice of partible inheritance, meaning that these leading men struggled to maintain their dignity.

It is also possible that the resource-hungry prince began to encroach on the privileges previously granted, claiming dues from land that had been granted free of them.[27] Furthermore, the ministers may have been alienated by Llywelyn's ambitious policies, and the calamities they had brought to Gwynedd; in such circumstances, the possibility of turning to the king of England as an alternative source of power and patronage may have been compelling. In the course of the thirteenth century members of the Welsh ministerial class had been to England on diplomatic missions, some had spent time there as hostages or captives, others had defected there, served the English king, taken his land and pensions, and married into the English nobility. According to Dr David Stephenson: 'Such a process of assimilation may have had as its consequence a decline in the significance of political frontiers towards England and her marcher satellites, and, correspondingly, a decline in the determination to maintain those frontiers by the class of Welshmen most affected.'[28]

The evidence from one leading man in particular is revealing, a person who shared the name of the prince: a Dominican friar from Bangor called Llywelyn ap Gruffudd. He had been one of the men sent by the prince to accompany Eleanor de Montfort on her 1275 journey from France and, as such, was privy to the Welsh leader's most intimate councils. Given his family background, this was unsurprising; the friar's father was Gruffudd ab Ednyfed, who was one of the prince's earliest adherents and who had served as his *distain*. Gruffudd ab Ednyfed's father was arguably the greatest of all the Gwynedd ministers, Ednyfed Fychan, the *distain* of Llywelyn ap Iorwerth. But Llywelyn ap Gruffudd ab Ednyfed defected to Edward's service at some time during the 1277 campaign in the middle march and then on 21 July – as the king closed in on Gwynedd itself – he was found to be assisting attempts to defect to the English by his brother Rhys, his first cousin Hywel ap Goronwy ab Ednyfed (who had also served as *distain* to the prince), plus Gruffudd ap Iorwerth, a member of a prominent Anglesey family.[29] Another of his brothers, Hywel ap Gruffudd ab Ednyfed, was also found in Edward's service during the 1277 campaign.

A letter sent by Bishop Anian of Bangor to Robert, the bishop of Bath and Wells, after the conclusion of the conflict gives further indication of the bitter civil splits created in Gwynedd: 'He [Anian] lost his brother, his sister's son, his cousin and kinsmen to the number of sixty in the king's service, and Llywelyn greatly rejoices at this misfortune. His tongue cannot suffice to tell his losses, the burnings of churches and the plundering of his property in this war.'[30] This valuable letter also gives a rare indication of the intensity of the 1277 conflict, both in regard to the number of casualties inflicted by Llywelyn's troops and in the fact that Edward's invading army had failed to respect the rights of the church.

The Treaty of Aberconwy

Having lost Anglesey and its harvest, and being unable to rely on the support of those closest to him, Llywelyn submitted; this was perhaps as early as 11 September, when we know that Edward had left Deganwy for Rhuddlan and there are signs that the English army was being disbanded.[31] By the middle of September the cavalry had been released, while infantry numbers had dropped to around 1,600. On 20 September permission was sent to the southern commander, Edmund, to return home, leaving Roger de Molis in command of the construction of Aberystwyth, while the king was happy to release those native lords of Deheubarth who had come to him to do homage for their lands. The Cinque Port ships were retained until the end of September, when they sailed for home.

Edward's reluctance to place Dafydd in power in Snowdonia may have influenced the king's decision not to press his invasion beyond the Conwy, and in the peace talks that followed it was again the position of Llywelyn's younger brother that was the chief obstacle to agreement. After protracted negotiations, the Treaty of Aberconwy – set out on 9 November 1277 in the shadow of the church that housed the remains of Llywelyn's ancestors – stripped away almost all the gains that Llywelyn had made in his years of ascendancy, leaving the achievements that had been acknowledged in the 1267 Treaty of Montgomery as nothing but a distant memory.

In the crucial matter of the patrimony of Gwynedd, Llywelyn was said to be holding a portion of Dafydd's patrimony west of the Conwy. When Llywelyn died, even if he had an heir, that portion would revert to Dafydd; its temporary retention by the prince was noted as a concession made by Edward to Llywelyn. The prince also had to agree that the same principle applied with regard to the rights of his youngest brother Rhodri to a share of the patrimony, although in this instance Llywelyn was allowed to complete a plan he had enacted in 1272, to buy Rhodri out of his share for £666. Owain's age and, perhaps, his state of health meant that the eldest brother's position was less of a problem; he was released from jail by Llywelyn and provided for in Llŷn. Owain passed away at some point within the next four years. The Gwynedd dynasty faced the likelihood of being fractured further, though, as Llywelyn was made aware that he would soon face a legal challenge for the right to rule Meirionydd from his fifth cousin, Madog ap Llywelyn. Madog was a direct descendant of Owain Gwynedd through his son Cynan (d. 1174); Llywelyn had driven Madog's father, Llywelyn ap Maredudd, out of Meirionydd in 1256, leaving Madog under the protection and sponsorship of the English king.

Llywelyn was allowed to retain Anglesey, although he was initially required to pay £666 a year for it, as well as being held liable for huge war reparations totalling around £50,000. In Gwynedd east of the Conwy Llywelyn was left with nothing. The English crown claimed two of the four *cantrefi* that made up the Perfeddwlad, Rhos and Tegeingl, with Dafydd given the other two, Dyffryn Clwyd and Rhufoniog, plus the lordship of Hope.

The title Prince of Wales remained accorded to Llywelyn, but this almost seemed in mockery as he had lost his claims to overlordship in south and central Wales, retaining only the homage of five minor Welsh lords. One of these was from Deheubarth, but Rhys Fychan ap Rhys ap Maelgwn had been entirely disinherited from his lands in Ceredigion. The other four ruled close to the English border in Edeirnion and included two sons of Owain ap Bleddyn. A close look at the backgrounds of the other two proves revealing; Elise ap Iorwerth and Dafydd ap Gruffudd ab Owain had both been imprisoned by Llywelyn in 1277, and their release was secured under the terms of the treaty, along with that of Owain ap Gruffudd ap Gwenwynwyn and members of the Gwynedd ministerial aristocracy who had been incarcerated by their prince, Rhys ap Gruffudd ab Ednyfed and Madog ab Einion. To ensure adherence to the terms of the treaty, Edward took hostages and sworn oaths from the leading Gwynedd dynasties, the oaths to be repeated on an annual basis.

The treaty was far from being the end of the prince's humiliation, as he now had to submit personally to Edward; to that end, he was escorted from Aberconwy on 10 November to face the king in his new castle of Rhuddlan. The site itself was both a symbolic and strategically important location in the many clashes there had been between English and Welsh. The Anglo-Saxons and Welsh had vied for control of north-east Wales for centuries, and we know of a clash of arms in the area in 796, the so-called battle of Morfa Rhuddlan. Welsh legend has associated this great Anglo-Saxon victory with the completion of Offa's Dyke, and it has also been suggested that Offa's death in 796 was in some way connected to the conflict. The Anglo-Saxons penetrated the area in the early tenth century, and there are references to their fortified burh at 'Cledemutha' (Rhuddlan) in the period 921–c.950. In the eleventh century it was reclaimed under Welsh rule and Gruffudd ap Llywelyn, the only king to rule all Wales, had a major court at the site of Twthill, 300m to the south-east of the greenfield site used for Edward's castle. Control of Rhuddlan and the surrounding territory fluctuated between English and Welsh throughout the eleventh, twelfth and thirteenth centuries, but the events of 1277 finally secured English rule.

Edward was prepared to demonstrate stage-managed magnanimity at Rhuddlan, pardoning Llywelyn the unrealistic £50,000 fine and the annual rent from Anglesey. Whatever the symbolic significance of Rhuddlan, though, this was not the place for Llywelyn to finally perform homage to Edward; this needed to be done in the heart of the king's domain, in London. On 20 November Edward left for England with Llywelyn trailing alongside; they reached the capital just before Christmas and, at Westminster on 25 December, the prince finally performed his homage before the assembled community of the realm.

Chapter 8

Wales Under the Heel of Longshanks

The conquests of 1277 left Edward with more land directly under his rule in Wales than any previous king of England. His increased interest in the country was reflected when, from November 1277, it was ordered that copies of all official correspondence relating to Wales be kept in separate government records, the Welsh Rolls. In 1279 his holdings increased further when he resumed control of Cardigan and Carmarthen from his brother, Edmund having been granted them in 1265. The king's arm would stretch into all aspects of Welsh life, and in 1280 one of his household servants, Thomas Bek, was made the new bishop of St Davids.

In terms of finance, Edward's victory in Wales had been won relatively cheaply, the cost of the campaign estimated at just over £23,000.[1] But it had taken nearly a year of his time and the king was determined to invest the significant additional funds that he hoped would make the settlement a lasting one. The process of road widening and forest felling was advanced, with responsibility being placed on Welsh and marcher lords in areas under their dominion; if they refused to comply, the king's agents would be brought in and would charge the local lords for the work.[2]

Edward's new castles after 1277

Other calls on Edward's resources included the significant rebuilding work that was required on Dolforwyn and on the fortifications of dispossessed lords of south Wales like Rhys Wyndod; despite his submission to Edward in 1277, he was forced to give up to royal control the castles of Carreg Cennen, Llandovery and Dinefwr. But the major work of construction was on the new castles at Builth, Aberystwyth, Flint and Rhuddlan, where temporary timber work was replaced with stone. The building was largely complete by 1280 at a cost of £25,000–£30,000, a figure well in excess of the entire cost of the 1277 war. According to Ifor Rowlands:

These four [castles] incorporated all that was best in contemporary military architecture: high and immensely thick curtain walling used in combination with projecting mural towers. Fighting platforms at wall-top level and arrow hoops set in curtain and tower enabled the garrison to bear both from above and across the flanks. Tower and curtain could thus be used to cover an entire site by integrating two or more enclosures or wards longitudinally or side by side, thus presenting a series of obstacles to the enemy; when an inner and more formidably defended circuit was enclosed by an outer ring of defences, the resulting concentric plan made these obstacles virtually insurmountable. The entrance was protected by placing it between two exceptionally strong projecting towers and great ingenuity was devoted to the defence of the massive gatehouses thus created.[3]

Master Bertram may have been in overall control of the early building work, and over the years Edward would employ other expert builders and engineers on his Welsh castles, including Manasser de Vaucoulers, Richard of Chester, Walter of Hereford, Henry of Oxford, Laurence of Canterbury and William of Drogheda. But the man brought in to mastermind the enormous construction programme was the famous Savoyard, Master James of St George. The king had met him when travelling through Savoy on his return from crusade, Edward being impressed by the new castle that Master James had designed near Lyon, St George de Espéranche. The master craftsman had long been in the employ of the counts of Savoy, but in 1275 he disappears from their records; he next appears in English records in April 1278, when he was sent to Wales 'to ordain the work of the castles there'.

The level of influence Master James had at Flint is unclear, work having started there in the summer of 1277 and being largely complete by 1280. A continental influence has often been cited in regard to the castle, but this was not necessarily from Savoy. It is regularly compared to Aigues-Mortes, which lies on the coast of southern France between Montpellier and Marseille; Edward had sailed from there in 1270, during his crusade. The core of Flint castle was an almost perfectly square enclosure with a round tower on each corner. The great south-east tower was a hugely enlarged structure that could serve as an independent keep (or donjon); this is often compared to the tower of Constance at Aigues-Mortes. Concentric fortifications were laid out around this powerful core, with a tidal moat adding to the defensive strength and ensuring that the castle could be supplied by sea. As the stone fortification was being built, a borough was laid out in a near-perfect grid pattern under its walls, defended by earthworks and timber palisades.

Impressive and elaborate as the work at Flint was, the king's major construction project was at Rhuddlan. In order to ensure that supplies could be

The view west from the top of the ruined Deganwy Castle, looking towards Aberconwy. The formidable river crossing was the bane of many English expeditions to Wales and the scene of a famous 1245 conflict, recorded in detail by Matthew Paris. (© *Tomasz Przechlewski, Flickr*)

Dolwyddelan (*below*), Cricieth and Dolforwyn were some of the stone castles built by the princes of Gwynedd. They serve as examples of the growing power and ambition of the rulers of Snowdonia as they competed with their Welsh and marcher rivals. (© *Dragon-tours.com*)

Cricieth (*above*) and Dolforwyn (*below*).

Mighty Caerphilly Castle was the first in Britain to be built fully in the concentric style. Constructed by Gilbert de Clare in the early 1270s, it crushed Llywelyn's ambitions in Glamorgan, reversing his unbroken success and signalling the slow retreat of his power throughout Wales. (© *Dragon-tours.com*)

In 1277 Edward rebuilt Builth Castle and began the construction of his great new works in Wales, the castles of Aberystwyth (*above*), Flint (*below*) and Rhuddlan (*opposite*). Each of the three was constructed on a greenfield site with access to the sea, and designed in the powerful, concentric style. (© *Dragon-tours.com* & (*opposite*) © *Julie Anne Workman, Wikipedia Commons*)

The elevated site of Denbigh Castle dominates the surrounding countryside. Dafydd ap Gruffudd led the Welsh resistance from here in 1282, defying Edward's forces for months. The commanding gatehouse was only built after the revolt of 1294, the Welsh having taken the castle in the course of that rising. (© *Dragon-tours.com*)

In 1282–3 Edward's forces on Anglesey crossed the Menai Straits using a pontoon bridge. They met disaster at the battle of Moel-y-don, but later crossed near Bangor. It was in the belfry of that cathedral that Llywelyn was said to have been betrayed by his own men. (© *Dragon-tours.com*)

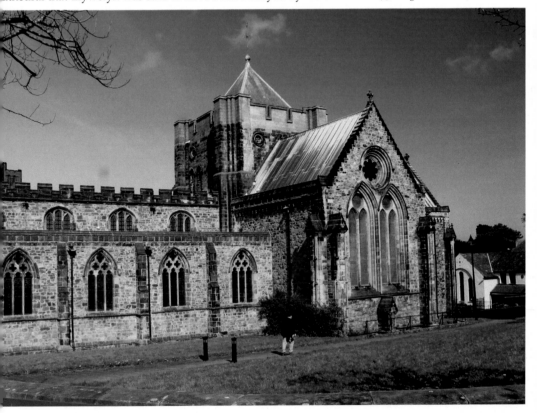

The view from the top of Builth Castle that Edward's army of the middle march would have seen as they awaited the approach of Llywelyn from the north-west. The prince reached as far as Llanganten and the church could have been where he heard his final mass. Betrayal may have played a large part in Llywelyn's death and local legend suggests that – after his head had been chopped off – Robert Body washed it in this well ('Ffynnon Llywelyn') before sending it to Edward. A monument now stands in the village of Cilmeri, next to the well, …

... and there is a heroic statue of the prince by Henry Pegram in Cardiff City Hall. Llywelyn's head was eventually taken to adorn the Tower of London, but the rest of his body is said to lie close to his grave slab in the abbey of Cwmhir. (© *Dragon-tours.com*)

Conwy Castle, built on the site of the abbey of Aberconwy, was the military key to the final subjugation of Wales, thrusting English military power across to the west bank of the river. Construction began towards the end of Edward's 1283 campaign and was continued at a frenzied pace. It was accompanied by the building of the powerful town walls, which run for over three-quarters of a mile. (© *Dragon-tours.com*)

Conwy Castle.

Construction of Harlech Castle also began in 1283. This mighty concentric fortification stands in stark majesty in remote Ardudwy, speaking volumes about Edward's desire to overawe the native Welsh. The formidable gatehouse was protected by a total of seven obstacles. (© *Dragon-tours.com*)

Caernarfon Castle was the jewel in Edward's iron ring of castles, built to choke the independence of Snowdonia. The imposing Eagle Tower and the banded curtain walls – perhaps built in imitation of Constantinople – reflect the site's Roman heritage and the imperial nature of Edward's ambition.
© Dragon-tours.com)

In the 1287 revolt in the south-west the Welsh unusually chose to try to withstand sieges from the English forces, first at Dryslwyn Castle (*opposite*) and then at Newcastle Emlyn. (© *Dragon-tours.com*)

Beaumaris Castle was the last and arguably the finest of Edward's fortifications in Wales. Construction started in 1295 but was not completed, the walls never reaching their intended height. Even so, it is regarded as one of the most perfect examples of concentric fortification ever built. (© *Dragon-tours.com*)

A sixteenth-century depiction of Cadwaladr the Blessed (d. 682) in Llangadwaladr Church, Aberffraw. Geoffrey of Monmouth claimed that Cadwaladr was the last of the 'Kings of the Britons' and that his death led the 'Britons' to take on the name 'Welsh'. This historic myth was widely accepted and is symbolic of the erosion of the status of – and respect for – Welsh leaders in the twelfth and thirteenth centuries. (© *Dragon-tours.com*)

brought to the castle by sea, the river Clwyd needed to be straightened with the cutting of a deep-water canal, 2 to 3 miles in length. Huge numbers of diggers – at one point numbering 1,000 – were set to work at this task for a period of three years. As noted, the castle itself was another concentric design, laid out on a greenfield site 300m north-west of the old Norman motte at Twthill. The early work at Rhuddlan may have been supervised by Master Bertram, but this castle was intended to be Edward's show-piece construction in Wales and responsibility was passed over to Master James. The intention to make this the main royal base in the region was reflected in the laying-out of a garden for the queen's pleasure, and the abortive plans to transfer the bishopric of the region from St Asaph to Rhuddlan. The inner ward was a striking diamond shape, with twin gatehouses to east and west and round towers at the other points. These towers dominated the outer ward, which had its own, lower curtain wall and was surrounded by a moat on three sides, with the river Clwyd to the west. A new, bastide-type town was laid out on the northern end of the castle, defended by banks, a ditch and timber palisade; work on castle and town was largely complete by 1281. Edward also arranged for the bridge across the Clwyd to be repaired, giving him easy access to Rhos, where little seems to have been done to repair the ruined fortification of Deganwy; the king's lack of interest in this site is best understood by a consideration of his campaign in 1282–3, when he would seek to cross the Conwy further up its valley to the south.

The legend of Arthur

Alongside these practical measures to secure the continued subjugation of Wales, Edward paid close attention to propaganda. In early 1278 the king and his court were at the Iron Age hillfort of South Cadbury (Somerset), an imposing site that was already associated with Arthur's Camelot. The royal party had moved on to Glastonbury in time for Easter, seemingly in order to fulfil the personal interests Edward and his wife had in the Arthurian legend, but also to reinforce the king's favoured interpretation of it.

If he existed at all, Arthur was, of course, a British leader who opposed the Anglo-Saxon invaders of the island, and the inheritors of this historical tradition – the Welsh – believed that the king had not died, that he was wounded and taken to the isle of Avalon after his final battle, and that he would return to reclaim Britain for his people. While English audiences loved the Arthurian tales, this aspect was always troubling to them, but in the late twelfth century Henry II and the monks of Glastonbury came up with an innovative solution to the problem. A tomb was 'discovered' at Glastonbury in 1184 that was said to contain the skeletons of Arthur and his wife

Gwenevere. This at once boosted the reputation of Glastonbury as a must-visit destination on the lucrative pilgrimage trail, while the confirmed news of Arthur's death helped Henry in his own propaganda wars with the Welsh. It was no coincidence that in 1278 Edward chose to visit the site to reopen the tomb, confirm the presence of the skeletons, and arrange for their reburial in a lavish ceremony. In case there should be any doubt about the mortality of Arthur, his skull and that of his wife were left outside the elaborate new tomb, clearly on display for any visitor to see.

The prince's marriage

While English subjugation of the lands that Llywelyn had previously claimed as part of his principality continued, the humbled leader remained under suspicion. But within a reasonably short period of time a measure of reconciliation was achieved, and at a court in Rhuddlan in the summer of 1278 the hostages he had given from Gwynedd were released. Plans were also put in place for Llywelyn's long-delayed wedding ceremony to the still-captive Eleanor de Montfort, although Edward's motives in this matter were much more than altruistic. The ceremony was arranged at Worcester in early autumn, was paid for from the royal coffers, and the bride was given away by her cousins Edward and Edmund. Dr Marc Morris called this 'an act of royal generosity, and the best dynastic match ever made by a Welsh ruler', but both those claims can be questioned;[4] Edward was publicly making clear the extent of his authority over Llywelyn, and of his superiority to the prince. Professor Rees Davies stated that:

> There was, of course, a political point to this public largesse: the prince of Wales was being married in the king of England's presence, by his permission, in a cathedral of his choice within his kingdom, and – with a nice and surely calculated sense of irony – on the feast-day of the Translation of Edward the Confessor, the patron saint of the English royal dynasty.[5]

If the outward appearances suggested good relations between king and prince, clear antagonism was brewing behind the scenes; Llywelyn would later describe a disturbing incident that occurred shortly before he walked down the aisle:

> On the day of the wedding, before mass, the king requested the prince to sign a letter concerning amongst other things that the prince would never maintain a man in his land against the king's will, which could have led to all the prince's faithful men being taken away from him. Compelled by fear the prince handed over the letter with his seal, even though

the peace treaty [Aberconwy] says that nothing ought to be demanded from him beyond what's contained in it.[6]

Other indignities followed for the Welshman, who would later make reference to matters like the hanging of two members of his household by English officials when they were under the protection of a royal safe conduct; the unwarranted arrest of his messengers at Chester; the impingement on his regal rights to shipwreck; and the harassment faced by his huntsmen from Meirionydd in the woods above Aberystwyth. The tension between king and prince would, though, be seen most clearly in the legal dispute over Arwystli (described below).

English finances

If the war of 1277 had been within the financial range of the king, peace and consolidation were proving expensive and Edward was again in need of funds. Reluctant to call a parliament – where he would face fresh questions and demands from his subjects – he turned to the well worn practice of distraint of knighthood; all landowners with property worth over £20 a year were forced to undergo the expensive and onerous process of becoming a knight, or else to pay a fine to avoid it (this was typically the preferred option). In addition, Edward reissued England's coinage: a popular and lucrative move that was long overdue, and that had long-term benefits for the economy of the land. In the course of this, the king launched a secret investigation into coinage offences such as the clipping of currency, an offence that carried severe penalties. Many Jews were involved in the metalworking trade and their unpopularity made them an easy target for the king's officials; around 600 men, every male adult Jew in the country, were seized and imprisoned. This targeting of the Jews has been described as 'one of the most exploitative and shameful acts of Edward's career'.[7] As a result of the coinage investigations, in early 1279 a total of twenty-nine Christians were hanged and around 300 Jews; the whole sorry episode raised the significant sum of £36,000 for crown finances.

The effective redress of fiscal matters was just part of a productive period for Edward's rule that included the agreement of friendly terms over Gascony with Philip III of France and Queen Eleanor's inheritance of the county of Ponthieu. Relationships with the church and the new archbishop of Canterbury, John Pecham, were generally good, the clergy agreeing to furnish the king with a tax in 1280. Dr Marc Morris describes a 'remarkably regular pattern' of government in England in the period 1278–81, with two parliaments held every year, no apparent cause of major problems or controversy, and plenty of time in the king's agenda for leisurely family down-time.[8] West of the Severn and Dee, though, life was very different ...

Crushed under the heel

Edward's castles would prove to be much more than military outposts, serving also as the heart of a new English administration in the conquered regions; the area under the control of Aberystwyth would, for example, answer to the new justiciar of west Wales, based in Carmarthen. It was the impact of the king's officers that would lead to renewed war, with the way they implemented the king's justice being the most sensitive and controversial of all issues. As early as January 1278 Edward had begun appointing justices and commissions 'to hear and determine all suits and pleas both of lands and of trespasses ... in the marches and in Wales and to do justice therein according to the laws and customs of those parts';[9] the most prominent of the commissions, the Hopton Commission, was named after its chief, Walter de Hopton. While there was no wholescale replacement of Welsh or marcher law, everything was brought under the overall jurisdiction of the English system. The weight of the new oppressions would fall most heavily on Deheubarth and the Perfeddwlad, where the new rulers would now remember the pre-1277 principality of Llywelyn as something of a golden age.

In the years to come, it was not just the native Welsh but also the marcher lords who would feel the pressure of central government. Perhaps the most famous example of this would be the handling of the trouble that arose between the earls of Gloucester and Hereford in 1289–92. The dispute was a territorial one, relating to the earls' positions as marcher lords of Glamorgan and Brecon and the border between those lordships in the region of Merthyr Tydfil. To assert his claim, de Clare began the construction of Morlais Castle, but de Bohun's retaliation resulted in a private war between the two. While this was allowable under marcher custom, the issue became contentious when Edward directly ordered the two earls to desist from conflict. The king insisted that the rights and dignity of the crown were superior to any marcher liberties, and emphasised his point by temporarily imprisoning both men and depriving them of their Welsh lands.[10]

The treatment of the native Welsh, though, had an added national and racial element, and multiple examples can be found of complaints against harsh English rule, the undermining of traditional rights, and the denying of Welsh custom, status and law. This impacted on the common people as well as the ruling classes, who were angered that kin were no longer able to redeem the lives of convicted criminals, who lost ancient rights to pasturage and forest, and who were denied promised compensation for land on which the new castles were built.

In many such instances it is not unrealistic to speak of apartheid, especially when considering the establishment of the new boroughs in the shadow of the castles of Aberystwyth, Flint and Rhuddlan, where the burgesses exploited the commercial privileges offered to them. Population pressure in England meant there were plenty of colonists ready to take up the terms on offer and live behind the protective walls of the towns, the newcomers also proving an additional military resource that could be used by the king and marchers in future conflicts with the Welsh. Indeed, many of the burgesses of the new towns were war veterans from 1277;[11] sheriffs of the border counties were told to find other settlers, offering attractive terms such as large land endowments and three years free of rent. The English saw the towns as a source of both civilisation and Anglicisation; the natural assumption was that the two went together.

The so-called 'plantation boroughs' were given a monopoly of wholesale trade in large areas of the surrounding countryside, with general orders for no Welshmen to trade outside the walls. In the years to come, the men of Rhuddlan would complain that 'so many Welsh are lodged near to the town on the outside that they disturb the profit and the market of the English, and give voice to much treason among them'.[12] Specific ordinances would be made against such things, such as one stating that all districts within 8 miles of Caernarfon would have to trade within the town walls. Such laws allowed the burgesses to gain control of the rural economy, running the fisheries and mills, and using their resulting fiscal power to buy up escheated land and further increase their wealth. Townsmen would refuse to use Welsh law and proclaimed proudly that they were 'the English burgesses of the English boroughs of Wales', emphasising their racial superiority to the Welshmen who were excluded from the privileges.

The Arwystli dispute

If a single case can be said to serve as an example of the irreconcilable differences between native Welsh rule and English overlordship, it is surely the interminable Arwystli dispute. This was a territorial conflict between Llywelyn ap Gruffudd and Gruffudd ap Gwenwynwyn which Llywelyn referred to the royal justices in February 1278, from which point the legal wrangling rivalled anything to be found in Jarndyce and Jarndyce.

The lordship of Arwystli was situated in the heartlands of mid-Wales at the top of the Severn valley – to the west of Newtown and to the east of Aberdyfi – centred close to Llanidloes and Llandinam.[13] In the early middle ages it may have been an independent kingdom, but from at least the eleventh century there was dispute as to whether the territory was part of Gwynedd or Powys.[14] Such historical wrangling was not the basis of the legal case that Llywelyn launched, though. Gruffudd ap Gwenwynwyn had held the land in 1274, but forfeited it to Llywelyn when he fled to England following the discovery of his part in the plot to take the prince's life. Gruffudd had been able to recover Arwystli in the course of the 1277 war, but Llywelyn argued that the forfeit still stood and that the lordship should be returned to him.

Despite the recent conflict, Edward was initially more than willing to receive Llywelyn's case; it was an example of the prince being prepared to recognise the authority of the king's jurisdiction, something Llywelyn continued to acknowledge throughout the course of the dispute that would find no resolution before the eventual conquest of Wales. According to the terms of the Treaty of Aberconwy, disputes in Wales should be subject to Welsh law and Llywelyn repeatedly asked for this to be respected, as in this 1279 letter:

> Prince Llywelyn declared that the fact that each province under the lord king's dominion – the Gascons in Gascony, the Scots in Scotland, the Irish in Ireland and the English in England – has its own laws and customs, according to the mode and usage of those parts in which they are situated, amplified rather than diminished the Crown. In the same wise he seeks to have his own Welsh law and to be able to proceed by it, especially as the lord king had of his own free will in the peace made between them, granted their own law to him and to all Welshmen. As a matter of common right the Welsh, like those other nations subject to the king's governance, ought to have their own laws and customs according to their race.[15]

Whilst acknowledging Edward's jurisdiction, if Llywelyn could get the decision from the royal officers that the case should be heard according to Welsh law, it would then take the ruling itself out of the hands of English royal officers. Gruffudd, though, said that he held Arwystli by barony from the king as a lord of the march and he wanted the case to be settled by English law. This caused huge delays and prevarications amongst the English judicial officers, who had a natural inclination to favour their reliable ally in Powys. When Gruffudd tried the same defence in a dispute with the king's favourite Roger Mortimer over land in Cydewain, though, the case was quickly dismissed as it was declared that the land was in Wales and the issue should be determined by Welsh law.

In the case of Arwystli, Edward did not dispute that the land was in Wales but – to the despair of Llywelyn – he placed the entire case within the framework of the English judicial system. As such, the prince was treated like any other litigant and told to secure writs, observe the due procedure of the king's court, abide by the summonses of the royal justices to their sessions, and work to their timescale. Arwystli was not a valuable lordship, but – above all else –

Llywelyn wanted Edward to make a clear ruling on the matter, as seen in this frustrated missive from 1280:

> [Llywelyn] begs the king to declare his will in the matter [of Arwystli], so that Llywelyn and his men be not burdened with trouble and expense in the matter any further. For it seems that three years should suffice for the settling of one article.[16]

If such a ruling were to go in favour of the prince, he would gain the lordship; if it went against him, he would win a propaganda battle that would reveal the nature of English rule in Wales on an issue that also affected the other native lords of the country. Edward was too canny to offer such a clear-cut decision – a fine example of the Henri Queuille quote that 'politics is the art of postponing decisions until they are no longer relevant' – and the king allowed the legal case to drag on, while Llywelyn continued to press for an answer. When the prince tried to widen the dispute with talk of the rights and customs of people and nations, the king began to question the status of Welsh law, saying he would only acknowledge what was 'just and reasonable', and that he would not allow a ruling to stand if it was to the detriment of his Crown and the rights of his kingdom; he stressed that, at his coronation, he had taken an oath to root out bad laws and customs. The increasingly tetchy nature of the correspondence between king and prince on the issue reveals much about the nature of the relationship between the two and their incompatible views of authority, justice and dignity.

Reginald de Grey

While the personal differences between Edward and Llywelyn loom large in the records, the prince was also aware of the ultimate weakness of his position, and he would not be the man responsible for the renewal of war between England and Wales in 1282. There were many reasons for the return to arms, but amongst them the individual actions of royal officers on the ground in Wales must be considered to have played a large part. The native population complained long and loudly about the activities of a large number of officials, men such as Roger Clifford, Roger Lestrange and Bogo de Knovill. But if an individual could be singled out as the man bearing the most responsibility for the renewed conflict, it must surely be Reginald de Grey.

De Grey's family could trace its descent from Anchetil de Greye, a Norman knight who was with William the Conqueror at Hastings in 1066, and Reginald's long service to the crown had included the holding of such iconic offices as sheriff of Nottingham. In November 1281 he was appointed as justice of Chester; if complaints from the native Welsh of the Perfeddwlad had been vociferous before this point, they now turned into an outraged wail.

The rule of de Grey impacted most directly on the *cantrefi* directly ruled by the crown, Tegeingl and Rhos, and those communities would find a native leader of impeccable heritage ready to champion their cause. That man was not Llywelyn, whose own rule west of the Conwy was isolated from the actions of de Grey. It was his brother Dafydd, who saw himself as an independent ruler within his Perfeddwlad *cantrefi* of Dyffryn Clwyd and Rhufoniog, but over whom de Grey felt he could claim jurisdiction. In late 1281 Dafydd was called to the county court at Chester to answer a territorial dispute raised by William de Venables, who claimed land in Hope and Estyn which the king had given to Dafydd in 1277. A previous ruling on the case had gone in Dafydd's favour, but it was re-opened by de Grey, something that sparked an outraged letter from Dafydd to Edward. 'Since the king is lord of various countries and various tongues, and various laws are administered in them and not changed, let the laws of Wales be unchanged like the laws of other nations.'[17] On attending the county court, Dafydd vociferously claimed that the land in dispute was in Wales, meaning that the court at Chester should have no jurisdiction in the matter; it clearly echoed the issues at stake in the Arwystli case.

Dafydd's problems with de Grey and his officers went far deeper than this, and similar grievances can be seen in the affairs of the likes of Rhys Wyndod in Deheubarth and a whole host of native Welsh lords who had proved amenable to Edward's will in 1277, but who now faced problems dealing with the king's officials. Rhys, for example, remained understandably aggrieved that: 'After Rhys granted his castle of Dinefwr to the king after the last peace agreement [in 1277], when Rhys was in the tent of Payn de Chaworth, six of Rhys' noble men were murdered, concerning whom he has never had amends or justice.'[18] Rhys was also frustrated in his legal attempts to regain the commotes of Hirfryn and Perfedd from the king's favourite, John Giffard; the interminable delays in the case were reminiscent of the Arwystli dispute. Meanwhile, Rhys' brothers Llywelyn and Hywel would maintain that in 1277 they had been faithful to their prince, as determined by the Treaty of Montgomery which had been agreed to by Edward; why, therefore, were they subsequently deprived of land?[19] Gruffudd ap Maredudd petitioned parliament in 1278, complaining that he had lost half his lands, despite the fact that he had served the king in Ceredigion, at his own expense, during the war.[20] Later, Gruffudd would make his own complaint about the lack of respect for Welsh law and custom that reflected the feelings of Llywelyn and Dafydd in north Wales:

> All Christians have laws and customs in their own territories and indeed the Jews living among the English have their laws, and the complainants

[the Welsh] and their predecessors had immutable laws and customs in their lands until the English took their laws from them after the last war.[21]

In a political sense, by 1282 there can hardly be said to have been a principality of Wales in existence. However, the nature of English overlordship and settlement in the country and the individual actions of the crown's officers on the ground had succeeded, to a considerable extent, in uniting the Welsh nation, something that cannot be said of the war of 1277. When the inevitable revolt came, the prince of Wales was not the man who initially planned or led it. But Llywelyn would become the focus of the resistance in both English and Welsh eyes, and his officers would prove to be the most eloquent source of its justification as the Welsh people pleaded their case in their brave, forlorn fight.

Chapter 9

1282–3: The War of Conquest

The storm of what was a popular and well planned rising against English rule broke late on 21 March 1282, the night before Palm Sunday chosen to increase the surprise.[1] The fighting in Easter week would be heavily criticised from the English side (who had themselves fought in Easter week in 1277); if this was a tactical decision, it appears to have been effective.[2] The attack was led by Dafydd, whose anger at English rule in the Perfeddwlad has been noted. His continued exclusion from power in Gwynedd west of the Conwy was another deep frustration, a feeling that would have been exacerbated by the news that Prince Llywelyn's wife Eleanor was pregnant. Dafydd and his followers targeted Hawarden Castle, 6 miles to the west of Chester. The land had been given to Roger Clifford in 1281 and he began work on the new fortification soon afterwards, suggesting that it was still under construction when attacked. Dafydd had been expected there as a guest for the Easter feast, his apparent friendliness signified by a recent gift of two salmon that he had made to Clifford. But Dafydd arrived in secret and in force a week early, the castle falling in a surprise night attack and being burnt to the ground. Clifford and Pain de Gamage were taken as captives, the rest of the garrison slain.

In the following days, more of the new English castles and towns through-out Wales were attacked. This indicates both that there was co-ordination between Dafydd and many of Wales' other native leaders, and that there was a desire to strike at these new centres of alien, intensified lordship before the fortifications were complete. On 22 March surprise assaults were made on Flint and Rhuddlan, although only the towns around the powerful castles fell. The town of Oswestry was assaulted on the same day, with particular fury, by Llywelyn ap Gruffudd Fychan of northern Powys; as has been seen, he was one of the first native princes to defect to Edward in the previous war, but his subsequent treatment at the hands of royal officials made him one of the most fervent of the king's enemies this time. Meanwhile in Ceredigion, Aberystwyth Castle was taken through subterfuge on 24 March, as described in a letter sent to Gilbert de Clare:

> Gruffudd ap Maredudd came to [Aberystwyth] alone and as though in peace, and sent to the constable of the castle and invited him to come to

town to dine with him. So the constable went. And the constable had adjourned to that same day his court for the king's men of that neighbourhood. So when they had dined, the constable wished to withdraw. And they ordered him to surrender, took him and raised the cry. And the king's men from the court came and slew the men of the town and entered the castle; but they have not demolished anything.[3]

The notice that 'they have not demolished anything' contradicts the evidence of the Welsh chronicle, which says that after the castle and town fell the Welsh troops 'burned them and destroyed the walls, but granted their lives to the garrison because of the imminence of the days of the Passion'.[4] Further south in the Tywi valley, Rhys Wyndod was able to recover Llandovery and Carreg Cennen on 26 March, but Dinefwr remained in English hands.

In the midst of this stunning Welsh rising Llywelyn, the Prince of Wales, was notable by his absence. This was apparently not realised in England, where the natural assumption was that he was behind the trouble. In a letter sent by Edward to Queen Margaret of France on 8 April, the king said that 'Llywelyn and his brother Dafydd' were waging war against him,[5] and there were terrified reports of the elder brother's sighting throughout the length and breadth of Wales, but there is little to substantiate these claims. The prince would later wash his hands of responsibility for the fighting in Holy Week because 'he was ignorant of this until after the event', although he stated that it was right for the rebels to have taken action 'lest they be disinherited and killed'.[6]

For all the humiliations Llywelyn was forced to endure in the period 1277–82, he was isolated from the direct rule of royal officers and the prince had been content to stay under the radar, following the example of his ancestors at times of English strength by consolidating his position in Snowdonia, waiting behind his mountain barrier for better times. The huge territorial losses of 1277 meant that Llywelyn had been removed from contact with his old marcher enemies, and an indication of improved relations with them had been seen on 9 October 1281 when the prince made a treaty of alliance with his most consistent opponent, Roger Mortimer. This may have been against the threat of their mutual neighbour, Gruffudd ap Gwenwynwyn, with the ageing Mortimer keen to secure the smooth succession of his eldest son, Edmund.[7]

Edward's response to the rising

The relaxed atmosphere of Edward's England in early 1282 has been noted, and the king was spending time with his family in their favoured manor of Down Ampney, Gloucestershire, when urgent messages began arriving (by 25 March) of the renewed trouble throughout Wales. Astonished by the Welsh 'treachery', especially the actions of Dafydd, the king had to act quickly; the contrast with the slow countdown to the war of 1277 could not have been more marked. Edward immediately called his council together and ordered the magnates to muster at Worcester in mid-May, while the ships of the Cinque Ports were told to prepare for service. The Riccardi of Lucca were alerted to the imminent need for credit, crossbowmen ordered from Gascony and horses purchased in France. The importance of supply meant that orders soon went out for food from Kent, Hampshire, Essex and Surrey, with further supplies requested from Ponthieu, Ireland and Scotland. We can trace demands for the service of 345 carpenters and over 1,000 labourers, the burden spread across twenty-eight counties. The demand for goods was endless, examples including iron, lead, hurdles to create palisades, crossbow bolts, arrows, bran to clean the king's armour, tents, carts, and cloth for armbands bearing the cross of St George. The part played in this by the magnates is largely hidden from us, but was surely substantial; for example, we have a list of the provisions offered by the earl of Norfolk, Roger Bigod, from just two of his Irish manors. He planned to supply 200 quarters of oats, 100 quarters of wheat, 57 pigs, 120 sheep, 77 beef cattle and 28 tuns of wine in an operation that cost £176.[8] In the course of the campaign, a new royal mill was set up at Rhuddlan, while the government made major efforts to encourage merchants and markets to come to the army, or at least to border towns such as Chester and Oswestry. Meanwhile, severe penalties were threatened on anyone daring to trade with the enemy.

Edward's campaign would largely follow the twelfth-century advice of Gerald of Wales on 'How the Welsh can be conquered'; so closely, in fact, that some have suggested that the king had read Gerald's book. While this is possible, I would suggest that the military realities of the situation were well known, but that Edward was the first English king with the time, determination and inclination to see a conquest of Wales through to the bitter end. Gerald wrote:

> Any prince who is really determined to conquer the Welsh and to govern them in peace must proceed as follows. He should first of all understand that for a whole year at least he must devote his every effort and give his undivided attention to the task he has undertaken. He can never hope to conquer in one single battle a people which will never draw up its forces to engage an enemy army in the field, and will never allow itself to be besieged inside fortified strong-points. He can beat them only by patient and unremitting pressure applied over a long period. Knowing the spirit of hatred and jealousy which usually prevails among them, he must sow

dissension in their ranks and do all he can by promises and bribes to stir them up against each other. In the autumn not only the marches but certain carefully chosen localities in the interior must be fortified with castles, and these he must supply with ample provisions and garrison with families favourable to his cause. In the meantime he must make every effort to stop the Welsh buying the stocks of cloth, salt and corn which they usually import from England. Ships manned with picked troops must patrol the coast, to make sure that these goods are not brought by water across the Irish Sea or the Severn Sea, to ward off enemy attacks and to secure his own supply lines. Later on, when wintry conditions have really set in, or perhaps towards the end of winter, in February and March, by which time the trees have lost their leaves, and there is no more pasturage to be had in the mountains, a strong force of infantry must have the courage to invade their secret strongholds, which lie deep in the woods and are buried in the forests. They must be cut off from all opportunity of foraging, and harassed, both individual families and larger assemblies of troops, by frequent attacks from those encamped around. The assault troops must be lightly armed and not weighed down with a lot of equipment. They must be strengthened with frequent rein-forcements ... Fresh troops must keep on replacing those who are tired out, and maybe those who have been killed in combat.[9]

Again Edward placed his household in the vanguard of the English forces, with about 200 cavalry drawing pay for service in Wales from early April, and about 300 by May. In addition, the king was soon paying to support various local levies as they took the fight to the Welsh.[10] One of the first household contingents in action was under the leadership of Amadeus of Savoy, who gathered a force at Chester before moving along the well prepared coast road to secure Rhuddlan; the castle and, especially, the town had suffered significant damage in the Welsh attack. The relief force left Chester about 21 April and quickly restored control, perhaps suggesting that they had need to clear Welsh insurgents from inside the town walls in order to reach the beleaguered garrison; the household troops were back in Chester by 25 April.

If the mobilisation of the household went smoothly, the initial request for the general muster at Worcester proved controversial. This was due to Edward's divergence from traditional feudal custom, his desire to escape the restrictions of forty-day service and to gather a more 'professional' force.[11] Six earls and 150 other named individuals were 'affectionately requested' to serve for pay, rather than by feudal obligation. It is unlikely that the king would have taken this course without a measure of agreement from at least some of those summoned, but hostility soon arose to the call that many magnates said made them 'mercenaries'; none of the earls would accept payment for the campaign. The opposition was led by the earls of Hereford and Gloucester, Humphrey de Bohun and Gilbert de Clare; de Bohun held the office of constable of England and may have insisted on the traditional rights associated with the position. Further resistance to Edward's plans may have been caused by the knowledge that this would be a war of conquest, with confiscated land to be distributed; a man serving by feudal custom would have a greater claim to such land than one who had served for wages.

Edward's recruitment innovation was soon set aside and new, more conventional writs sent out ordering the muster at Rhuddlan for the beginning of August; timing that would again allow maximum use of the forty-day service period during the best campaigning season. Ever bullish in the knowledge of his own power and status, de Clare insisted on taking on the leadership of the southern army in place of Robert Tibetot. As in 1277, Edward planned a three-pronged attack, with Roger Mortimer leading the army of the middle march from Shrewsbury and the king heading north to Chester by early June to lead the largest force. Edward also arranged for the excommunication of the Welsh rebels; in contrast to 1277, this did not include the personal censure of Llywelyn. Bishop Anian of Bangor soon complied and enacted Edward's excommunication order, although his namesake at St Asaph – who had experienced the hand of Reginald de Grey's direct rule – would prove less accommodating to the king's will than he had five years previously.

Advances in north-east Wales

In contrast to the first Welsh war of 1277, in 1282–3 the opposition to the invaders was sustained and widespread throughout the country. Dafydd, the instigator of the rising, had based himself at his castle of Caergwrle (Hope), just a few miles from the border and directly in Edward's firing line. This fortification was on an old Iron Age site, a steep hill above the river Alyn, the castle including two apsidal towers and one giant round tower. It was probably incomplete in 1282, and the round tower may never have been finished. That Dafydd was able to operate here, just 12 miles from Chester, for a period of three months was an indication of the careful, methodical preparation undertaken by the English.

The king arrived in Chester in early June, ahead of the main muster, and soon afterwards Reginald de Grey advanced into the Perfeddwlad with an army of 7,000 men, including large numbers of archers. Dafydd did not defend Caergwrle; within days of the English advance he had abandoned and slighted the fortification, its new occupiers having to clear the wells and pull down an unsafe tower as part of repair work that continued throughout July and August. Hugh de Pulford was appointed constable of the castle, commanding thirty-six cavalry, thirty crossbowmen and 2,600 footsoldiers, while workmen were drafted in from the midlands and the north; John Morris calculated an initial 430 woodmen, followed by another 300 in July, plus 340 carpenters and forty masons.[12] Over the next few months, cavalry numbers increased to sixty-three and crossbowmen to sixty, while infantry numbers dropped to 960. This would suggest that the initial sweeping and clearing work of the hostile countryside was first completed by the footsoldiers, allowing a smaller, more mobile and elite force to take on the management of the region from bases in the captured and repaired fortifications; the area around Ewloe and Hawarden had certainly been secured by the end of June.[13] Tight English control of this geographically small region of north-east Wales meant that the familiar invasion route from Chester along the north Wales coast had been secured ahead of the gathering of the feudal muster.

Also in early June English forces began to advance up the Dee into northern Powys (Powys Fadog); the lord of southern Powys, Gruffudd ap Gwenwynwyn, had again remained loyal to Edward. An indication of the progress made in northern Powys was the grant of the lands of what would become the lordship of Chirk to Roger Mortimer Jr;[14] the native lord of this region, Llywelyn ap Gruffudd Fychan, had attacked Oswestry on the first full day of the revolt and would be found at the side of his namesake from Gwynedd, Prince Llywelyn, when he was killed. The land that would become the lordships of Bromfield and Yale had also been conquered by Edward's forces, and this area was temporarily granted to de Grey. The native heirs to this land were two young sons of Madog ap Gruffudd, Llywelyn and Gruffudd, but they died in mysterious circumstances before the autumn of 1282; later sources claim that they were drowned in the river Dee at Holt bridge by their guardians, John de Warenne and Roger Mortimer Jr, both of whom would later profit with land in this region. The only native lord of Powys Fadog to survive the war of 1282–3 would be Gruffudd Fychan, who lost his land of Glyndyfrdwy to the king but would later have it restored. His direct descendant was Owain Glyn Dŵr, the great rebel leader of the fifteenth century who would be proclaimed Prince of Wales.

Welsh success in Deheubarth

English progress in the south was anything but smooth, with Brycheiniog up in arms and keeping de Bohun fully engaged. Aberystwyth was recaptured in April, though, probably by sea. Master James arrived there in the middle of May to inspect the damage which had been inflicted both by the Welsh rebels and by the waves, some of the original masonry having been positioned too close to the water. Soon afterwards, de Clare was told to find new burgesses willing to come to the town, while orders went out for masons from

Gloucester and Somerset to gather at Bristol; at the end of June they set sail for Ceredigion. Work would continue on Aberystwyth until 1294 at a cost of at least £4,300.[15]

Many of the English failings elsewhere in Deheubarth can be attributed to de Clare, who on 11 June set out from Dinefwr with a force of 100 cavalrymen and 1,600 infantry. Within five days the troops had achieved their goal of recovering Llandovery and Carreg Cennen, but as they incautiously retraced their steps back down the Tywi valley, they fell into a well laid Welsh ambush near Llandeilo, close to the site of the 1257 battle of Cymerau. The invading force lost a large number of footsoldiers, plus five prominent knights including William, the son of William de Valence and a cousin of the king. A furious Edward was forced to divert a portion of his cavalry to the southern theatre; the knights of the south-western counties of England were told to muster at Carmarthen, while those of the midlands were ordered to Montgomery. Meanwhile, de Clare was summoned north to explain himself to the king; on 6 July he was stripped of his southern command and replaced by William de Valence, who was thus given the chance to avenge the death of his son.

Llywelyn joins the fray

It is likely that an awareness of the undistracted strength of England had played a part in Llywelyn's reluctance to support the Welsh resistance. His age was possibly another factor – he may have already passed sixty – but hope for the future of his line remained, as Eleanor was heavily pregnant. On 19 June personal tragedy would overwhelm the prince; his wife died while giving birth to their child, a daughter, Gwenllian. With no male heir to follow him, the mercurial Dafydd was the only real choice as the future of the Gwynedd dynasty, and soon after Eleanor's death Llywelyn would join his brother in the great rising against Edward. It has been noted that earlier apparent sightings of Llywelyn as the leader of the Welsh rebel forces are unreliable, but a more credible account places him in Deheubarth in early August; Professor Beverley Smith suggests that, as in 1257, he headed there in the wake of the victory of his allies in the Tywi valley.[16]

The tide was already starting to turn in the English favour in south Wales, though, with royal forces beginning to arrive and, more importantly, a huge build-up of marcher military strength, particularly from the lands surrounding Deheubarth: Gower, Kidwelly, Emlyn and Cemais. Rhys ap Maredudd had been vexed by the behaviour of royal officers in the years after 1277, but he was the only major native lord of Ystrad Tywi to choose to stay loyal to the king in 1282, and his men played an important role in local recovery operations in Ceredigion. The gathering of troops continued in Cardigan and Carmarthen, and in August these forces were prepared for a rumoured attack from Llywelyn. When it failed to materialise, de Valence advanced from Carmarthen into the Tywi valley, where – as in 1277 – the army of the west would join up with an allied force marching from Brecon and Builth in the east. Rhys Wyndod suffered under the weight of this dual onslaught and would complain to Archbishop Pecham of the brutality of the invading force and its flaunting of expected codes of military conduct:

> The English have committed injuries in Rhys' land, especially in respect of churchmen; at St David's church, Llangadog, they have made stables and stationed prostitutes and carried away all goods that were kept there and burned all the houses; in the same church, by the altar, they also struck the chaplain on his head with a sword and left him half-dead ... In the same region they have plundered and burned the churches of Llandingad and Llanwrda, and have plundered other churches in those parts of their chalices, books and all other ornaments.[17]

The English advance was eased considerably by the help of the troops of Rhys ap Maredudd from his castle at Dryslwyn; in return for his assistance, Rhys was granted the lands of many of his rebel kinsmen. With Ystrad Tywi largely tamed, de Valence's force was able to head north and west into Ceredigion, moving from Lampeter to Tregaron, then on to Aberystwyth by early September. Troops from Cardigan had already begun the subjugation of the native Welsh of the area and de Valence soon moved back south to join them. Late in the month, the value of Rhys ap Maredudd's local knowledge would again be evident, his spies discovering that Gruffudd ap Maredudd and his brother Cynan were at the small castle of Trefilan. Rhys joined royal forces on a secret night march that led to them surprising and routing their enemies, freeing eighteen prisoners, burning the castle and seizing a reported 3,000 head of cattle; Gruffudd and Cynan barely escaped.[18] There were still fears of Welsh risings in the Aeron valley and elsewhere in Ceredigion, but ultimately the only help Llywelyn could offer the native Welsh resistance in Deheubarth was a shelter for disinherited lords in Gwynedd.

Edward advances in the north

On 6 July, the same day that Edward removed de Clare from command of the southern army, the king began his advance from Chester, progressing along the well prepared coast road towards Rhuddlan. If the road clearance work that had been done served the king well, so did the expensive engineering project to straighten the river Clwyd, as the forty-ship Cinque Port fleet was able to sail up to the walls of Rhuddlan, bringing the men and material necessary for repair work on the castle. From this secure base, Edward was once again contemplating the conquest of Anglesey in the west, but a tougher target lay up the Clwyd valley to the south. After abandoning Caergwrle, Dafydd had moved into the wooded depths of Dyffryn Clwyd and established his campaign base at Denbigh. With heavy fighting in prospect, Edward was glad to see the feudal cavalry arrive at Rhuddlan in early August to accompany an infantry force that had grown to around 6,000.

The king was again eager to secure Anglesey before the gathering of the harvest, and to that end despatched a force of 200 cavalry and 2,000 infantry under Luke de Tany, the former seneschal of Gascony. After meeting little opposition and gathering in the crops, Edward's next plan for the forces on the island demonstrated the extra ambition he would show in this campaign as compared to 1277. This time, Llywelyn would not be left untouched in his mountain stronghold and the formidable natural citadel of Snowdonia would be breached; to that end, men from the Cinque Ports had been summoned to Chester by 23 June to build a fleet of flat-bottomed boats, a project requiring vast amounts of rope, timber, iron and nails. The vessels were taken to Rhuddlan, then on to Anglesey, where de Tany oversaw the construction of a bridge of boats that would span the narrow channel separating the island from Snowdonia; hundreds of carpenters began work on the pontoon in September. The king may have taken inspiration for the plan from his copy of Vegetius, the Roman author having written of the efficacy of pontoon bridges of this sort.

Atrocities in the subduing of the Perfeddwlad

The inability of the Welsh to defend Anglesey against a numerically superior enemy with control of the sea had also been evident in 1277, but much tougher fighting awaited the king's forces as they attempted to move south from Rhuddlan, deeper into the Perfeddwlad. This had been the cradle of the revolution, a community outraged and united by the royal administration, and a people that had found a highly capable military leader in Dafydd. Edward's easy advance to Rhuddlan had been along his well prepared military highway, skirting the rebel heartlands, but now the fighting would become intense and ugly.

The royal forces followed the Clwyd south, through St Asaph. As noted, the loyalties of Bishop Anian are uncertain in this war and Edward's men claimed that his cathedral church was being used to shelter Welsh rebels; consequently, the church was burnt and further depredations committed on its lands. As discussed below, the Welsh leaders in the war would later produce extensive evidence of atrocities committed by their enemies that included

the devastation and burning of churches and killing of ecclesiastical persons, that is, of male and female recluses and other religious, and of women and infants at the breast and in the womb, the burning of guest-houses and other religious buildings, homicide in cemeteries, churches and on altars and other acts of sacrilege horrible even to the ears of pagans ... Who truly delights in the shedding of blood is clear from the facts: for the English have spared neither sex nor age nor feebleness and have shown no regard for any church or sacred place.[19]

Anian wanted to excommunicate the English soldiers responsible, but Pecham urged caution, claiming that the incidents were 'characteristic of war in Wales'. The archbishop did later write to express his concern that 'certain clerks at Rhuddlan, in contempt of the church, are put to death along with robbers and other malefactors'.[20] After the war, the archbishop soon petitioned the government for the damages suffered by a large number of churches in the St Asaph diocese.[21] Over 100 claims were made and by November 1284 over £1,730 had been paid in compensation.

The advance south continued, the king's forces moving through Llandyrnog. By 28 August they had reached Ruthin, which may have been fortified by Dafydd, meeting up with the force led by de Grey that had been subduing northern Powys and the south-east of the Perfeddwlad. The slow, methodical movement is emphasised by the presence of siege engines given names such as Howans and Pyceyns; these were taken from Chester to Ruthin and then on to Derwen Llanerch by 23 August. We have little evidence for the nature of the Welsh resistance, but what we do have suggests its fierceness, persistence and professionalism. For example, English officers in Penllyn were amazed at the stockpile of corn and the number of animals that the resistance forces had been able to build up, while on 27 October Edward noted that the military cemetery at Rhuddlan was full to capacity. After the war Denbigh, Dyffryn Clwyd, Bromfield and Yale would be subject to some of the more widespread attempts at English peasant colonisation and corresponding Welsh disinheritance. It could be suggested that this was both a result of the Welsh resistance in the area and of the opportunities presented by the casualties inflicted in the war. Up until early October, Dafydd maintained himself at his campaign base of Denbigh. The English forces edged around this elevated stronghold and looked to isolate it, but were very hesitant to engage it directly. It is quite possible that the later English castle at Denbigh was founded on a structure that Dafydd had built and occupied, but it was not fear of such a fortification that delayed the English engagement; rather, it was Dafydd's control of the difficult surrounding territory, including treacherous moorland, that saw his enemies advance with extreme caution.

The royal army's long, methodical advance west across hostile territory may have begun from Derwen Llanerch, but Denbigh was skirted. Edward's sweeping, destructive encompassing of the country was accomplished by splitting his host into three columns that crept forward, eliminating opposition in their path. The standard organisation of infantry units was to place twenty men under the command of a vintenar and to group five of these units under the leadership of a centenary. In Wales in 1282 and 1295, though, there is evidence for a departure from standard practice with the use of larger units of 1,000 men;[22] such a force was, perhaps, more effective at sweeping the countryside in a campaign where there was no large opposing army capable of offering battle. Particular problems were noted in Penllyn and Rhufoniog, but by mid-September the royal forces had entered Rhos Is Dulas, the eastern half of Rhos opposite Rhuddlan, and established themselves at Llangernyw, working with forces from Dyffryn Clwyd to snuff out remaining Welsh resistance in Rhufoniog. That *cantref* would then serve as the base for a further advance into Rhos Uwch Dulas (western Rhos), which would leave the eastern bank of the Conwy at the mercy of the king along its entire length; royal forces would eventually take control of Llanrwst and Betws, opening the southern route across the Conwy and into Snowdonia. These movements are indicative of the fact that Edward considered a crossing of the Conwy in the north, near its estuary at Deganwy, as too dangerous, and he had no intention of wasting his time there as his father had in 1245 and 1257.[23]

The king was not yet ready to take on Llywelyn's mountain citadel; he sent spies into Snowdonia, but by early October he had returned east to Rhuddlan, where he began the process of doling out conquered territory to his loyal followers. English activity in Denbigh is only evident from mid-October, at which point there was still Welsh resistance in the surrounding moorlands. Dafydd had escaped, but his former lordships were now in enemy hands, Dyffryn Clwyd going to the hated de Grey. Henry de Lacy, the earl of Lincoln, received Rhos and Rhufoniog, while the earl of Surrey, John de Warenne, got Maelor and Iâl.

Clerical intervention

Despite English successes, Dafydd had now joined Llywelyn in Snowdonia and – with winter fast approaching – the king faced the unattractive prospect of having to challenge the brothers in their last and strongest mountain redoubt. While the idea was daunting, it was not a challenge that a king as determined as Edward would shy away from and, with his mind set on the final resolution of his Welsh problem, he was eager to push ahead with the required military action. Given that, the arrival on the scene in late October of the archbishop of Canterbury was surely an unwanted distraction, but Pecham was resolved to try to find a peaceful end to the conflict.

While the haughty archbishop himself would have more than his share of conflicts with Edward, he was also well known for disparaging views of Welsh culture, society and behaviour and his intervention could barely be considered impartial. He wrote to the Welsh, urging them to recognise his intercession and offer their unconditional surrender as their only hope, while stressing that England enjoyed the papacy's special protection and noting that Rome would not tolerate anything that was damaging to the status of the English kingdom. He condemned what he called the cruel excesses of the Welsh and their treacherous revolt in Holy Week, saying that they were, in some ways, 'worse than Saracens'. Llywelyn and his allies, the rebel native nobility of Wales, responded to Pecham at detailed length with complaints (*gravamina*) that included an eloquent statement of their rights and of the atrocities that had been committed by the English forces, notably against the church:

[Llywelyn stresses his desire for peace and thanks the archbishop for his efforts, especially as they were undertaken against Edward's will] ... Though the kingdom of England is specially suited to the Roman curia, when the pope and curia hear how many wrongs have been inflicted on us by the English, namely that the peace first made was not observed towards him; then, the devastation and burning of churches and killing of ecclesiastical persons, that is, of male and female recluses and other religious, and of women and infants at the breast and in the womb, the burning of guest-houses and other religious buildings, homicide in cemeteries, churches and on altars and other acts of sacrilege horrible even to the ears of pagans, as set out more fully in other rolls Llywelyn is sending for the king's inspection ... Who truly delights in the shedding of blood is clear from the facts: for the English have spared neither sex nor age nor feebleness and have shown no regard for any church or sacred place; the Welsh have not done such things. Moreover, since he greatly grieves if one held to ransom is killed, he does not protect the killer, who wanders in the woods like a thief ... Concerning those who began the war at an unsuitable time, Llywelyn was ignorant of this until after the event ... It is right for them [the Welsh] to defend them-selves lest they be disinherited and killed ... He [Llywelyn] has waged war because necessity compelled him. For he and all the Welsh were oppressed, despoiled and reduced to servitude by royal justices and bailiffs, contrary to the peace agreement and all justice, even more than if they were Saracens or Jews, as he has often informed the king. Nor has he had any amends, but always more ferocious and crueller justices and bailiffs were sent; and when these were sated by their unjust exactions, others were sent anew to despoil the people, to such an extent that the people preferred to die than to live ... The archbishop ought not to believe all the words of Llywelyn's enemies; just as they have oppressed and oppress him in deeds, so they defame him in words, alleging what they will.[24]

Faced with this account, Pecham was bold enough to suggest to Edward that the charges needed addressing. Such issues had the potential to instigate debate about whether or not the conflict could be regarded as a just war: a debate that Edward would have no truck with, the king being of the opinion that he was putting down a treacherous rebellion, not engaging in a war between nations whose leaders and rights could be regarded as being of an equal status. Rejecting Pecham's suggestion entirely, Edward also refused the archbishop's request that the Welsh should be freely allowed to come and go from his court to discuss terms. He then disapproved of Pecham's alternative plan to travel into Snowdonia for discussions; ignoring the king's will, the archbishop went anyway, crossing the Conwy in early November. He travelled to Llywelyn's campaign base in his hall at Garthcelyn near Abergwyngregyn, a strategic spot on the north Wales coast that allowed the prince to keep watch on the English force on Anglesey, monitor movements east of the Conwy, block the coast road west from Aberconwy and control the important pass of Bwlch y Ddeufaen – the key to movement north from the Conwy valley.

Despite Edward's intransigence, Pecham took with him a secret deal that had been proposed by some of the king's leading nobles. If Llywelyn were to submit and 'place the lord king in absolute, free and perpetual possession of Snowdonia', they offered to intercede with Edward on the prince's behalf; they were convinced that they could then persuade the king to 'honourably provide [Llywelyn] with land worth £1,000 ... in any place in England'.[25] Dafydd was offered his life if he would depart for the Holy Land, never to return unless the king granted permission. There is little to suggest that such an offer would receive even the slightest consideration from Llywelyn and Dafydd, but if there was a chance for peace it was shattered by events elsewhere at the time of the archbishop's visit that both increased Welsh military confidence and destroyed any belief that they may have had in English good faith.

The bridge of boats

After months of risk-free, methodical campaigning by Edward's forces in the north, the invaders were finally tempted into a rash, dangerous move – a decision for which they would pay a heavy price. The reason for their action is unclear, but may be related to the need for speed with winter fast approaching, or to Edward's impatience after the unwanted interference from Pecham. Certain sources, including the chronicler Thomas Wykes, suggest opportunism and treachery on the English part; the attack was made at the same time as the ongoing peace talks with Pecham.[26] It is also possible that the hasty move had nothing to do with Edward at all and was made, without his permission, at the direction of Luke de Tany, as the strike came from Anglesey.

The bridge of boats had finally been completed by early November, spanning the Menai Straits to a stepping-off point that was most probably close to Bangor; Professor Beverley Smith notes, though, that an alternative site is also possible, de Tany's pontoon perhaps stretching from his army's camp at Llanfaes to the sandbank opposite.[27] Llywelyn's court of Garthcelyn was opposite Llanfaes and just 5 miles east of Bangor on the north Wales coast. On 6 November de Tany crossed the bridge in force. Whether the assault was ordered by the king or by local commanders on the ground, the prospect of capturing the prince and his supporters – a move that would surely have ended the war – was just too tempting to ignore. A variety of sources narrate the events that followed and not all of them can be reconciled, but perhaps the most famous account comes from Walter of Guisborough:

> When [de Tany's force] had reached the foot of the mountain and, after a time, came to a place at some distance from the bridge, the tide came in with a great flow, so that they were unable to get back to the bridge from the depth of the water. The Welsh came from the high mountains and attacked them, and in fear and trepidation, for the great number of the enemy, our men preferred to face the sea than the enemy. They went into the sea but, heavily laden with arms, they were instantly drowned.[28]

The clash has traditionally been called the battle of Moel-y-don, a name that would fit with a crossing close to Bangor, and if this was the stepping-off point de Tany's men would have then moved along the narrow coast road towards Llywelyn's court. Soon, though, a much larger Welsh force swept down the hillside to outflank them, while the changing tide made flight back to the bridgehead impossible. The invading force broke in chaos, with large numbers of armoured men plunging suicidally into the sea. Otto de Grandson and the household knight William Latimer were amongst the fortunate survivors, their horses strong enough to swim to safety, but at least sixteen knights were killed. The victims included the host's leader, de Tany, as well as Roger Clifford, the son of the Roger Clifford taken captive at the outset of the revolt. Other high-profile victims included Hywel ap Gruffudd ab Ednyfed and two relatives of the chancellor Robert Burnell; these were either his nephews or his illegitimate sons.

Brutus and the Trojans

It was in this blood-fuelled atmosphere that on 11 November the final letters from Llywelyn to the English were sent. Although addressed to Pecham, the prince's impassioned words were surely meant for the ears of Edward and contain some of the clearest examples of his perception of the political relationship between England and Wales – a viewpoint that was entirely irreconcilable with that of his enemy. The fact that no peace deal was realistically possible would have been clear from some of the opening remarks, where Llywelyn said that if there were peace talks his council would permit no challenge to his right to rule Anglesey or the Perfeddwlad – regions firmly under Edward's military control – because 'those *cantrefi* belong purely to the prince, and the princes and their predecessors from the time of Camber son of Brutus have had the sole right to them', a supposed fact that was said to have been acknowledged in the Treaty of Montgomery.[29] Such an opening was provocative enough, but Llywelyn then proceeded to address openly and directly the secret offer of land worth £1,000 in England:

> The prince is not obliged to abandon his inheritance and that of his ancestors in Wales since the time of Brutus, and confirmed to him by the papal legate [Ottobuono at Montgomery], and receive land in England where he is ignorant of the language, manners, laws and customs, and where certain things could be maliciously imposed upon him by the inveterate hatred of the neighbouring English, who would be deprived of that land forever ... As the king proposes to deprive the prince of his original inheritance, it does not seem commendable that the king should allow him to have land in England, where he seems to have no right. And if the prince is not even permitted the barren and uncultivated land due to him by hereditary right from ancient time in Wales, he would not be permitted cultivated, fertile and abundant land in England ... As regards the demand that the prince give the king absolute and perpetual seisin of Snowdonia, since Snowdonia belongs to the appurtenances of the principality of Wales, which he and his predecessors have held from the time of Brutus, his council does not permit him to renounce this and receive a place to which he is not entitled in England ... The people of Snowdonia say that, even if the prince wished to give seisin of them to the king, they do not wish to do homage to a stranger of whose language, manners and laws they are entirely ignorant, since they could be captured and treated cruelly, just as the other *cantrefi* everywhere were treated more cruelly

than the Saracens by the king's bailiffs and other royal officers, as is clear from the rolls which they have sent to the archbishop.[30]

Dafydd was not to be outdone and included his own open letter of rejection of the secret deal that had been proposed: 'When [Dafydd] wishes to go to the Holy Land he will do so voluntarily, for God, not for man. He will not travel there against his will, as he knows that forced services are displeasing to God. If he should later go to the Holy Land, he and his heirs shouldn't be disinherited because of this, but should be rewarded.'[31] Llywelyn's younger brother was also keen to base his reasons for initiating the war on the injustices perpetrated by English officers in Wales and to highlight the atrocities that had been committed by Edward's troops in the course of the war:

> Since the prince and his supporters did not wage war out of hatred or a desire for riches by invading foreign lands, but rather by defending their own patrimony, rights and liberties, and the king and his supporters made war on the prince's lands out of inveterate hatred and avarice, Dafydd believes that they are fighting a just war and that God will help them by bringing divine vengeance upon the devastators of churches who have burned churches to the ground, robbed them of their sacraments, killed clergy and religious as well as the blind, deaf and dumb, suckling infants and the weak of both sexes and committed other enormities, as contained in the rolls sent to the archbishop. Therefore the archbishop should not pronounce any sentence against any other than those who have committed these actions. Those who have thus suffered from the king's supporters hope that the archbishop will give them remedy, and turn his attention to those who have committed sacrilege and their supporters, lest for lack of correction or vengeance the aforesaid evils provide an example to others forever ... Though it is hard to live in war, it is harder for a Christian people, which seeks only to defend its rights, to be utterly destroyed and reduced to nothing. Necessity compels Dafydd and the greed of enemies offends him. Reminds the archbishop that he said in Dafydd's presence that he would pronounce sentence on all who prevented peace because of hatred or avarice; yet it is clear who wages war for those reasons. Fear of death, imprisonment or perpetual disinheritance, non-observance of agreements and charters, tyrannical domination and many other similar things compel Dafydd to war.[32]

Ending 'the malice of the Welsh'

It was at this time that Llywelyn was excommunicated by name and, if there was even the slightest doubt that negotiations were over, it would have been ended by Pecham's reply to the prince, his brother and their supporters.[33]

The archbishop said that he had previously treated the Welsh as erring sheep, but now he rebuked their obstinacy, saying that if they were descended from the Trojans, it meant that they were friends of the adulterer Paris, something that could account for the laxity of Welsh law when it came to legitimacy and marriage.[34] Their complaints about the Anglo-Saxons having conquered their land were dismissed; hadn't the Welsh themselves conquered Britain from the giants? Pecham claimed that English and canon law were clearly superior to Welsh law, Hywel Dda's only authority being the devil. In a final insult, the archbishop said that the Welsh were so ignorant that, outside of England, the only people who knew of their existence were a few Welsh beggars in France.

The robust written response was matched by military preparations. The defeat of the force from Anglesey had been a major English setback and after such a blow, with winter at the door, the example of previous expeditions would have suggested it was time for a retreat from the banks of the Conwy, leaving Snowdonia untouched for another campaign season. But if Llywelyn's letter was an example of the hardening of attitudes on the Welsh side, Edward was equally determined to take things further and force a solution by striking into the bowels of the Gwynedd dynasty in Snowdonia. It would not be easy; the size of both his cavalry and infantry forces was dropping, the period of obligatory feudal service having long since elapsed. But the king had moved from Denbigh to Rhuddlan after de Tany's defeat and on 24 November sent writs to all corners of England, to laymen and churchmen, outlining his intentions:

> The king proposes ... to put an end finally to the matter he has now commenced of putting down the malice of the Welsh, as Llywelyn ap Gruffudd and other Welshmen, his accomplices, have so many times disturbed the peace of the realm in the king's time and the time of his progenitors and they persist in their resumed rebellion and the king conceives it to be more convenient and suitable that he and the inhabitants of his realm should be burdened on this occasion with labours and expenses in order to put down wholly their malice for the common good.[35]

Edward was in need of more troops – cavalry, infantry and crossbowmen – and widespread calls for reinforcements went out in November and December, for soldiers who would be available by mid-January. But, above all else, the king needed the money to pay for his campaign, war having come upon him so quickly that he had had no time to ask for a general taxation. His currency reserves and the credit offered by the Riccardi of Lucca had proved more than adequate in 1277, but the increased demands of the second Welsh war had stretched his finances beyond breaking point. While the first conflict had cost just over £23,000, the estimated cost of the 1282–3 campaign would be over £150,000.[36] In the summer of 1282 Edward had received a variety of cash gifts and had taken emergency loans from English towns and cities, including £4,000 from London.[37] Those closest to the Welsh border proved most generous and a total of £16,535 was raised by these methods, but the only option for covering his outgoings was another general taxation. To that end, two great assemblies were called for January 1283, one in Northampton and one in York. These would be the largest parliaments that had ever been held, with calls for the attendance of four knights from every county, two men from every town, plus every landowner with an income of over £20 a year.[38]

In the build-up to these assemblies, Edward's attention to propaganda regarding the 'malice of the Welsh' would play a key part. His infantry marched behind their dragon-slaying patron saint's banners and with the cross of St George sewn into their armbands. The conquest of Wales was partly fuelled by religious fervour, and in its aftermath Pecham would claim that – had Edward's efforts proved unsuccessful – the church of Rome would have mustered all its efforts for a crusade against the country. It was in such an atmosphere that the parliaments showed their support for the king through their approval for a general taxation of a thirtieth, with further funds being rather more reluctantly dragged out of the church via a clerical tax.[39]

The death of Llywelyn

Aware of the overwhelming superiority of his enemy's resources, Llywelyn knew that he had to do more than sit in Snowdonia and await the gathering storm. November had been a good month for the Welsh resistance, with renewed risings in south, west and mid-Wales, as well as the great victory over de Tany's force at the Menai Straits. The most promising theatre appeared to be in the middle march, where the death in late October of the old warrior Roger Mortimer (from natural causes) opened up a multitude of opportunities. Llywelyn, apparently hopeful of winning over converts to his cause after Mortimer's death, set out for the middle march with a significant force, leaving Dafydd in charge of the defence of Gwynedd.

The situation in the area was intriguing, Roger Lestrange having taken over leadership of the forces of the middle march after Mortimer's demise. This may not have pleased Mortimer's heir Edmund, whom Edward further slighted by keeping possession of his lordship for a month. The reason for the delay, which caused upset in a strategically crucial section of the campaign theatre, is difficult to fathom, especially when the king had shown notable favour to Edmund's younger brother Roger, with the award of conquered Welsh land that created the lordship of Flint. It has been seen that Llywelyn had arranged a treaty of alliance with Roger Mortimer Sr in 1281 and –

unlikely as it may seem – the prince's move south may have been made with the belief that he could win support from Edmund in the middle march.

The possibility of this is increased by the Welsh chronicle's rather cryptic account of events: 'And then was effected the betrayal of Llywelyn in the belfry at Bangor by his own men.'[40] The prior of Bangor was Llywelyn ap Gruffudd ab Ednyfed, the prince's former servant who had defected to Edward in 1277, and who would be found in the king's service soon after the conquest. The friar's brother Hywel had helped lead the king's forces in the conquest of Anglesey and was then killed in the November battle at the Menai Straits, while another brother, Rhys, was also with Edward's army. It is highly unlikely that the prior had the prince's ear in 1282, but it is probable that he had close connections with many other men who were on his war council. There are also further suggestions of intrigue; Pecham had left clerics in Snowdonia after his peace mission to Llywelyn, including a certain Brother Adam of Nannau. On the day that Llywelyn died, the archbishop – who was in close proximity to the slaying, at Sugwas to the west of Hereford – immediately sent messengers ordering Adam to return to him 'without delay'; he would also show concern at the end of the war for the protection of clerics in Snowdonia.[41] After the prince's death, Edmund Mortimer's men were in close enough proximity to gather Llywelyn's personal effects, including his seal and a letter that hinted at a treacherous plot. Pecham felt obliged to write to the king to tell him of the existence of this letter, which apparently indicated that 'certain magnates in the neighbourhood of the Welsh are not too loyal to the king', perhaps suggesting that he needed Edward to know of this because the allegations in the letter were not true, but part of the plot against Llywelyn.[42] While no definitive conclusions can be drawn, the possibility exists that the prince was encouraged to leave Gwynedd by the false suggestion that Edmund Mortimer could be won over as an ally. It is also possible that, when Llywelyn left Snowdonia, information on his movement was passed to his enemies.

As Llywelyn moved south, Lestrange had detailed knowledge of the prince's location and also proved to be aware of the wider Welsh backing that the prince was again gathering. Llywelyn garnered support from those responsible for the continued unrest in Ceredigion, Lestrange reporting on the strength of the Welsh presence in the Berwyn and Pumlumon mountains, areas he would not dare to penetrate at this point in the war. The loyalties of the Welsh of Elfael and Brycheiniog were wavering, and by 11 December Llywelyn had reached as far south as Llanganten – about 3 miles west of Builth and close to the village of Cilmeri – where he took the homage of many of the Welsh of the area. But the prince found that at Builth itself the whole might of the middle march was waiting to challenge him, a formidable army including Lestrange, Edmund Mortimer, Roger Mortimer Jr, Gruffudd ap Gwenwynwyn, John Giffard, Reginald FitzPeter and Peter Corbet.

Llywelyn's force occupied the high land between the rivers Wye and Irfon, to the north-west of Builth, with the river waters separating the prince from his enemies. Producing a definitive account of the events that followed on the fateful day of 11 December is made impossible by the contradictions that exist in the multiple sources, but common themes are that the prince was separated from the main body of his army before he was killed, and that there was a separate, larger battle in which the main Welsh force was defeated and took heavy casualties. If we accept that a conspiracy had played a part in Llywelyn's decision to come south, it lends credence to chronicle accounts that he had detached himself from the main body of his army in order to come to a pre-arranged meeting with Edmund Mortimer. It is otherwise hard to understand why the Welsh chose to await the assault of a superior force, rather than retreating to the uplands where their enemies would find it hard to follow. The poet Gruffudd ab yr Ynad Coch says that the prince was accompanied by just eighteen men when he fell, and we know that Edmund Mortimer's servants were close at hand after his death; they recovered the prince's seal, and also delivered to their lord the 'treasonable letter, disguised by false names' mentioned by Pecham. It was Lestrange's men who landed the sword blows that actually killed Llywelyn and who then decapitated him, respon-sibility for the deeds falling to Stephen de Frankton and/or Robert Body;[43] both were Shropshire men with close connections to Lestrange. The larger Welsh force that had been left without its leader was defeated in a clash vari-ously referred to as the battle of Orewin Bridge or the battle of Irfon Bridge. Responsibility for the English victory is traditionally attributed to a local Welshman, Helias Walwyn, who showed Lestrange's men a ford in the river that enabled them to get in behind the prince's army. Lestrange wrote a bare letter of triumph to the king:

> Informs the king that the troops under Roger's command fought with Llywelyn ap Gruffudd in the land of Builth and that Llywelyn ap Gruffudd is dead, his army defeated, and all the flower of his army dead.[44]

The fervent, crusading spirit that the Welsh war had engendered in England was reflected in the decidedly non-clerical language of a letter from Stephen of St George, a clerk serving Edward in Orvieto, when he heard the news some weeks later:

> Glory to God in the highest, peace on earth to men of good will, a triumph to the English, victory to king Edward, honour to the church,

rejoicing to the Christian faith ... and to the Welsh everlasting dam-
nation.[45]

A monastic annalist in the border city of Chester chose to record the death of
Llywelyn with a nod to the conflicting reactions of the peoples of England
and Wales to the news:

> Llywelyn, prince of Wales, was killed with a few followers in the land of
> Builth, and his head was brought to the king, upon whom two religious,
> one an Englishman, the other a Welshman, wrote [epitaphs]. The
> Welshman as follows:
>
>> 'Here lies of Englishmen
>> The tormentor, the guardian of the Welsh,
>> The prince of the Welsh,
>> Llywelyn the example of manners,
>> The jewel of his contemporaries,
>> The flower of the kings of the past,
>> The model of those of the future,
>> The leader, the glory, the law, the light of the people.'
>
> The Englishman thus replied:
>
>> 'Here lies the prince of deceptions
>> And the plunderer of men,
>> The betrayer of the English,
>> A livid torch, a school of the wicked,
>> For the Welsh a deity,
>> A cruel leader, a murderer of the pious,
>> [Sprung from] the dregs of the Trojans,
>> From a lying race, a cause of evils.'[46]

The glory taken by the victors in the defeat of Llywelyn had a gory aftermath,
reminiscent of the treatment of the remains of Simon de Montfort after his
defeat at Evesham. The prince's head was sent to Edward by Lestrange, the
king then despatching it to Anglesey to raise the spirits of the troops on the
island after their recent, costly defeat. From there, the skull was sent to
London, where its arrival was greeted by a fanfare of trumpets. It was carried
through the streets of the capital on a lance, before being placed on an iron
spike on the Tower of London. As a final insult, Llywelyn's head was given
a crown of ivy, a mocking reference to the Welsh mythology that claimed a
Welshman would one day wear a crown in London.

Professor Frederick Suppe has described how, in Celtic tradition, decapitation could be a sign of respect for an honoured foe if it occurred during
combat. However, cutting off the head of a captive or corpse was demeaning

and galling.[47] The sense of outrage that would have been felt in Wales at this treatment of Llywelyn's remains is suggested by the lament of the prince's poet, Gruffudd ab yr Ynad Coch:

> Leaving me a head, with him headless.
> Head that slain made fear unhateful,
> Head that slain made surrender best,
> Head of a soldier, head of praise,
> Head of a duke, a dragon's head,
> Head of fair Llywelyn, sharp the world's fear,
> An iron spike through it,
> Head of my lord, harsh pain is mine,
> Head of my spirit left speechless,
> Head that had honour in 900 lands,
> Nine hundred feats for him,
> Head of a king, his hand hurled iron,
> Head of a proud hawk, he forced a breach,
> Head of a kingly wolf thrust foremost,
> Head of kings, heaven be his haven![48]

The rest of the prince's broken body is believed to have been buried in an unmarked grave in the Cistercian abbey of Cwmhir, within the lordship of Maelienydd where he had campaigned for so many years. The sense of disaster and despair that Llywelyn's death brought upon the Welsh resistance is again reflected most clearly and most famously in Gruffudd ab yr Ynad Coch's lament for his lost leader:

> See you not the rush of wind and rain?
> See you not the oaks lash each other?
> See you not the ocean scourging the shore?
> See you not the truth is portending?
> See you not the sun hurtling the sky?
> See you not that the stars have fallen?
> Have you no belief in God, foolish man?
> See you not that the world is ending?
> Ah God, that the sea would cover the land!
> What is left us that we should linger?[49]

The last prince of Wales

There still remained a prince in Wales, though, Dafydd having taken on the title as he assumed the leadership of the remaining resistance. Llywelyn's younger brother continued to issue sealed charters that purported to have impact as far afield as Deheubarth and the middle march. There are also suggestions that he made an approach to Edward for peace, perhaps sending the captive Roger Clifford as an envoy. A generous appraisal of his motives could see it as a desire to minimise the suffering of his people, a pragmatic move in view of the overwhelming odds now facing the Welsh. Dafydd, though, had repeatedly acted in his own self-interest, and the suspicion must be that – having finally inherited the rule of his dynasty's heartland in Snowdonia – he may have sought a deal similar to the one gained by Llywelyn in 1277, a settlement that would allow him to build and consolidate, whatever the immediate losses he may have to concede to Edward.

If this was Dafydd's hope, the king would have no truck with it and his future dealings with the new prince reveal the feelings of betrayal he held towards the instigator of the revolt, a man he had previously sheltered and assisted. Above and beyond such personal motivations, Edward's tactical position had greatly improved since the wobbly days of November, and not only because of Llywelyn's defeat and death. Ships were arriving at Rhuddlan from as far afield as Gascony and Ireland, bringing plentiful supplies of food and ammunition – 70,000 crossbow bolts is one stand-out number. The ships also brought a huge, highly prized mercenary force from Gascony and the Basque country, comprising forty-seven knights, 121 mounted crossbowmen and 1,430 foot crossbowmen. Many of these men had previously been regarded as rebels by Edward when they opposed him in Gascony, but they had served him in Wales in 1277 and were brought back in 1283. Their involvement in bitter fighting – and the continued resistance of the Welsh – is indicated by the high level of casualties, with many of the Gascon contingents losing between 33 per cent and 50 per cent of their number. The most famous leader was Imbert de Monte Regali, whose forty mounted crossbowmen served for a full year, drawing wages of £979.[50] The majority of Gascons served for around three months (inclusive of the long journey each way), the total wages paid to them amounting to £7,618. Two of their number, Arnold de Monteny and Arnold Guillaume, would go on to join Edward's royal household.

Edward's forces would continue to grow, with the knights of south-west England ordered to assemble at Carmarthen, and additional infantry joining both the northern and southern armies in January. At the beginning of January – far away from the regular summer campaign season – the English forces of both north and south Wales were ready to advance. William de Valence led 1,500 infantry from Carmarthen to Aberystwyth, while Edward took 5,000 men south-west from Rhuddlan to campaign bases at Llanrwst and Betws, showing that the upper Conwy had been crossed. Welsh resistance in this area was organised from Dolwyddelan, a castle crowning a small, rocky hill on the flank of Moel Siabod that was close to the birth-place of Llywelyn ap Iorwerth. A large, rectangular keep crowned the highest point, supplementing the defence offered by a low curtain wall, second tower and weak gateway, surrounded by a rock-cut ditch. Of more importance than the castle's rather light defences was its strategic position, controlling the southern entry to Snowdonia and standing on the watershed of valleys leading to Conwy, Cricieth and Harlech. The location was the focal point for mobile defensive forces to cover the militarily vital surrounding region, as indicated by the ten vaccaries that the princes of Gwynedd had established nearby, which were capable of supporting 552 cattle year-round.

As early as December, though, there had been talks between Edward and Dolwyddelan's constable, Gruffudd ap Tudur. By 18 January the fortification was in the hands of an English garrison, most probably following a deal that had been negotiated before the advance of the royal forces. By this time, the English troops on Anglesey – now led by Otto de Grandson – had also suc-ceeded in entering Snowdonia, stepping off the newly repaired bridge of boats near Bangor. Another detachment of the English army had moved north along the western bank of the Conwy to Aberconwy, which Edward would establish as his main base by March, camping his army in the grounds of its Cistercian abbey where the ancestors of the Gwynedd dynasty were buried.

The handing over of Dolwyddelan was symbolic of the fact that the heart had been ripped out of the Welsh resistance and their will to resist. The castle's new English garrison was supplied with white clothing to camou-flage them as they engaged in mid-winter raids into the surrounding country-side. Edward's confidence was shown as he was now ready to release the majority of his footsoldiers and mercenaries, despite the fact that his financial worries were easing; on the last day of February orders were sent out for the collection of the tax that had been granted by the January parliaments. Even as he reduced the manpower of his army, on 13 March Edward began to move into the deepest depths of Gwynedd in earnest; the roads were now open to Caernarfon and Cricieth, and by the end of the month the king's forces were also penetrating deep into Ardudwy and Penllyn. Edward's thoughts were turning to the occupation of the all but conquered country, and on 14 March new writs were sent to his magnates for musters at Montgomery and Carmarthen, as well as for the gathering of a new contingent of 5,000 infantry, the army of occupation.

'The last of a family of traitors'

Dafydd, of course, was still on the loose, but he was not on hand to defend the heartland of Snowdonia. The Welsh leader had moved south into Meirionydd, where he holed up for a time in the fortress of Castell y Bere, close to Llanfihangel-y-Pennant and overlooked by Cader Idris. This was the largest and most elaborate of the native Welsh castles, perched on a jagged, inaccessible rock which was enclosed by an eclectic collection of towers and connecting walls and further protected by a rock-cut ditch. The position was threatened from the south, where de Valence had secured Ceredigion by early January. As the weather improved in April he moved north, reaching Castell y Bere by the 15th of that month. He was joined there on 21 April by the forces of the middle march led by Lestrange, who was more comfortable with an advance through the mountains of mid-Wales following the victory at Builth in December. All told, a force of around 3,000 was ready for the assault on the castle, including the siege engineer Master Bertram. Again, though, the garrison would not defend such a hopeless cause, and a date of 25 April was agreed when the constable, Cynfrig ap Madog, received payment in return for the surrender of the castle.

Much to the king's annoyance, Dafydd had already departed and a search for the prince was conducted across the length and breadth of Wales. Perhaps predictably, he had fled to the wilds of Snowdonia, but the English advances meant that this could now hardly be called a safe haven. In the middle of May Edward led 7,000 men south from Aberconwy along the length of the Conwy valley to Dolwyddelan, while peeling off forces to search into the interior of Snowdonia. Even this effort failed to find the prince, and it was surely a frustrated king who made his way back to Conwy in early June, then on to Rhuddlan in time for his birthday. It was a week later that he received the belated present he desired: Dafydd had been captured in Llanberis, below Snowdon itself, where he was betrayed at the last by his own men. On 28 June Edward sent a letter of celebration back to the earls and barons of England:

> The tongue of man can scarcely recount the evil deeds committed by the Welsh upon the king's progenitors and him by invasions of the realm from time within memory ... but God, wishing, as it seems, to put an end to these evil proceedings has, after the prince had been slain, destined David, as the last survivor of the family of traitors aforesaid, to the king's prison after he had been captured by men of his own race.[51]

Dafydd's sons, Llywelyn and Owain, were also hunted down, captured and imprisoned in Bristol. Llywelyn, the eldest, died in 1287, while the records reveal a longer, if hardly happier, life for Owain; he remained imprisoned, with reports of nights spent in a bound iron cage. A plea for him to be given more food and clothing, and to be able to play in the castle's courtyard, was blankly refused by the king.[52] The last known reference to Owain comes in 1325, when he was still incarcerated. Dafydd's daughters, meanwhile, were forcibly placed in nunneries in Lincolnshire, the same fate that awaited Prince

Llywelyn's only known child, Gwenllian; the Welsh chronicle records that 'before her coming of age she was made a nun against her will', and she was kept in the Gilbertine priory at Sempringham until her death in 1337.[53]

If the treatment of Llywelyn's remains after his death had been horrific, the punishment meted out on the live body of his brother was far worse. In September Dafydd was taken from Rhuddlan to Shrewsbury, where a parliament of magnates plus representatives of the shires and boroughs had been called to rule on Edward's contention that the prince was guilty of treason. The exclusion of the clergy was surely deliberate, as they could not take part in a judgement of blood. While treason was an ancient crime, to use the accusation against a vassal who had been in rebellion – and to use it against a noble of such high rank – was a novel interpretation. To the surprise of nobody, the parliament concurred with Edward's judgement, and on 20 October the unfortunate Dafydd would suffer a gruesome, four-fold punishment. Firstly, for the crime of treason, he was dragged through Shrewsbury to the scaffold by a horse's tail; secondly, for homicide, he was hanged alive; thirdly, for committing crimes in Holy Week, he was disembowelled and had his entrails burnt; finally, for planning the king's death, he was cut into quarters, with the parts sent to the four corners of the kingdom. An unseemly argument broke out between York and Winchester over who would get the right shoulder, the northern city triumphing, while the left shoulder went to Bristol. Of the lower torso, Northampton claimed the right leg and hip, Hereford the left. Dafydd's head was always destined for London; it was bound with iron to prevent it falling to pieces from putrefaction, then put on display next to that of his brother.[54]

Chapter 10

Castles, Colonisation and Rule

The English effort in the war had been enormous and Edward was deter-mined to both savour the victory and ensure that the Welsh were aware of its totality. He spent two months touring the long-defiant land of Snowdonia, taking submissions from the crushed community, with large numbers of hostages from there and the rest of Wales being sent back to English prisons. It was the end of August – the conclusion of over a year of campaigning – before he finally returned to England, the king then setting out on a thanks-giving circuit around the churches of his homeland.

Territorial dispossession and distribution

The disaster that had fallen upon the native aristocracy of Wales can be com-pared to that inflicted on the Anglo-Saxon ruling class following the Norman conquest of England in 1066. The extent of their disinheritance was such that it is easier to name the survivors than those who lost out, starting with perhaps the most consistent royalist supporter, Gruffudd ap Gwenwynwyn of southern Powys. He gained little in terms of new territory from the war of 1282–3, but was simply happy to have won victory in his rivalry and land disputes with Llywelyn ap Gruffudd. Gruffudd ap Gwenwynwyn's son and successor, Owain, would further integrate his lands into the English adminis-trative system, effectively turning it from a Welsh lordship to a marcher lordship and taking on the name Owen de la Pole of Welshpool; depending on perspective, it could be argued that the rulers of southern Powys proved the most successful of all the Welsh dynasties.

Apart from Gruffudd ap Gwenwynwyn, the only surviving native lord of significant power was Rhys ap Maredudd, whose loyalty to Edward was rewarded with control of almost all of Cantref Mawr in Ystrad Tywi, plus the gift of two rebel commotes in Ceredigion, Gwynionydd and Mawbynion. Most of the rest of the native dynasty of Deheubarth had capitulated to the king in time to save their lives, but not their lands. Rhys Wyndod and his brothers were sent to English prisons, while other members of the Deheubarth dynasty would serve in Edward's armies in the years to come, some earning distinctions and royal pensions.

In northern Powys, the five surviving heirs of the dynasty were summarily dispossessed; this applied whether they had been part of the Welsh resistance or not. When Gruffudd Fychan was later restored to Glyndyfrdwy, it was stressed that this was only by the king's concession and grace. A variety of lesser Welsh lords and dynasties also survived throughout the country, including native rulers in the middle march, but their status was much reduced and they would prove all but defenceless against future encroachments from the marchers.

Below the level of the native aristocracy, there was not a systematic dispossession of Welshmen's lands, but there were specific and significant attempts to create enclaves of English peasant settlement within Wales. This was seen most notably in the lordship of Denbigh, with similar, smaller-scale projects in Dyffryn Clwyd, Bromfield and Yale; it is unlikely to be a coincidence that these areas had been at the heart of conflict and community resistance in the recent war. In the lordship of Denbigh – made up of Rhos, Rhufoniog and Dinmael – at least 10,000 acres were transferred from Welshmen to new native settlers, especially around the castle borough and the fertile lowlands of the Vale of Clwyd. Some of the Welsh were simply dispossessed, while others were compensated with land of poorer quality on more marginal terrain, something that would predictably be the source of enduring bitterness; there would be major resistance in this area in the rising of 1294. The peasant settlement was accompanied by a great expansion in the number and size of plantation boroughs; in addition to Aberystwyth, Rhuddlan and Flint, in the years after the conquest towns would be established and/or fostered in locations including Caernarfon, Conwy, Harlech, Holt, Denbigh, New Mostyn, Caerwys, Cricieth, Castell y Bere, Dinefwr, Ruthin, Overton, Newtown, Dryslwyn and Beaumaris.[1] The alien colonisers on the ground included soldiers, adventurers, workmen brought in for the construction of Edward's castles and roads, plus landless and desperate men looking for opportunities. The size of these boroughs and the success they achieved varied considerably, but to give an indication of their scale, in the early 1290s there were seventy-four taxpayers at Flint and seventy-five at Harlech; in 1298 there were sixty-two taxpayers at Caernarfon and 110 at Conwy.[2]

The major territorial settlement to the king's followers had been determined in the early part of 1282, with favourable grants going to Edward's loyal deputies. Reginald de Grey was given Dyffryn Clwyd and Ruthin, Earl Warenne received Dinas Brân and the lands of Bromfield and Yale, while the lordship of Denbigh went to the earl of Lincoln, Henry de Lacy. Roger Mortimer Jr profited with the lands of Llywelyn ap Gruffudd Fychan plus the castle of Chirk, and Roger Springhouse, the sheriff of Shropshire, was awarded land in Mechain Iscoed. Further south, the exchanges of land were less widespread and dramatic, but John Giffard received Cantref Bychan, giving him control of the land south of the Tywi. All of these territorial settlements were made as marcher lordships, but a clear distinction can be drawn between these 'new' marcher lordships and the 'old' ones; the conquest had been won by the Crown and the new lordships were granted by the king's gift, under defined, feudal terms.

The Statute of Rhuddlan

When it came to conquered territory the Crown was by far the greatest beneficiary, its acquisitions adding to those of 1277 and leaving the king as by far the most powerful landholder in Wales. Indeed, the fact that so much land had been retained by Edward seems to have been a source of discontent amongst many of the magnates who had served him without territorial reward. Edward's view of the legal position was quite clear; the Welsh prince and other leaders had held their land of him by feudal right and, because of their rebellion, the territory had now escheated to the Crown. For the time being there was no mention of the Principality of Wales, only the 'land of Wales'. The people who lived there were a conquered race who could make no legal appeal to native laws, customs or liberties; any such things that were conceded were by the king's grace. After the war Edward retained all Gwynedd west of the Conwy – which would answer to the newly created office of justiciar of north-west Wales – plus the forfeited lands of Ceredigion. He ensured that he kept control of strategically important territory such as Faenol, and was particularly keen to secure the north Wales coast road; he would retain Flint, Hope, the marshland of the Clwyd around Rhuddlan and the commote of Creuddyn, on the eastern side of the Conwy estuary and containing the abandoned castle of Deganwy. In the south, Edward disappointed his ally, Rhys ap Maredudd, by making him quitclaim Dinefwr to the Crown, further lengthening the royal reach into the Tywi valley.

In the spring of 1284 Edward was back at Rhuddlan to determine the legal settlement that would be imposed on the conquered territory. On 19 March the Statute of Rhuddlan – also known as the Statute of Wales – set out the constitutional basis for the government's rule of the conquered lands in the north. For all its wide-ranging clauses, it is important to stress that this was not an act of union. One of the reasons for this may have been Edward's belief that Wales had already been a part of his domain before the war; why, then, would he need an act of union? But of more significance was the complexity that would have been involved in trying to impose such a union on the diverse patchwork of lands that made up Wales in 1284; the societies of native Wales, the march and England were not yet ready for this. Although there were significant exemptions, what the statute did do was to extend the English legal and financial system to Wales, as most obviously seen with the adoption of the shire system and the corresponding offices of sheriff, coroner and bailiff. Ruthless and capable royal officers would impose the English administration, a colonial rule with an almost total absence of Welshmen in higher office, and with the dues of government returned to the royal exchequer in London.

The Statute of Rhuddlan itself can be seen in a somewhat more favourable light than the officers who implemented it, with Edward – the great lawmaker who has been called 'the English Justinian' – able to turn his talents in this area towards Wales. The king's disputes with Llywelyn had revealed his attitude towards the law of Hywel Dda; he was not overtly hostile to it, but he had no doubt about the superiority of English law and customs, a belief that only grew as he learnt more about Welsh institutions. Such an attitude would have been fuelled by his archbishop, John Pecham, who had been studying the Welsh laws and was increasingly outraged by what he read. Welsh legal traditions would all be subject to the scrutiny of the king, and to his personal judgement of what was 'just and reasonable'. Edward would retain certain native practices, such as the settling of disputes over territory by the appointment of mutually agreed arbitrators. In a land that lacked reliable documentary evidence this could be seen as a sensible move, as could the retention of the practice of settling disputes over movable goods through proof by witnesses or wager of law. In other areas the king would modify existing Welsh legal practices; for example, the custom of partible inheritance between male heirs would be continued, but illegitimate children were now specifically excluded. The most wholesale changes occurred in the area of criminal law, with the king insisting that English common law was used for all major felonies. Such offences were to be punished by the king's officers as a breach of his peace; they were not matters that could be settled privately between kin members.

Edward's iron ring of castles

The centres for the new government of Wales – administrative, financial and judicial – were, of course, the castles. In 1282, with the war still raging, repair work had started at Hope, and the king's magnates had begun building at Ruthin, Holt and Denbigh. As Edward moved into Gwynedd west of the Conwy for the first time, his men occupied, repaired and improved Llywelyn's castles of Dolwyddelan, Castell y Bere, Cricieth and Dolbadarn. But the crowning achievement of Edward's castle building would be the new fortifications he would construct in western Gwynedd, and the three crucial works were started as the war drew to a close, between March and June 1283.

The ambition revealed in the construction project would outshine even that shown in the building of Builth, Flint, Aberystwyth and Rhuddlan after 1277. Snowdonia would be placed within the noose of Edward's famous iron ring of castles, Conwy, Harlech and Caernarfon, each one a state-of-the-art fortification built with easy access to the sea to ensure a source of supply that would sustain the garrisons through even the most relentless Welsh assaults.[3] In 1283–4 about 4,000 carpenters, masons, diggers, carters and quarrymen were employed on these three fortifications, the men drawn from almost every county in England. While the programme was masterminded by Master James of St George, numerous other experts were brought in from the continent, including Stephen the Painter from Savoy and Master Manasser from Champagne, who was in charge of the diggers at Caernarfon and later became a burgess there.[4] Craftsmen who had worked on major projects in England were also utilised, including Master Nicholas Durnford and Master Walter of Hereford. The scale was gargantuan and involved the deployment of resources from throughout the king's realms, including iron and steel from Newcastle-under-Lyme, timber from Liverpool, lead from the Isle of Man and rope from Lincolnshire. The scope of the construction work has been questioned, it being pointed out that the crushed Welsh resistance would have struggled to mount sophisticated siege operations and that more modest fortifications would have sufficed. But the intention to overawe the native population involved more than just military might, while we may imagine a desire within both Edward and Master James of St George to outdo the magnificence of their previous construction as they approached each new fortification.[5]

Conwy Castle

As will be seen, Caernarfon was regarded as the jewel in this iron necklace, but militarily the crucial construction was Conwy. The barrier of the mighty Conwy river had, time and again, proved too formidable for invading English forces, this typically being the crucial factor in determining that a negotiated settlement would be made between English and Welsh that left the Welsh princes in control of their Snowdonia heartland. This had proved to be the case in 1277, and even in 1282 the English invasion had faltered at this hurdle in the November cold. It was the slaying of Llywelyn, the phenomenal logistical and financial commitment made by Edward in the depths of the winter of 1282–3, and the decision to cross the river to the south that finally saw the Conwy breached, and the king was determined to now ensure an unshakeable English presence on the western side of the river's estuary.

The broken castle on the forlorn twin peaks of Deganwy clearly had no future; it was on the wrong side of the river and could not be directly supplied from the sea. It was perhaps from those ruins in 1277 that Edward had looked greedily across the water to the Cistercian monastery at Aberconwy, and this would be his chosen location for a new castle and town. The monks were treated with care and respect, elaborate plans enacted to relocate their abbey and community 7 miles upriver at Maenan.

The initial work on Conwy began in March 1283 under the direction of Richard of Chester, although overall responsibility again belonged to Master James. The importance of the defensive site meant that this was the main priority for Edward's builders and the castle was largely completed inside four-and-a-half years. The rectangular shape of the rock on which the castle was built meant that this would not be a concentric fortification, the elevated ground enclosed instead by a high curtain wall that was controlled by eight formidable round towers, with lower barbican outworks at either end. The main entrance was defended by a long, stepped entrance ramp, leading up to a drawbridge and portcullis. A cross wall separated the two sections of the inner ward, which could be held independently of one another.

The initial phase of construction was accompanied by the building of Conwy's remarkable stone town walls, which stand at a height of 9 metres, include twenty-one towers and three gatehouses, and run for over three-quarters of a mile. A ditch offered further protection to the north and west, with the rivers Gyffin and Conwy covering the south and east walls of town and castle and offering the crucial benefit of direct access to the sea. As will be seen in other aspects of Edward's settlement of Wales, the king was keen to associate himself with the right to rule of the princes of Gwynedd, and in the construction of Conwy Castle this was reflected in the dismantling of one of Llywelyn's nearby halls which was then reconstructed within the walls; this may well have been the hall from Garthcelyn, 10 miles to the west, which the prince had used as his campaign base in 1282.

Harlech Castle

If the strategic importance of Conwy is obvious, the same can hardly be said of Harlech, situated on Tremadog Bay on the west coast of Ardudwy, a little below Traeth Mawr. The construction of such a formidable fortification at such a remote location speaks volumes about Edward's desire to overawe the population of all Gwynedd with his majesty and might. Perched atop an imposing rock and with direct access to the Irish Sea via a gated, fortified stairway, Harlech was at the cutting edge of military thinking, a concentric design with the huge inner ward defences dominating the outer works. Both Harlech and the later Beaumaris on Anglesey show the logical conclusion of thinking with regards to concentric fortifications: the development of the keepless castle; the real defensive strength was in the curtain walls and hugely imposing gatehouses, meaning that there was no need for a classic donjon. The natural shape of the rock at Harlech meant that the only feasible direction of attack was from the east, and the formidable gatehouse here was protected by a total of seven obstacles, including three portcullises. As at Conwy, Edward appropriated a nearby hall of Llywelyn's, dismantling the structure at Ystumgwern 5 miles to the south and rebuilding it within the castle walls. Most of the construction work at Harlech was completed in the period 1285–7, and the castle would be given a continental twin in 1305 when Master James built Villandraut in the Gironde for Pope Clement V.

Caernarfon Castle

For all the stark majesty and military effectiveness of Conwy and Harlech, Edward had something even more ambitious in mind for Caernarfon. This was a key strategic and administrative site, located on the Gwynedd mainland at the mouth of the river Seiont, an important connecting point between Anglesey, the mountainous heartland of Snowdonia and the rich Llŷn peninsula. Perhaps even more significant, though, were the historical and legendary associations of the site. The area had been important in Roman times, the remains of the imperial military presence still evident at the ruined camp of Segontium, half a mile south-east of where the castle was built. This importance was embellished in Welsh mythology, as most clearly seen in the famous prose tale *Breuddwyd Macsen Wledig* (*The Dream of Macsen Wledig*). Macsen was the fourth-century Roman general Magnus Maximus, who was proclaimed emperor in Britain and used troops from the island to cross to the continent and rule a portion of the western empire. In the Welsh legend it was as emperor of Rome that Macsen dreamt of a woman who stole his heart, leading him on a quest to find the lady of his dreams – she turned out be Helen, the daughter of a chieftain named Euaf ap Caradog who was based in Caernarfon. Macsen's vision of Helen's home may have been a further inspiration for Edward's builders and is described thus:

> He saw himself coming to the fairest island in the world [Britain], and having crossed the island from one sea to the other he could see, at the far end of the island, steep mountains and lofty crags, and rough, rugged terrain, the like of which he had never seen before. From there he saw an island in the sea, facing that rugged terrain, and between him and the island he saw a land whose plain was the length of its sea, whose forest was the length of its mountain. From that mountain he saw a river crossing the land, making for the sea, and at the mouth of the river he saw a great castle, the fairest that anyone had ever seen, and he saw the castle gate was open, and he came into the castle. He saw a hall in the castle. He thought that the roof tiles of the hall were all of gold. The side of the hall

he thought to be of valuable, sparkling stones. The floors of the hall he imagined to be of pure gold, with golden couches and silver tables.[6]

Macsen had been deeply embedded in the mythology of Wales, symbolic of the inherited right to rule that passed from Rome to the Brythonic leaders. It was he who was said to have established Caernarfon as the chief fort of Britain, the island being given to Euaf to rule. The work of Geoffrey of Monmouth helped to spread the legend of Macsen, and the genealogies of a number of princely lines proudly listed the emperor as their ancestor. An erroneous but widespread belief also named Macsen as the father of Constantine the Great, while Geoffrey claimed that Constantine was the grandfather of Arthur. In the course of Edward's 1283 campaign in Snowdonia, the king had 'discovered' the body of Macsen at Caernarfon, an act as fortuitous and well timed as that of the monks of Glastonbury who had 'found' Arthur and Gwenevere in the twelfth century.

It is with this mythology in mind that we must consider the unusual and beautiful construction of Caernarfon Castle, which was built on the site where the late eleventh-century Norman adventurer Robert of Rhuddlan had established a motte and bailey castle. If Caernarfon is compared to Harlech and Conwy, the first thing that strikes the observer is that the seven towers are not round, but polygonal. A round tower is more effective militarily, offering a better field of fire for defenders and making the wall more difficult to undermine. But the polygonal towers were built in deliberate imitation of Roman works, perhaps even of the Theodosian walls of Constantine's great city of Constantinople; the Roman link is emphasised by the visually striking banded masonry seen on the southern walls of the castle. This was a fortification built to overawe the native population with more than military might; it was an imperial statement made by a king determined to assume the mythical rights to rule of the Welsh, soon after he had wiped out their native leaders and crushed their martial independence.[7] To further emphasise the imperial message, in time a statue of the English king was carved above the main gate and the castle's grandest tower, the Eagle Tower, was crowned by three turrets, each of which had a stone eagle atop.[8]

This was not a concentric fortification; as at Conwy, the design was determined by the natural lie of the land, which dictated a narrow, figure-eight shape, with two separate enclosures. The battlements and firing galleries built into the curtain walls and towers offered fearsome, projecting offensive power, with further protection offered by the water to the south and west and a deep ditch below the landward-facing walls. A water gate at basement level gave crucial sea access to the garrison. Much of the shell of the castle was constructed in the period 1284–6, with the elaborate interior worked on in

1287, but from the earliest phases of construction the building was connected with the raising of impressive stone walls for the new town. These stretched for almost half a mile, including eight towers and two medieval gatehouses. Although impressive, the fact that these remained the main defence of the unfinished castle on its northern side would prove to be a weakness that could be exploited.

*   *   *

The new royal castles that accompanied the conquest of Wales were part of an unprecedented and unparalleled burst of building in the country. The construction programme after 1283 helped inspire new, non-royal castles such as Chirk, plus the extensive rebuilding of old sites like Chepstow, Usk, Brecon, Kidwelly, Laugharne and Llansteffan, leaving the country more locked down than ever before. Such security came at a price, though, and it has been estimated that by the time Edward appointed his son Edward to his lands in Wales in 1301, the king's new castles in the country had cost him about £80,000.[9]

In addition to the construction costs, the ongoing garrisoning of the fortifications was a considerable burden on royal finances. This was despite the fact that garrisons were comparatively small, their military purpose essentially being to hold the strategic locations until more formidable forces of relief and subjugation could arrive. Numbers could, though, be quickly expanded in times of hostility, meaning that the castle garrison could then also serve as an attacking force. Such a strategic threat would remain in existence behind enemy lines, a troubling presence that the Welsh would be all too aware of. In 1283 the garrisons at each of Conwy, Cricieth and Harlech castles numbered thirty men, with forty at each of Castell y Bere and Caernarfon.[10] About a third of the personnel were crossbowmen, a reflection of the effectiveness of that weapon in a siege situation. The potential to expand numbers in times of conflict was seen at Dryslwyn in 1287, where the English garrison comprised two knights, twenty-two men-at-arms, twenty crossbowmen and eighty archers, while at Flint in 1294 numbers were increased to twenty-four cavalrymen, twenty-four crossbowmen and 120 archers. The military potential of the population of the boroughs outside the castle walls was also utilised, although this would then bring the burden of more mouths to feed; in Harlech in 1294–5 the twenty-man garrison was inflated by the people of the town, bringing the manpower total to thirty-eight. In addition, sheltered behind the castle walls were seven women and five children who were connected to the garrison, plus another twelve women and twenty-one children from the town.[11]

The appropriation of mythology

Following the pronouncement of the Statute of Rhuddlan, Edward spent the spring and summer of 1284 in a determined effort to appropriate the rights to rule that had been claimed by the native dynasty of Gwynedd, the men who saw themselves as the rightful inheritors of the 'kingdom of the Britons'. In addition, the royal party were simply enjoying the fruits of their victory, wallowing in the legends of the ancient land they had conquered, fuelled by the dreamy stories that had been popularised throughout Europe by Geoffrey of Monmouth.

Edward was in Conwy on 26 March, but made a determined effort to get to Caernarfon by early April. Eleanor was heavily pregnant, and there is little doubt that the king wanted his wife to give birth at this mythologically loaded location; a son, the future Edward II, was born on 25 April. A later story, first recorded in the sixteenth century, would claim that the king had promised the Welsh 'a prince born in Wales, who did not speak a word of English', and it was as such that he presented his infant child; but the unlikeliness of this is suggested by the fact that the young Edward would not be given the royal lands in Wales until 1301, at the time of his birth he was not the king's heir, and the royal language was French. It was at Caernarfon, though, that Edward was presented with a key piece of paraphernalia associated with Llywelyn's right to rule his principality: a gold coronet known as 'Arthur's crown'. This was sent back to London, where it was presented to the king's eldest son, Alfonso, at the shrine of Edward the Confessor in Westminster Abbey.

The royal court spent much of June, including the king's forty-fifth birthday, at Llyn Cwm Dulyn, a lake in the mountains of Snowdonia that was said to have mystical properties. The use of the courts of the former princes was part of a deliberate attempt to emphasise both the humiliation and replacement of the old dynasty.[12] In July the court had moved to another such court, Nefyn on the Llŷn peninsula, the place where Gerald of Wales claimed to have discovered a copy of the prophecies of Merlin. Here, the royal party chose to further indulge their Arthurian fascination by holding a tournament that was referred to as a 'Round Table'. Determined to explore the extremities of his newly conquered domain, by early August Edward had reached the far tip of the Llŷn, taking in the tiny islands off the coast before returning to Caernarfon by 13 August, and to the English borderlands by 22 August.

It was around this time that messengers arrived to tell Edward and Eleanor that Alfonso had died, but the royal couple chose to continue their victory tour rather than attending their eldest son's funeral in London. On 1 September the monks of the new abbey of Vale Royal were presented with a silver chalice made from the melted seal matrices of Dafydd, Llywelyn and his wife Eleanor de Montfort; it has been suggested that this may have been the so-called Dolgellau Chalice that is now in the queen's private collection.[13] Heading back towards the border, Edward's court at Overton was said to have been entertained by 1,000 Welsh minstrels, and in early October the king had re-entered Wales to inspect the work at his new castles of Conwy, Caernarfon and Harlech. In November the royal party headed south to Aberystwyth, Cardigan and St Davids, then in December travelled east to Cardiff, Caldicot and Chepstow. In Glamorgan there was a hint of future trouble as de Clare, proud of his rights as a marcher lord, acted almost like a sovereign lord; Edward was said to have been 'received with the greatest honour, and conducted to the boundary of his own lands by the earl at his own expense'.[14] Finally, about 21 December, Edward was ready to return to England, taking a ship across the Severn to celebrate Christmas at Bristol.

If the king's attention now began to turn to other matters – plans for a new crusade were foremost on his mind – his appropriation of Welsh royal prerogatives also continued. At a parliament in London in May 1285, the king's first appearance in the capital for three years, Edward led a procession of his magnates past the severed heads of Dafydd and Llywelyn, carrying the princes' most precious relic, the Croes Naid, said to be a piece of the true cross of Christ.[15] This was placed on the altar of Westminster Abbey, and later gifted to the nuns of St Helena at Bishopsgate, Helena being the mother of Constantine the Great, who claimed to have discovered the true cross. Towards the end of the summer Edward staged another 'Round Table' tournament; held at Winchester Castle, this was a much grander affair than the event at Nefyn and may have been the occasion for the creation of the famous round table that hangs in the castle's great hall today.[16]

Chapter 11

Resistance and Submission

If Edward's military campaigning and consolidation in Wales had effectively crushed the resistance of the country, it would only increase the latent discontent amongst the population. Many of the complaints that arose would be familiar from the period before the conquest, 1277–82: a disregard of the status, laws and customs of the Welsh; removal of their rights to pasture and forest; judicial innovations; the financial demands of zealous royal officers; and territorial resettlements to make way for new towns and castles. After 1283 the numbers of these new towns and castles increased greatly, with additional anguish caused by land dispossessions in favour of English peasant colonists. The commercial monopolies and other privileges enjoyed by the alien settlers intensified the nature of colonial rule, with attitudes hardened by the recent experience of bloody war. Welshmen had to sell their goods in the market towns but could not hold land in them or bear arms in them; they were not allowed to give hospitality to strangers for more than one night; they were prohibited from holding gatherings without royal permission and in the absence of royal officials. The king would also soon be demanding a return from his new lands in Wales; as early as June 1283 he was ordering valuations of his estates ('extents') to be prepared for north-west Wales, and the extensive documentation was ready by March 1284. While the castles and other instruments of conquest would initially be a major drain on royal finances, by 1300 the Crown would be drawing handsome returns from Wales.

The revolt of 1287

Amidst all the other sources of oppression pillorying the people of Wales, the piqued feelings of surviving native nobles who had not gained all they had hoped from their support of the conquerors were unlikely to elicit much sympathy. This, though, was the main cause of the first serious trouble in the country after 1283 – a localised revolt led by Rhys ap Maredudd of Deheubarth, a man who had previously proved to be one of Edward's most reliable allies.[1] As has been seen, after the conquest he had received some small grants of land and signs of favour, but he had been forced to yield the ancestral seat of Dinefwr to the Crown. He also saw Cantref Bychan granted to the royal favourite, John Giffard; in 1279–81 Rhys had been embroiled in a bitter dispute with Giffard for control of land around Llandovery, and Edward had now decisively ruled in Giffard's favour.

It was a combination of personal animosity towards the justiciar of west Wales at Carmarthen, Robert Tibetot, and associated legal disputes that finally sent Rhys into revolt. Royal control of Dinefwr left the Welsh leader having to deal with Edward's officials to the east of his main castle at Dryslwyn, as well as to the west in Carmarthen. A series of arguments led to Rhys refusing to attend the court at Carmarthen and writing to Edward in Gascony with details of his complaints. The king was too distant to be aware of the seriousness of the situation, and in any case would surely have seen the refusal to attend the court as a direct denial of his jurisdiction. On 8 June 1287 Rhys chose to resort to arms, his first blow falling on Giffard's land in Llandovery. The castle was quickly taken, along with those at Dinefwr and Carreg Cennen, the constables being killed along with many of the garrisons.

While it is difficult to imagine much popular support for Rhys, given his loyalty to Edward in 1277 and 1282–3, a measure of the discontent in the country was seen in the fact that the revolt touched on Aberystwyth, Carmarthen, Swansea and Brecon. Even so, the trouble sparked what can only be described as a massive over-reaction from the regency government in London. With memories of the life-or-death struggles of 1282–3 fresh in the mind, 24,000 men were mobilised to crush the Welsh opposition, over half of them coming from Wales and the march. In Edward's absence, his brother Edmund took charge. With the royal household also in France, he was without the help of the Wardrobe for organising his war finances and would place a heavy reliance on the Italian bankers, the Riccardi of Lucca.

For the first and only time in this series of wars between England and Wales, the Welsh made concerted attempts to defend castles, Rhys initially holing up in his impressive fortification of Dryslwyn; perhaps the restricted geographical area he was operating in reduced his options. The formidable, natural site of Dryslwyn, on a rocky hill above the Tywi, was built upon in stone in the 1220s, and Rhys had continued to strengthen, enlarge and improve the castle in the years after 1283. A round keep was at the heart of the structure, with a curtain wall enclosing the polygonal ward. A projecting chapel tower was included in the eastern wall, and there was a basic gatehouse to the north-east.

Imposing as the site was, it had little hope of holding out against the forces ranged against it, and Edmund commanded an army of 11,000 men below the castle walls for a siege that began in the second week of August. Troops were drawn from all corners of Wales, including the north, where craftsmen were diverted from work on the king's new castles. They helped to construct the most formidable of all medieval siege engines: a trebuchet made of timber, hides, rope and lead at a cost of £14. Twenty quarrymen and twenty-four carters were employed to shape and move the large stone balls that were needed as ammunition; two of these, each measuring over sixteen inches in diameter, were recovered in archaeological excavations and can now be seen in Carmarthenshire County Museum (Abergwili).[2] Additional effort was put into undermining the vulnerable chapel tower, and it was here that the besieging force suffered its greatest setback when a wall collapsed, crushing to death a number of nobles who were inspecting the work, including the earl of Stafford, Sir William de Monte Caniso, and Sir John de Bonvillars.

Despite this severe blow, the castle was captured by 5 September after a siege of three weeks. The badly damaged fortification was repaired and heavily garrisoned, with plans soon laid out for a new plantation borough at the foot of the hill. Rhys had somehow managed to slip away, but his wife and son were captured. This did not end his rebellion, and in November he resurfaced in Cardiganshire, where he was able to take the castle of Newcastle Emlyn by surprise; the castellan was taken captive and the rest of the garrison slaughtered. The fall of the fortification was the trigger for renewed outbreaks of trouble throughout much of Deheubarth.

By the beginning of January Rhys was besieged in Newcastle Emlyn and accounts of subsequent events are dominated by the logistical efforts required to bring up the trebuchet from Dryslwyn and get it ready for action. The machine was given an escort of twenty cavalry and 463 infantry as it was hauled in five days from the Tywi valley to St Clears, then on to Cilgerran and Cardigan. After being taken across the Teifi it was repaired, before sixty oxen dragged it to Newcastle Emlyn, and the engine was ready for action by 10 January. In the meantime, bridges and hurdles had been prepared for the assault, while the men of Cardigan were employed to gather 480 stones from the nearby beach that would be suitable to serve as ammunition for the trebuchet. These were transported upriver to Llechryd, where 120 packhorses were used to drag them the remaining 8 miles to the siege camp. The castle had capitulated by 20 January, and the fact that no men were lost from the besieging force would suggest that it was surrendered on terms; either the trebuchet had done considerable damage or the very threat of its presence was enough to convince the garrison to give in. In the aftermath the thanks and monetary rewards given to the men of Cardigan for their efforts on Edward's behalf are an indication of the lack of widespread support felt for Rhys and his rebellion amongst the native Welsh.

Again, though, Rhys had been able to slip away from the siege. The failure to pursue him to the bitter end may have been related to pleas made on his behalf by his marcher friends and relatives, notably Gilbert de Clare who, it was rumoured, may have helped Rhys to flee to Ireland. He remained at large until 1292, when he was captured 'through the treachery of his own men' in the woods of Mallaen, to the north of Llandovery; he was taken to York for trial, where the inevitable verdict of treason was returned, before he was dragged through the streets of the historic city to his execution. Putting down his revolt had cost the government an estimated £10,000, the Riccardi of Lucca providing at least £8,288.[3] In the aftermath the six commotes of Cantref Mawr were incorporated into the county of Carmarthen.

The revolt of 1294–5

If the 1287 revolt had been a limited, local affair, the wider build-up of anger at English rule and administration continued apace. The pressure of taxation grew significantly in the early 1290s, and fell harder on the poor, impoverished people of Wales than on the king's subjects elsewhere. It has been estimated, for example, that in 1292 the average Merioneth taxpayer was asked for 4 shillings 3 pence, while his Colchester counterpart would have had to find 1 shilling 9 pence.[4] The 1292 tax demanded the astronomical sum of £10,000 from Wales and exchequer records show that just over £3,000 was paid; the exactions of corrupt, colonial officials in Wales probably meant that the actual amount levied on the people was much more. The final instalment of this hated tax was due at the time the 1294 revolt broke.

The weight of the fiscal demands on the conquered lands of Wales was emphasised in a comparative study by Professor James Given of two territories that had been taken under outside rule in this period. He examined the revenues taken by the English government from the principality of north Wales in 1306–7, comparing them to the revenues gathered by the French government in Languedoc in 1293–4. Although many of the figures are highly speculative, the overall impression is revealing; for example, the average return per 1,000 inhabitants in Gwynedd was estimated at £44.6, that of Languedoc at £13.[5] With the native nobility of Wales having been wiped out in 1282–3, the dues were going directly to the officers of the Crown and on to London, meaning that wealth was stripped from an already poor region: 'The Welsh – forced to pay higher rents and dues; compelled to buy access to the upland pastures and forests of the region; mulcted by the courts, tax collectors and military arrayers – saw the resources of their country stripped to supply the needs of their foreign masters.'[6]

Edward's distractions

If such conditions created a powder-keg atmosphere in Wales, the mid-1290s may also be considered a propitious moment to have mounted a rebellion. From the Welsh perspective, a characteristic of both the 1277 and 1282–3 wars was their astonishingly bad timing. The leaders of Gwynedd had to face an undistracted England under a young and capable king, who had access to plentiful credit and supplies. By the mid-1290s, though, aspects of Edward's reign had begun to turn sour. On top of the costs of the Welsh war and the expenses involved in the subsequent castle building and settlement of the country, major problems were brewing in Scotland with the succession crisis that resulted from the death of the 'Maid of Norway' in 1290. Of more immediate concern were problems in France, where Edward had been out-manoeuvred in humiliating fashion by Philip IV.

Edward had been experiencing some of the problems that had been faced by his old enemy Llywelyn, finding himself in the position of being an overlord of a land (Gascony) that was also subject to a superior overlord (the king of France). The situation had led to countless disputes, with Edward's vassals in Gascony able to appeal any decisions they disliked direct to the French royal court in Paris. For decades, any problems relating to such issues were eased by the good relations that existed between the English and French royal houses, a cordiality that was helped by close familial ties with frequent inter-marriage between the dynasties. The English royal family, though, seems to have failed to grasp the change that had been brought about by the accession of the clever, calculating Philip IV to the French throne in 1285.

In 1294, in the course of another of the regular disputes, Edmund negoti-ated a secret deal whereby Edward would surrender Gascony to Philip as part of a face-saving exercise for the French king. Personal promises were made to Edmund and Edward that the duchy would then be immediately handed back to English control, but no sooner was the deal signed than French troops began to move in. It was a huge and embarrassing diplomatic blunder that Edward had to personally explain to a parliament that believed the king had lost his mind and, having succeeded in winning back trust, he then needed to secure his realm's backing for a huge, daunting campaign to Gascony that offered few guarantees of success.

Finance was, once again, the major issue, the king's plan to use the funds that had been amassed for a crusade being just one part of a huge, protracted row with the church. Edward's long-running and successful relationship with the Riccardi of Lucca fell apart when they were unable to secure the crusade funds for the king; the bankers had invested them overseas, but Philip IV ensured that the money could not be retrieved. Despite the ever-growing list of problems facing the expedition, Edward did receive plentiful popular support in light of the French treachery, and a muster was ordered at Ports-mouth which was to be ready to sail on 1 September. The force gathered would not, though, include any feudal contingent serving forty days at their own cost; the magnates argued that such service was not owed overseas and that it would exceed the forty-day limit, and their resistance – probably on a passive basis – forced the king to change his recruitment methods.[7]

Bad weather led to the delay of the muster until the end of the month, and a large infantry levy that was being raised in Wales was ordered to be at Shrewsbury by the end of September. But events were overtaken by more weather delays and the arguments over feudal service, meaning that 5,000 Welsh infantry who had been ordered to march to Westminster were now told to turn around and head for home. If the English authorities had any inkling of what was about to happen, the return of such large numbers of trained, armed Welshmen to their homeland would surely not have been allowed.

A national rising

Amidst all of the problems Edward was facing in 1294, the news that some of the Welsh infantry that had been summoned to Shrewsbury had revolted on 30 September was probably low down the list of his priorities. By early October, though, more worrying news arrived, indicating that this was not a localised disturbance but part of a national uprising throughout Wales. If the situation in the country was already combustible, further tinder had been added to the mix as the garrisons of the formidable castles that kept the native population in check had been stripped to provide troops for the planned expedition to Gascony. It was against this background that Welsh troops were mustered for that same unpopular expedition, meaning that the most militarily capable members of society were armed, organised and brought into close association.

When the inevitable storm broke, the baronial castles of Ruthin, Mold, Hawarden and Denbigh quickly fell, while the great new royal fortifications of Builth, Aberystwyth, Flint, Harlech and Conwy were besieged, along with Castell y Bere. Royal officials were slaughtered, including Roger Puleston (the sheriff of Anglesey) and Geoffrey Clement (the deputy justiciar of south Wales). The insurgents targeted the levers of government, destroying records as a symbol of the colonial rule. The news that must surely have sent Edward into an apoplexy of rage was the fact that his great showpiece, imperial castle of Caernarfon had been taken, its walls thrown down and the surrounding town burnt to the ground. The delays in building the north curtain wall and the reliance placed on the town defences had cost the king dear.

If any of Edward's wars in Wales can be said to have a truly national, England *v* Wales context, it was that of 1294–5. The impassioned language that had been used by the native nobility in their November 1282 letters to Archbishop Pecham may have had popular support amongst the people of the land, but it was the colonial rule that those people had endured under

Edward's alien officials that lit the fire of patriotism. The rising was far more widespread than even 1282–3, spreading throughout the royal lands of Wales, the 'new' marcher lordships such as Denbigh and Dyffryn Clwyd, and the 'old' marcher lordships such as Brecon and Glamorgan. But if the popular support was undoubted, the rising now lacked natural leaders with the power, experience and authority of the previous wars, making it harder to maintain a sustained, organised resistance against their enemies. These shortcomings were, of course, exacerbated by the new castles and towns that rooted the English in even the deepest reaches of the country. If Llywelyn ap Gruffudd and his allies had never chosen to defend their own native castles to the death, they had used the strategic sites as bases for the organisation of mobile defence. In 1294–5 such sites were almost all in the hands of the English, the garrisons sitting secure in well fortified safety, able to await relief and – when the time was right – harass their enemies behind the lines.

The revolt in Gwynedd was led by Madog ap Llywelyn, wrongly identified by many contemporaries and later historians as an illegitimate son of Prince Llywelyn ap Gruffudd. A direct descendant of Owain Gwynedd (d. 1170), Madog was actually head of the Meirionydd line that had previously found sponsorship from the English king as it sought to press its claims to rule parts of Gwynedd in the face of hostility from Llywelyn. He may have expected to gain Meirionydd after 1283, but the king retained this territory as part of the new royal lands in Wales, Madog having to be content with the grant of a small estate on Anglesey. In 1294 the disappointed Welshman would take on his fifth-cousin's old title of Prince of Wales, and he would be acknowledged as the most prominent leader of the revolt. Madog seems to have been in overall control of the resistance in the north and the middle march.

Although there was some co-ordination among the Welsh resistance, Madog does not seem to have had any real authority over the leaders elsewhere in the country. Included amongst these men were Maelgwn ap Rhys Fychan of Genau'r Glyn, who could claim descent from the Lord Rhys of Deheubarth (d. 1197). Troops in Ceredigion besieged the castle of Aberystwyth, attacked royalist forces in Cardigan and launched significant raids into Carmarthen and Pembroke. An obscure minor noble named Cynan ap Maredudd took the lead in the Brecon and Elfael region; Builth was besieged for six weeks, and he attacked the castle of Cefnllys. The most prominent leader in the south was Morgan ap Maredudd, a Welsh noble from the dynasty of Gwynllŵg (Machen and Caerleon). He had been disinherited by Gilbert de Clare and his quarrel was on more of a local than a national level; he called it 'a war against the earl' and would later transfer his homage from the earl of Gloucester to Edward. An attack on de Clare's new castle of Morlais was part of the revolt in the region.

Above all else, though, this was a popular rising driven by community leaders, the rebellious mood of the country perhaps forcing the hand of the surviving Welsh nobility. This is suggested by a study of the so-called Penmachno Document of December 1294, the only known, surviving act made by Madog; it is a letter patent in which he confirms land grants to Bleddyn Fychan.[8] At the time, Madog was in no practical position to enforce such a grant and both Bleddyn and the named witnesses of the act – important Welsh nobles, including several of the line of Ednyfed Fychan – had a history of service to the English Crown. In the period 1283–94 Bleddyn had received signs of the king's friendship and had worked closely with Henry de Lacy, his lord in Denbighshire; this included the removal of tenants from Bleddyn's lands of Archwedlog in order to create a forest. The families of Bleddyn and of the key witnesses to the Penmachno letter would prosper in the years after the end of the revolt as landholders and local officials, suggesting that they had been in no way fully committed to the rising. It may be that the document was made by Madog at the request of Bleddyn as an insurance policy; Bleddyn and some of the witnesses to the document may not have played any part in the rebellion, but they wanted an agreement in place with Madog in the event that he found success, a deal that would allow them to keep their positions of local power and influence under a native prince of Wales.

The English response

As in 1282, Edward had been taken completely by surprise, but he again quickly grasped the scale of the trouble and reacted skilfully, putting his continental plans on hold and diverting troops from Portsmouth to Wales. Reginald de Grey was also characteristically effective, boosting the garrisons of Flint and Rhuddlan and undertaking emergency work to strengthen the defences there.[9] But localised attempts to quell the trouble would only show how urgently royal intervention was needed. On 11 November Henry de Lacy tried to advance to relieve Denbigh, but was attacked by his own tenants and made to flee. There was also a failed attempt to relieve the siege of Castell y Bere; archaeological evidence suggests a fire at the site about this time, and after the revolt the castle was abandoned by the English. There was better news for Edward further south, where John Giffard was able to relieve the siege of Builth in mid-November, on his fifth attempt to break through to the garrison.

If the earlier muster for the war in Gascony had helped the Welsh organise their forces, it also speeded up the English response, with the war funds that had been gathered for the continental expedition readily available for use in Wales.[10] There was a swift and smooth gathering of cavalry, infantry, work-men, material and supplies, the whole operation having been described as 'a well-oiled war machine in operation'.[11] Edward was forced to moderate his usual domineering manner towards his magnates in order to ensure their support, something that included the abandonment of the *Quo Warranto* inquiries that had been a major bone of contention between king and nobility; de Clare was at the heart of the opposition to this. The chronicler Pierre Langtoft hints at further discord between the king and his leading magnates, suggesting that the Welsh trouble could have been put down much more quickly if Edward had been prepared to grant conquered land to his followers.

The king did enjoy a large measure of popular support from the English community that was outraged by another example of the 'treachery' of the Welsh and, with the support of his realm behind him, Edward gave his forces a now-familiar three-pronged disposition. Assembling at Worcester on 21 November, he assigned armies to south, mid- and north Wales, with campaign bases at Chester, Montgomery, Carmarthen and Brecon. Leadership in the south was given to William de Valence and Roger Bigod, earl of Norfolk, while in the middle march the earl of Hereford, Humphrey de Bohun, was assisted by John Giffard, Roger Lestrange and Edmund Mortimer. The king took his usual position at the head of the army of the north and the scale of the effort dwarfed even the 1282–3 campaign, with total troop numbers estimated to have been around 35,000. Ships were commandeered from as far away as Bayonne, the fleet needed to deliver the huge volumes of supplies required by the armies, while the besieged castles of Aberystwyth, Harlech and Cricieth were soon resupplied from the Irish Sea.

The main sphere of activity was, again, in north Wales, where 16,000 troops advanced along the coast road to join de Grey in Rhuddlan, while Edward led another 5,000 into the interior of the Perfeddwlad. The king had arrived in Chester by 4 December and had advanced to Wrexham by 8 December, targeting the areas where the earl of Lincoln had encountered so many problems. One source from Lincolnshire, the Hagnaby Chronicle, suggests that 10,000 Welshmen in the north-east submitted to the king and promised to bring in Madog and his followers, and then to serve Edward in France. They were despatched to secure Madog, but when they found the Welsh leader he was able to win them over so that they vowed they would 'rather die in their country than elsewhere' and attacked the English who had accompanied them.

The number of Welsh involved in this incident – and so the extent of the English setback – has almost certainly been exaggerated. Edward's forces moved through Llandegla – crossing the watershed between the Dee and Clwyd – then on to Derwen, which he had reached by 17 December. By 19 December – the date of the Penmachno letter – he was at Llech in the commote of Ceinmeirch, suggesting that he had been able to bring to heel the rebel centres of Ruthin and Denbigh. At Denbigh Henry de Lacy set in motion the extensive rebuilding work that included a massive new gatehouse, plus taller and thicker curtain walls, and the integrated 1,100 metres of town walls. The royal army continued its progress north and was at Abergele by 23 December; the size of the invading army, the English fortresses that had been constructed in the preceding decades and the road-widening and forest clearing that had been undertaken meant that advance to the Conwy was rapid, and Edward soon crossed the river to celebrate Christmas at his formidable new castle on the western bank.

Once more, Edward's skill as an organiser and a calculating, methodical general had been apparent, but on 7 January 1295 he made one of the hasty, careless moves that had been a sporadically recurring theme of his military career. At Lewes in 1264 his rash cavalry charge had cost the royalists the battle, and in November 1282 it was, perhaps, his order that led to the costly defeat of Luke de Tany's force from Anglesey. Now, with the Welsh opposition being slowly, relentlessly ground down, the king made a swift, ill-considered advance from Conwy Castle into the depths of Snowdonia. Perhaps the reason for Edward's hasty action can be traced to the news of trouble in Scotland, resistance to English influence there encouraged by the problems the king was facing in both France and Wales.[12]

It was mid-winter and the bulk of the king's forces were on the opposite bank of the treacherous river, and hardly had the king left the shelter of his castle walls than his baggage train was ambushed, the invading force being on the receiving end of major losses. Edward's main column was too powerful for the Welsh to challenge, though, and the king was able to advance through Bangor (8 January) and Llanwnda (9 January), then on to the Llŷn peninsula, reaching as far as Nefyn (12 January). But few gains came from this reckless thrust and by 20 January the royal force was back at Conwy, where it found itself dangerously short of supplies. Great care had been taken to ensure that the castle could be supplied from the sea, but appalling mid-winter storms meant that the ships could not dock, and the king and his men suffered significant hardship until finally, in early February, a break in the weather allowed the arrival of boats from Chester, Lancashire, Bristol, Dorset, Ireland and Gascony.

Despite the build-up of men and supplies, and the calls for action in France and Scotland, the king now proved far more reluctant to move from the safety of Conwy. Instead, ecclesiastical weapons were brought into play with the help of Robert Winchelsey, the new archbishop of Canterbury. On 6 February he wrote to the bishop of St Asaph, Llywelyn, telling him to excommunicate Madog and his 'wicked, degenerate and mad' followers and to interdict their lands if they did not stop their 'sedition, conspiracies, machinations, killings and arson'.[13] These penalties were enacted by 3 March, although the arch-bishop followed up with an immediate offer to lift them should the Welsh come to the king's peace.

It was not until the middle of March that Edward's stir-crazy infantry managed to persuade him to allow them to begin raiding. A mixed force including cavalry, archers and crossbowmen left the safety of the castle walls, surprising the Welsh while they were sleeping and recapturing much of the baggage train; according to the Hagnaby Chronicle, this took place on 10 March and the Welsh dead numbered 500. The news coming in from the rest of Wales was also positive for Edward, his troops at Rhuddlan under de Grey having struck out into the Perfeddwlad at the beginning of March and begun clearing Welsh resistance out of the deep forests. In the south Humphrey de Bohun had recovered Abergavenny in the middle of February and gone on to inflict other reverses on the Welsh.

It was once again in the middle march where the decisive defeat of the Welsh occurred; on 5 March at Maes Moydog, 8 miles north-west of Mont-gomery and 4 miles west of Welshpool, Madog ap Llywelyn was engaged by the earl of Warwick, William de Beauchamp, in a pitched battle.[14] Such an encounter is unlikely to have been of Welsh choosing, and we know that spies had come to Warwick when he was at Oswestry, giving him detailed knowl-edge of the advance of his enemy into Cydewain. Warwick quickly moved his forces back to Montgomery by 4 March and was then able to surprise the Welsh leader with a rapid, night march, apparently surrounding Madog with a detachment of his army, cutting off the Welsh escape route to the west, up the Banwy valley.

Warwick's army was said to be quite small, but with around 119 cavalry and 2,500 infantry his force would have heavily outnumbered that of his opponent, who is likely to have commanded somewhere between 1,000 and 1,500 men. One account of the battle suggests that the English interspersed their cavalry with archers and crossbowmen, something that has been inter-preted as a novel tactic that would be repeated – with much success – in the Hundred Years War. The sources do not seem strong enough to warrant such an interpretation, though, and the pay rolls only list thirteen archers and crossbowmen in Warwick's army (although the numbers listed under the generic description of 'infantry' are likely to have included many more archers).[15] On an open battleground that was not of his choosing, and with no option to flee, Madog – who was, we are told, accompanied by 'the elite of his Welshmen' – arranged his forces effectively and fought bravely, even winning the admiration of his enemies. He organised his troops into an infantry square, with their spears used to repulse the English cavalry: a sensible tactic for an outnumbered force that was likely to have conceded major advantages to its enemies in terms of cavalry and heavy armour, but something that could only delay inevitable defeat. A newsletter account of the engagement has been preserved in the Hagnaby Chronicle:

> The prince's host awaited our men on open ground and they fought together, our men killing a good 600. Then our men from Chesseweit [Llystynwynnan] joined battle with those who were transporting the prince's victuals, and killed a good 100 and took from them over six score beasts laden with foodstuffs. And we lost only one esquire, the tailor of Robert FitzWalter, and six infantrymen, but a good ten horses were killed. For the Welshmen held their ground well, and they were the best and bravest Welsh that anyone has seen.[16]

The loss of his baggage train in the secondary clash at 'Chesseweit' – tentatively identified as Llystynwynnan[17] – is the evidence for the belief that Madog was surrounded and forced to give battle, and it is also this source that allows a discussion of the Welsh army numbers. The need for '120 beasts laden with foodstuffs', indicates an army of significant size, while two separate sources claim that 700 Welsh were killed in the fighting. If Madog's army was surrounded, it would suggest that not many of his men escaped from the English and, if the figure of 700 dead does not include other wounded, an army size of close to 1,500 would seem likely. If, on the other hand, the Welsh wounded were slaughtered, a figure closer to 1,000 may be more appropriate. Madog himself did manage to slip away in the chaos, probably fleeing to Snowdonia and/or Meirionydd, but his defeat ripped the heart out of the resistance. When he heard the news, Edward almost immediately began redirecting supplies from Wales to his troops in Gascony.

Beaumaris Castle

The king still had business with the Welsh, and targeted the cradle of the revolt in the north: Anglesey. As has been seen, the island was always strategically vulnerable and – with the help of ships, a pontoon bridge and siege engines built by Master James of St George – it was quickly overrun in early April. At the outset of the insurgency the English sheriff Roger Puleston had been killed in Llanfaes, and on 10 April Edward was at the burgeoning town, ready to take his revenge. The settlement was razed to the ground and the population moved to the site of Rhosyr on the other side of the island, which would be known as Newborough Llanfaes. A new town would be raised on the old site of Llanfaes and would be protected by the final, and in some ways the finest, castle that Edward and Master James would build in Wales: Beaumaris.

Work started on the castle in April 1295 and in two seasons of frenzied building the structure that stands today was largely completed. In the first summer an average of 1,800 workmen, 450 stonemasons and 375 quarrymen were employed, the wage bill amounting to around £270 a week. The huge demand for resources would prove hard to justify in more settled times, and on 27 February 1296 Master James and Walter of Winchester would write to Edward pleading for the funds to continue their great work: 'As to how things are in the land of Wales, we still cannot be any too sure. But, as you well know, Welshmen are Welshmen, and you need to understand them properly; if, which God forbid, there is war with France and Scotland, we shall need to watch them all the more closely.'[18] A busy and productive summer of work followed in 1296, but the pace then dropped dramatically, proceeding slowly until Master James' death in 1309 and dragging on under Nicholas Durnford until 1331.

The castle was never completed, the walls not reaching their intended height, but what was left was arguably the most perfect example of concentric fortification ever built. Constructed on a low-lying, marshy site, it relied upon the strength of the walls rather than any natural defences. The castle was dominated by an inner ward with six huge towers and two D-shaped gate-houses, every wall and tower provided with formidable projecting firepower. Outside this was an outer curtain wall strengthened by twelve towers and two gatehouses, all surrounded by an 18-feet-wide, water-filled moat that allowed sea access to the south gate. The water approach was protected by another wall and firing platform that is thought to have carried a trebuchet.

The collapse of the resistance

By April 1295, when Edward began the work at Beaumaris, Welsh resistance was close to being extinguished, the improving weather adding to the English advantages. The king began receiving large numbers of submissions and taking hostages; a total of 250 would be sent back to English prisons from the royal lands in Wales alone. The marcher lords would follow Edward's example and take submissions and hostages on their territory, while Welshmen seeking the king's peace would also be subject to heavy fines and the taking of recognizances as a guarantee of future good behaviour. To secure such submissions, Edward headed south from Anglesey, crossing the Menai Straits to reach Bangor on 6 May, then visiting Cricieth and Harlech, castles that had been held throughout the revolt by their garrisons, which had been kept well supplied by the royal fleet. The king continued south, getting to within 10 miles of Aberystwyth, where he met the troops from Rhuddlan led by Reginald de Grey, plus the earl of Warwick's victorious army. This would be an unfortunate time for the Cistercian abbey of Strata Florida, the community of which had been stalwart supporters of Welsh culture. Its abbot had promised Edward that he would bring in the leading native rulers of the region to his peace, but when they failed to appear the king ordered that the abbey should be burnt to the ground. He would later claim that his soldiers had misunderstood his orders and that the destruction was 'contrary to his wishes'.

Edward kept moving south to Cardigan, then east to Carmarthen, Dryslwyn and Brecon. He was in Glamorgan by the middle of June, visiting Morlais and being delighted to be able to end the rebellion that the lord of the region, his old rival de Clare, had been unable to snuff out. The king showed Morgan ap Maredudd favour and took him into his peace 'against the earl's wishes'; Morgan would later serve as a squire of the royal household in Flanders and elsewhere. Edward also determined that de Clare had failed in his duty to deal with the trouble and so confiscated Glamorgan from him for a time; perhaps the king's vindictiveness was in revenge for the earl's opposition in 1294 that had led to the abandonment of the *Quo Warranto* proceedings. The outrage felt by the earl may have contributed to his death on 7 December, at the age of 52.

Edward headed back northwards along Wales' eastern border, passing through Montgomery, Welshpool, Oswestry and Chirk. By the end of June the king was back at Conwy, the token military force accompanying him an indication that the revolt was all but over. Madog was still at large, but surrendered unconditionally in either late July or early August. John de Havering received a £333 reward for securing the Welsh leader, but the man responsible would seem to have been Enyr Fychan of Meirionydd; he would later claim that he held the office of *rhaglaw* ('sergeant') of Talybont as a reward for his capture of Madog. The prisoner was taken to London but escaped a traitor's death, instead being kept in captivity in the Tower for the rest of his life; we know that he was alive in 1312, as were his sons, and there are indications that they were treated with honour and respect. This is perhaps an indication of the fact that Edward realised that Madog and the other Welsh nobles had been thrust to the forefront of a popular rising caused by the misrule of the country. The other main leaders of the revolt did not fare so well, though. Maelgwn ap Rhys Fychan was killed in fighting with de Clare's men near Carmarthen on 7 June; his brothers, Rhys and Gruffudd, are known to have been held in the king's prison of Norwich in 1308. Cynan ap Maredudd was captured in Hereford in the summer of 1295 and then hanged on 14 September, along with two close associates.

It had not proved possible to sustain the popular rising against a king as determined as Edward, and one with so many resources to call upon. The sovereign had, though, been forced to endure eight uncomfortable months in

Wales, distracting him from his other pressing concerns at a financial cost of around £55,000 that would contribute to a huge English fiscal crisis. It was only at this point that the king chose to return to the ruins of his prized castle at Caernarfon. There, Edward ordered the investment of huge sums, determined to rebuild and heighten the damaged castle and town walls, with major construction work continuing until 1300. This was an indication of his commitment to the task, at a time when urgent calls on his time and resources were coming from Gascony and Scotland. The haste with which the work was ordered was also an indication that the possibility of future trouble in Wales continued to loom large in the king's mind.[19] The grandiose structure was largely complete by 1301, when the king's 16-year-old son Edward of Caernarfon effectively became the new Prince of Wales when he was endowed with the royal lands in the country.[20] While much of the life and career of the future Edward II would be disastrous, that cannot be said of his relations with the Welsh; the native gentry were glad to have a new prince who would serve as an accessible source of petition and patronage, something that would begin the process of restoring a pathway to political power and influence for Welshmen.

If the elder Edward's determination and indomitable will were evident in his completion of construction at Caernarfon, the practical realities of his situation in 1295 demanded the abandonment of one of his prized projects at the site: the imperial, banded walls that resemble Constantinople were forgone on the damaged sections of the walls, meaning that they are only present on the southern side of the castle. The dominating, flawed and incomplete remains of Edward's grand design can be seen today, an appropriate symbol of the king's achievement in conquering the Welsh.

Chapter 12

A United Kingdom?

A royal commission was set up to look into the causes of the revolt of 1294–5, but the onerous financial exactions continued; in 1300 the collection of a tax of a fifteenth brought in £2,776 from Wales (excluding marcher territories).[1] Wales was crushed and if 1295 was effectively the end of Edward's Welsh wars, the remaining twelve years of his reign would see an enormous increase in the scale and intensity of his military activity. Wars in Scotland and France would dwarf the efforts and resources the king had expended in Wales, any achievements coming at almost incalculable cost. It was in this period that the chronicler Pierre de Langtoft compared Edward favourably with the legendary Arthur, who so clearly fascinated the English king:

> Ah God! How often Merlin said the truth
> In his prophecies, if you read them …
> Now are the islanders all joined together
> And Albany [Scotland] united to the regalities
> Of which king Edward is proclaimed lord.
> Cornwall and Wales are in his power
> And Ireland the great at his will.
> There is neither king nor prince of all the countries
> Except King Edward, who has thus united them
> Arthur never held the fiefs so fully.[2]

Whatever the king's obsession with mythology, though, it was the imposition of an English mythology, not an attempt to create a pan-British one. According to Professor Rees Davies:

> The power which Edward I exercised in 1296 was *not* that of monarch of the whole of Britain, either in name or in substance, but rather that of the king of England who had brought the four countries of the British Isles more or less under his power. The consequences of that fact, and of the way in which the power bloc had been assembled, cast their shadow over the history of the British Isles for generations, indeed centuries, to come. In a power bloc constructed from England, outwards, the status of the other countries and peoples of the British Isles was likely to be at best problematic, at worst inferior.[3]

While historical, cultural, political and economic realities played a part in creating this state of affairs, a large measure of responsibility must also lie with Edward himself. According to his biographer, Professor Michael Prestwich: 'He was very well aware of his own honour and his own rights, but invariably lacked awareness of the susceptibilities of others ... He placed the Welsh princes, and the Scottish leaders, in a position where they had little option, as they saw it, but to have recourse to arms, even though this had not been Edward's intention.'[4]

By 1305 it did seem that Edward had accomplished his goals in Wales, Scotland and France. To achieve this position, Dr Marc Morris estimates that Edward had spent well over £1m and: 'To raise it he had resorted to terrible expedients – visiting violence on the clergy, seizing the goods of his subjects without their consent, and even trying to impose taxation against the will of parliament.'[5] If resulting problems were clearly evident in England, they were far more so in Wales and Scotland, where the loss of life, destruction of property, seizure of land, and policies of apartheid and cultural appropriation would create lasting legacies of bitterness and resentment.

The burgeoning power of the kingdom of France meant that English gains on the continent were always likely to be challenged. Such trouble overseas would also help the Scots in their struggles with England, while the size of Scotland, the number of its inhabitants, its rugged nature, its distance from London and the growing Scottish nationalism that had been fostered by Edward's wars all played a part in the destruction of Longshanks' plan for a permanent conquest there.

In Wales, though, Edward's enormous war efforts and subsequent investment in towns and castles helped ensure that his conquest would be permanent. His actions built on the legacy of Anglo-Saxon and Anglo-Norman overlordship of Wales and on the work of the marcher lords in the two centuries since the Norman Conquest, continuing to exploit the rivalries that existed within the native Welsh dynasties. Under such pressures Brythonic/ Welsh political power had declined inexorably in the course of over 800 years from the days of Roman Britain; by the thirteenth century, it is hard to argue with the conclusion of Professor Rees Davies that: 'There could be no way, it seems to me, in which the vision of Llywelyn as it had been defined over the years 1255–77, that of the ruler of a virtually independent principality of native Wales, could be squared with the ambitions and assumptions of Edward I.'[6]

While the irreconcilable ideological arguments between Llywelyn and Edward, the red dragon and the white, loom large, it is well to remember the sufferings inflicted upon the ordinary people of Wales in these wars. The grievances outlined at Nancall in 1283 speak loud of how their traditional way

of life had been impacted upon by Llywelyn's desire to develop his principality, and hint at how things would only get worse under Edward's colonial
regime. Perhaps ultimately, it was the steady advance of England's lowland
civilisation into the rugged uplands of Wales that marked the real conquest of
the country, although the work of modern-day Welsh bards indicates that the
process remains far from complete:

> They don't care about
> You and me, obviously
> No not us
> We're the mountain people ...
> They'll seek us in the valley
> They'll seek us on the plain
> They own the milk and runny honey
> And they're not quite the same ...
> From a distance, I can see them
> Pacing upstream, slowly, ruthlessly
> Onwards, steady, nets and cages
> Open, ready, long term memory
> Soothes me, worry, take me, break me
> Any way you fancy.[7]

Notes

Chapter 1: The Red and the White Dragons

1. Walter Map, *De Nugis Curialium/Courtiers' Trifles*, ed. and trans. M.R. James, C.N.L. Brooke and R.A.B. Mynors (Oxford, 1983), pp. 193–5. The writer of this account was, appropriately, a man of the border, a twelfth-century Herefordshire cleric named Walter Map who had Welsh heritage and who worked in English royal service. The location is an ancient ferry crossing that is now spanned by the original Severn Bridge road crossing.

2. *Acts*, p. 543.

3. Translation of the Latin is from the J.A. Giles edition and can be found in full at http://legacy.fordham.edu/halsall/basis/nennius-full.asp.

4. See D.P. Kirby, 'Hywel Dda: Anglophil', *WHR*, 8 (1976–7), 1–13. For the original text, see *Armes Prydein: The Prophecy of Britain*, ed. I Williams, Eng. vers. R. Bromwich (Dublin, 1972).

5. These are the leaders accorded the title 'King of the Britons' in the Welsh-language versions of the native chronicle known collectively as the *Brutiau*, which shows bias towards an extended dynastic tree that includes Maredudd ab Owain and Bleddyn ap Cynfyn. Earlier, Latin texts of the chronicle – known collectively as *Annales Cambriae* – have a more select list of four leaders referred to as 'King of the Britons', omitting the names of Maredudd and Bleddyn.

6. John of Salisbury, *Policraticus*, ed. C.J. Nederman (Cambridge, 1990), p. 114.

7. *Description*, II, 7, p. 266. No examples of the inscribed stones described by Gerald have ever been found.

8. See my *The First Prince of Wales? Bleddyn ap Cynfyn, 1063–1075* (Cardiff, 2016).

9. ASC 'D', s.a. 1063.

10. See W.R. Jones, 'The image of the barbarian in medieval Europe', *Comparative Studies in Society and History*, 13 (1971), 376–407; also his 'England against the Celtic fringe: a study in cultural stereotypes', *Journal of World History*, 13 (1971), 155–71; R.R. Davies, *Domination and Conquest* (Cambridge, 1990), pp. 21–3; J. Gillingham, 'The context and purpose of Geoffrey of Monmouth's *History of the Kings of Britain*', *ANS*, 13 (1990), 99–118; also his 'The beginnings of English imperialism', *Journal of Historical Sociology*, 5 (1992), 392–409; and his 'Conquering the barbarians: War and chivalry in twelfth-century Britain', *Haskins Soc. Journal*, 4 (1992), 67–84; F.C. Suppe, 'The cultural significance of decapitation in high medieval Wales and the Marches', *BBCS*, 36 (1989), 147–60; R. Bartlett, *Gerald of Wales, 1146–1223* (Oxford, 1982), pp. 158ff; J. France, *Western Warfare in the Age of the Crusades, 1000–1300* (London, 1999), pp. 187–203.

11. *Brut (Pen 20)*, 1114.

12. *Brut (RBH)*, 1114.

13. H. Pryce, 'Owain Gwynedd and Louis VII: The Franco-Welsh diplomacy of the first Prince of Wales', *WHR*, 19 (1998), 1–28.

14. *LapG*, p. 27.
15. *Age*, pp. 292–3.
16. *LapG*, pp. 19–20.

Chapter 2: English and Welsh Military Institutions

1. *Description*, I, 1, p. 220.
2. *Journey*, p. 182.
3. *Age*, p. 9.
4. For further discussion, see I.W. Rowlands, 'The Making of the March: Aspects of the Norman Settlement in Dyfed', *ANS*, 3 (1980), 142–57.
5. As an indication of English settlement in this period, it has been estimated that there are 350 '-ton' settlement names in Wales. Such names typically date from the medieval period, and two-thirds of the ones in Wales are found in Glamorgan and Pembrokeshire; see R.R. Davies, *The First English Empire: Power and Identities in the British Isles, 1093–1343* (Oxford, 2000), p. 154.
6. R.R. Davies, *The First English Empire: Power and Identities in the British Isles, 1093–1343* (Oxford, 2000), p. 19.
7. Roger of Wendover, *Flowers of History*, ed. and trans. J.A. Giles, 2 vols (London, 1849), II, p. 509.
8. MP, I, p. 372.
9. MP, III, p. 200.
10. *Age*, pp. 146–7. Davies also estimates that the population of Scotland was approximately 1 million.
11. *Age*, p. 216.
12. *LapG*, p. 246.
13. *Journey*, pp. 187, 194.
14. *Brut (RBH)*, 1211.
15. *Age*, pp. 162–3.
16. H. Pryce, 'Frontier Wales, *c.*1063–1282', in P. Morgan (ed.), *The Tempus History of Wales* (Stroud, 2001), pp. 77–106, esp. 89–90.
17. *LapG*, pp. 249–51.
18. *Great and Terrible*, p. 136.
19. *Edward I*, p. 401.
20. As noted by David Stephenson: 'From the close of the principate of Llywelyn ap Iorwerth the support of the bishops of Bangor and St Asaph for the rulers of Gwynedd was at best uncertain and frequently non-existent'; *Political Power in Medieval Gwynedd: Governance and the Welsh Princes* (Cardiff, 2014), p. 181.
21. Benedict Wiedemann claims that Dafydd always knew such a ruling would go against him and that his appeal was made as a cunning way of delaying the pious Henry from launching his campaign against Wales; see B.G.E. Wiedemann, '"Fooling the court of the lord Pope": Dafydd ap Llywelyn's petition to the Curia in 1244', *WHR*, 28 (2016), 209–32.
22. *LapG*, p. 532.
23. *Description* II, 3, pp. 259–60.
24. *Description* II, 8, p. 268.
25. *Description* II, 10, p. 273.
26. *Description* I, 8, p. 233.

27. D. Stephenson, *Political Power in Medieval Gwynedd: Governance and the Welsh Princes* (Cardiff, 2014), p. 15.
28. D. Stephenson, *Political Power in Medieval Gwynedd: Governance and the Welsh Princes* (Cardiff, 2014), p. 5.
29. See D. Stephenson, *Political Power in Medieval Gwynedd: Governance and the Welsh Princes* (Cardiff, 2014), p. 89.
30. D. Stephenson, *Political Power in Medieval Gwynedd: Governance and the Welsh Princes* (Cardiff, 2014), p. 91.
31. D. Stephenson, *Political Power in Medieval Gwynedd: Governance and the Welsh Princes* (Cardiff, 2014), p. 93.
32. D. Stephenson, *Political Power in Medieval Gwynedd: Governance and the Welsh Princes* (Cardiff, 2014), p. 93.
33. For further discussion, see D. Stephenson, *Political Power in Medieval Gwynedd: Governance and the Welsh Princes* (Cardiff, 2014), p. 130.
34. An agreement made between Llywelyn and Richard, the bishop of Bangor, at Rhydyrarw on 29 April 1261, states: 'As regards men of the bishop unfit for war, neither military service nor its commutation should be exacted from those younger than the lawful age of 14 years; but let older men perform military service or pay the commutation'; *Acts*, p. 514.
35. For discussion, see *LapG*, pp. 293–5.
36. *Acts*, p. 483.
37. MP, III, pp. 217–18.
38. *Calendar of Ancient Correspondence Concerning Wales*, ed. J.G. Edwards (Cardiff, 1935), p. 15.
39. *Calendar of Ancient Correspondence Concerning Wales*, ed. J.G. Edwards (Cardiff, 1935), p. 18.
40. For further discussion, see *Edward I*, pp. 134–69; also his *War, Politics and Finance*, pp. 41–66.
41. *Edward I*, p. 147.
42. Owain was the son of Gruffudd ap Gwenwynwyn.
43. *Edward I*, p. 148.
44. *Edward I*, p. 193.
45. Sums paid to the earls of Norfolk, Lincoln and Warwick in the 1282–3 conflict are thought to have been for infantry forces; *Edward I*, p. 485.
46. *Edward I*, p. 564.
47. *War, Politics and Finance*, p. 67.
48. *Edward I*, p. 406.
49. For further discussion of distraint of knighthood and the changes it made on England's military forces, see D. Simpkin, *The English Aristocracy at War: From the Welsh Wars of Edward I to the Battle of Bannockburn* (Woodbridge, 2008).
50. According to Professor Michael Prestwich: 'It seems unlikely that these rates reflected the real cost of military service: a more realistic figure is suggested by agreements made by military contractors to provide the military service owed by ecclesiastics, which show that it cost £100 to provide five knights for forty days, or 10 shillings a day each.' *Edward I*, p. 485.
51. In theory, the king would not have to pay for the victuals of troops he was giving wages to, but in practice the burden of supply tended to fall on him.

52. *Welsh Wars*, p. 90.
53. *War, Politics and Finance*, p. 101.
54. *War, Politics and Finance*, p. 97.
55. *Edward I*, p. 401.
56. B.S. Bachrach, 'Military Logistics During the Reign of Edward I of England, 1272–1307', *War in History*, 13 (2006), 423–40.
57. *Welsh Wars*, p. 107.
58. *Great and Terrible*, p. 100.
59. Partial translation taken from T.R. Phillips, *The Roots of Strategy* (London, 1943), p. 67.
60. Partial translation taken from T.R. Phillips, *The Roots of Strategy* (London, 1943), pp. 92–3.
61. R.R. Davies, *Domination and Conquest* (Cambridge, 1990), pp. 39–40; Davies refers to the argument set out for Europe by R. Bartlett in 'Technique militaire et pouvoir politique, 900–1300', *Annalés Economies, Sociétés, Civilisations*, 41 (1986), 1138–59. Bartlett expanded his views in *The Making of Europe* (London, 1993), contending that *c.*950–1350 the nobility from the 'heartland' of Frankish and German Europe used their advanced military technology to make conquests on the 'fringes' of the continent. The three main components were missile weapons, castles and heavy cavalry.
62. J. France, *Western Warfare in the Age of the Crusades, 1000–1300* (London, 1999), pp. 32–3.
63. See, for example, J. Bradbury, *The Medieval Siege* (Woodbridge, 1992), p. 333; M. Strickland, *War and Chivalry: The Conduct and Perception of War in England and Normandy, 1066–1217* (Cambridge, 1996), p. 50.
64. See my *Welsh Military Institutions, 633–1283* (Cardiff, 2004), pp. 242–7.
65. *Brut (Pen. 20)*, 1210.
66. The only known departures from this general strategic approach occurred (unsuccessfully) in the revolt of 1287–8.
67. At the height of his power, Llywelyn ap Gruffudd (and/or his allies) also seems to have been responsible for the construction of stone castles in other outlying territories, near Clun, Sennybridge and Caerphilly; see *LapG*, p. 252.
68. Although the military role of vaccaries has been frequently highlighted, it is important to note that they were also of major economic importance. The relative importance of military and economic needs associated with their creation cannot really be judged.
69. *Mabinogion*, ed. and trans. J. Gantz (Harmondsworth, 1976), pp. 125–6; for discussion of siege warfare, see J. Bradbury, *The Medieval Siege* (Woodbridge, 1992); E. McGeer, 'Byzantine siege warfare in theory and practice', in I.A. Corfis and M. Wolfe (eds), *The Medieval City Under Siege* (Woodbridge, 1995), pp. 123–9; J. France, *Western Warfare in the Age of the Crusades, 1000–1300* (London, 1999), pp. 107–27.
70. For further discussion of Welsh siege warfare, see my *Welsh Military Institutions, 633–1283* (Cardiff, 2004).
71. See M. Strickland, *War and Chivalry: The Conduct and Perception of War in England and Normandy, 1066–1217* (Cambridge, 1996), p. 335.
72. See my *Welsh Military Institutions, 633–1283* (Cardiff, 2004), pp. 247–58.
73. *Acts*, p. 515. The same document outlines cases of fighting in the churches of Bangor, Rhosyr and Talybolion, for which fines for sacrilege were to be paid to the bishop.
74. MP, II, pp. 46–7.

75. In *The Dream of Rhonabwy*, for example, Rhonabwy and his companions, who were mere footsoldiers, were captured by a knight who regarded them as hostages for booty; *Mabinogion*, ed. and trans. J. Gantz (Harmondsworth, 1976), p.180.

76. *Acts*, pp. 617–18.

Chapter 3: The Rise of a Prince

1. By this time it was said that the three chief courts of Wales were Aberffraw (Gwynedd), Dinefwr (Deheubarth) and Mathrafal (Powys). Although many claims were made for the antiquity of this tradition, it only seems to have emerged in the twelfth century.

2. *Description*, II, p.273.

3. *LapG*, pp. 8–9.

4. *LapG*, p. 10.

5. *LapG*, p. 13.

6. See D. Stephenson, *Political Power in Medieval Gwynedd: Governance and the Welsh Princes* (Cardiff, 2014), p.153.

7. R.F. Walker, 'The Anglo-Welsh wars, 1217–67; with special reference to English military developments (unpublished D.Phil. thesis, Oxford University, 1954), p. 3.

8. *LapG*, pp. 37–8 notes the possibility that Senana was not Llywelyn's mother, with some late genealogies naming as his mother a woman called Rhunallt, the daughter of the king of Man. Professor Beverley Smith is confident that this claim is erroneous and that Senana was the mother of all four of Gruffudd's known sons, although he is less certain that she was the mother of Gruffudd's daughters, Gwladus and Margaret. The birth date of Llywelyn's younger brothers, Dafydd and Rhodri, are unknown, but neither seems to have come of age before 1246. They were most likely conceived in the period 1234–39, when their father was at liberty.

9. For discussion, see *LapG*, pp. 40–1.

10. *LapG*, pp. 42–3.

11. *LapG*, p. 45.

12. *MP*, I, p.372.

13. *MP*, I, p.373.

14. *Acts*, p. 474.

15. L. Alcock, 'Excavations at Degannwy Castle, Caernarfonshire, 1961–6', *Archaeological Journal*, 124 (1967), 190–201, esp. 190.

16. *MP*, I, pp. 487–8.

17. *MP*, II, p. 110.

18. *Brut (Pen. 20)*, 1245.

19. *MP*, II, p. 115.

20. *MP*, II, pp. 114–16.

21. *MP*, II, p. 141.

22. *LapG*, pp. 66–7.

23. *LapG*, p. 67.

24. *Age*, p. 318; *HW*, II, p. 258.

25. J.P. Clancy, *The Earliest Welsh Poetry* (London, 1970), p. 170.

26. No mention is made at this stage of Owain, Llywelyn and Dafydd's other brother, Rhodri. He may have been in the king's custody, and all parties involved will have realised the potential for further division of Gwynedd should his claims be pressed.

27. *Brut (Pen. 20)*, 1255.

28. Quoted from *LapG*, p. 72, fn. 142.
29. Quoted from *LapG*, p. 75, fn. 153.

Chapter 4: The Young Panther

1. For fuller discussion of Edward's early years, see *Great and Terrible*, pp. 6ff.
2. *Great and Terrible*, p. 6.
3. Quoted in *Great and Terrible*, p. 75.
4. M. Prestwich, *The Three Edwards* (London, 1980), p. 295.
5. The figure of 200 was given by Matthew Paris, but Professor Michael Prestwich says that this was 'surely an exaggeration on the chronicler's part'; *Edward I*, p. 15.
6. MP, III, p. 201.
7. MP, III, p. 201.
8. MP, III, p. 205.
9. D.A. Carpenter, *The Struggle for Mastery: Britain 1066–1284* (London, 2003), p. 362.
10. *Edward I*, p. 17.
11. *LapG*, pp. 87–9.
12. *Brut (Pen. 20)*, 1256.
13. MP, III, p. 204.
14. MP, III, p. 204.
15. MP, III, pp. 200–1.
16. *Brut (Pen. 20)*, 1256.
17. MP, III, p. 218.
18. MP, III, p. 233.
19. The exact locations of Coed Llathen and Cymerau have not been established.
20. MP, III, p. 238.
21. MP, III, p. 304, 1258; *Brut (Pen. 20)*, 1258; J.P. Clancy, *The Earliest Welsh Poetry* (London, 1970), p. 170.
22. MP, III, pp. 311–12.
23. MP, III, p. 312. In the previous year (1257), Llywelyn had written to Richard of Cornwall in an attempt to secure a permanent peace deal, offering money and land concessions in north-east Wales, or £1,000 for a seven-year truce; *Calendar of Ancient Correspondence Concerning Wales*, ed. J.G. Edwards (Cardiff, 1935), pp. 50–1.

Chapter 5: The Road to Montgomery

1. *Acts*, p. 503.
2. For discussion of the six-week service issue on this campaign, see D. Stephenson, *Political Power in Medieval Gwynedd: Governance and the Welsh Princes* (Cardiff, 2014), p. 90.
3. N. Bosco, 'Dafydd Benfras and his Red Book poems', *Studia Celtica*, 22 (1987), 49–117, esp. 103.
4. *Brut (Pen. 20)*, 1260.
5. *Acts*, p. 508.
6. *Brut (RBH)*, 1262. See also Matthew of Westminster, *The Flowers of History*, ed. and trans. C.D. Yonge, 2 vols (London, 1853), II, p. 402; *Acts*, p. 527.
7. *Calendar of Ancient Correspondence Concerning Wales*, ed. J.G. Edwards (Cardiff, 1935), p. 15.
8. *Acts*, p. 527.

9. Matthew of Westminster, *The Flowers of History*, ed. and trans. C.D. Yonge, 2 vols (London, 1853), II, p. 403.

10. *Great and Terrible*, p. 53.

11. See D. Stephenson, *Political Power in Medieval Gwynedd: Governance and the Welsh Princes* (Cardiff, 2014), p. 16.

12. *Brut (RBH)*, 1263.

13. Matthew of Westminster, *The Flowers of History*, ed. and trans. C.D. Yonge, 2 vols (London, 1853), II, pp. 403–4.

14. *Great and Terrible*, p. 58.

15. L. Alcock, 'Excavations at Degannwy Castle, Caernarfonshire, 1961–6', *Archaeological Journal*, 124 (1967), 190–201, esp. 192.

16. For further discussion, see *LapG*, pp. 166–9.

17. *Acts*, pp. 546–7. The settlement of the territorial agreement for Dafydd would drag on and was not granted until 1269.

18. J.P. Clancy, *The Earliest Welsh Poetry* (London, 1970), p. 167.

Chapter 6: The Phoney War

1. *LapG*, p. 345.

2. The Treaty of Montgomery had made provision for this, with Llywelyn to pay £3,666 for the homage if Henry agreed to it. It is unclear whether the sum was ever paid. Maredudd died a year later and was succeeded by his son Rhys.

3. *Great and Terrible*, p. 127.

4. J.P. Clancy, *The Earliest Welsh Poetry* (London, 1970), p. 170.

5. Humphrey de Bohun would succeed his grandfather as earl of Hereford in 1275 and was determined to win back territory that had been ceded to Llywelyn in Brycheiniog.

6. *LapG*, pp. 355–8. Both in Brycheiniog and Deheubarth, Llywelyn felt the need to take prisoners, hostages, sureties and solemn pledges from the native communities.

7. G.R.J. Jones, 'The military geography of Gwynedd in the thirteenth century' (unpublished MA thesis, University of Wales Aberystwyth, 1949), p. 104.

8. Gruffudd may have been further disgruntled by the likelihood that Dolforwyn was built on top of a site that had previously been fortified by the rulers of Powys.

9. *Acts*, p. 543.

10. *Acts*, p. 554.

11. Quoted in *Great and Terrible*, p. 115.

12. R.R. Davies, *The First English Empire: Power and Identities in the British Isles, 1093–1343* (Oxford, 2000), p. 22.

13. R.R. Davies, *The First English Empire: Power and Identities in the British Isles, 1093–1343* (Oxford, 2000), p. 13.

14. *Acts*, pp. 555–6.

15. *Age*, p. 216.

16. *Great and Terrible*, p. 137.

17. D. Stephenson, *Political Power in Medieval Gwynedd: Governance and the Welsh Princes* (Cardiff, 2014), pp. xxxiii–xxxiv.

18. *LapG*, pp. 364–6.

19. See above, pp. 20–1.

20. *Littere Wallie preserved in Liber A in the Public Record Office*, ed. J.G. Edwards (Cardiff, 1940), l–li.

21. *Great and Terrible*, p. 123.
22. *War, Politics and Finance*, p. 207.
23. See *Edward I*, p. 239; *Great and Terrible*, pp. 270–1.
24. *Brut (Pen. 20)*, 1274.
25. *Acts*, pp. 562–3.
26. *LapG*, pp. 367–9.
27. *Brut (Pen. 20)*, 1275.
28. *Treaty Rolls, 1234–1325*, p. 54; translation from *Age*, p. 327.
29. *Flores Historiarum*, ed. and trans. C.D. Yonge, 2 vols (London, 1853), II, p. 469.
30. *Brut (Pen. 20)*, 1275.
31. *LapG*, p. 398, discusses the legally binding nature of Llywelyn's marriage to Eleanor in 1275.
32. *Calendar of Ancient Correspondence Concerning Wales*, ed. J.G. Edwards (Cardiff, 1935), p. 82.
33. *Welsh Wars*, pp. 120–1.
34. *Brut (Pen. 20)*, 1276.

Chapter 7: 1277: The War of Domination

1. *Great and Terrible*, p. 144.
2. *LapG*, p. 416.
3. A. Taylor, *The Welsh Castles of Edward I* (London, 1986), p. 1.
4. For further discussion of his career, see A. Taylor, 'Master Bertram, *Ingeniator Regis*', in C. Harper-Bill (ed.), *Studies in History Presented to R. Allen-Brown* (Woodbridge, 1989), pp. 289–304.
5. *Calendar of Ancient Correspondence Concerning Wales*, ed. J.G. Edwards (Cardiff, 1935), pp. 30–1.
6. *Calendar of Ancient Correspondence Concerning Wales*, ed. J.G. Edwards (Cardiff, 1935), p. 31.
7. I have chosen to use Aberystwyth throughout, although government records consistently refer to the nearby, established settlement of Llanbadarn.
8. For further discussion, see R. Griffiths, *Conquerors and Conquered in Medieval Wales* (Stroud, 1994), pp. 309ff.
9. This ruler may also be referred to as Llywelyn ap Gruffudd Maelor, or as Llywelyn ap Gruffudd ap Madog.
10. *Welsh Wars*, p. 128.
11. *Calendar of Ancient Correspondence Concerning Wales*, ed. J.G. Edwards (Cardiff, 1935), p. 67.
12. *Calendar of Ancient Correspondence Concerning Wales*, ed. J.G. Edwards (Cardiff, 1935), p. 83.
13. I. Rowlands, 'The Edwardian conquest and its military consolidation', in T. Herbert and G.E. Jones (eds), *Edward I and Wales* (Cardiff, 1988), p. 48.
14. *Great and Terrible*, p. 149.
15. These were the preparations Llywelyn had made to meet Henry III's advance in 1257, as quoted above, from MP, III, p. 238.
16. *Great and Terrible*, p. 154.
17. R.F. Walker, 'William de Valence and the army of west Wales, 1282–3', *WHR*, 18 (1997), 407–29, esp. 423.

18. *Annales Monastici*, ed. H.R. Luard, 5 vols (Rolls Series, London, 1864–9), IV, p. 272; quoted in *Welsh Wars*, p. 130.
19. *Welsh Wars*, p. 132.
20. *Edward I*, p. 230.
21. *LapG*, p. 428.
22. Plans for a royal castle at Ruthin in Dyffryn Clwyd would suggest that at this time Edward still intended to make provision for Dafydd in Snowdonia; see A. Taylor, *The Welsh Castles of Edward I* (London, 1986), p. 35. At the end of the campaign Dafydd was instead provided with Dyffryn Clwyd, meaning that the royal castle at Ruthin was not continued.
23. *Great and Terrible*, p. 156.
24. *Welsh Wars*, p. 132.
25. *LapG*, p. 256.
26. J.P. Clancy, *The Earliest Welsh Poetry* (London, 1970), p. 169.
27. D. Stephenson, *Political Power in Medieval Gwynedd: Governance and the Welsh Princes* (Cardiff, 2014), p. 102.
28. D. Stephenson, *Political Power in Medieval Gwynedd: Governance and the Welsh Princes* (Cardiff, 2014), p. 129.
29. Llywelyn had taken sureties for the good behaviour of Rhys ap Gruffudd ab Enyfed as early as 1269.
30. *Calendar of Ancient Correspondence Concerning Wales*, ed. J.G. Edwards (Cardiff, 1935), p. 112.
31. *Great and Terrible*, p. 157.

Chapter 8: Wales Under the Heel of Longshanks

1. *War, Politics and Finance*, p. 170.
2. *Age*, pp. 339–41.
3. I. Rowlands, 'The Edwardian conquest and its military consolidation', in T. Herbert and G.E. Jones (eds), *Edward I and Wales* (Cardiff, 1988), p. 45.
4. *Great and Terrible*, p. 162. The issue of the 'greatest dynastic match' is certainly a subjective one, but, as one alternative example, I would cite the marriage *c.*1057 of Gruffudd ap Llywelyn to Ealdgyth, the future queen of England.
5. R.R. Davies, *The First English Empire: Power and Identities in the British Isles, 1093–1343* (Oxford, 2000), p. 23.
6. *Acts*, p. 622.
7. *Great and Terrible*, p. 170. All remaining Jews were eventually expelled from England in 1290, an act that resulted in Edward being granted another huge tax by his grateful people.
8. *Great and Terrible*, p. 172.
9. *Calendar of Welsh Rolls*, p. 163; translation from *Age*, p. 340.
10. For further discussion of this case, see *Great and Terrible*, pp. 255–6.
11. T. Herbert and G.E. Jones (eds), *Edward I and Wales* (Cardiff, 1988), p. 53.
12. *Edward I*, p. 217.
13. See A.D. Carr, 'A debatable land: Arwystli in the middle ages', *Montgomeryshire Collections*, 80 (1992), 39–54.
14. See my *The First Prince of Wales? Bleddyn ap Cynfyn, 1063–75* (Cardiff, 2016), p. 109.
15. *Welsh Assize Roll, 1277–84. Assize Roll No. 1147*, ed. J.C. Davies (Cardiff, 1940), p. 266.
16. *Calendar of Ancient Correspondence Concerning Wales*, ed. J.G. Edwards (Cardiff, 1935), p. 89.

17. *Acts*, p. 648.
18. *Acts*, p. 240.
19. *Acts*, pp. 241–2.
20. *Rotuli Parliamentorum*, 7 vols (Record Commission, 1783–1832), I, 5.
21. *Acts*, p. 212.

Chapter 9: 1282–3: The War of Conquest

1. Accounts differ in suggesting either late in the night of 21 March or early in the morning of 22 March, Palm Sunday.
2. The English were certainly militarily active in Holy Week in 1277, as shown by the letter of Henry de Lacy to Edward detailing the start of the siege of Dolforwyn 'on the Wednesday in Easter week'; *Calendar of Ancient Correspondence Concerning Wales*, ed. J.G. Edwards (Cardiff, 1935), pp. 30–1.
3. *Calendar of Ancient Correspondence Concerning Wales*, ed. J.G. Edwards (Cardiff, 1935), pp. 44–5.
4. *Brut (Pen. 20)*, 1282.
5. *Calendar of Ancient Correspondence Concerning Wales*, ed. J.G. Edwards (Cardiff, 1935), p. 67.
6. *Acts*, p. 618.
7. *LapG*, p. 461.
8. *Edward I*, p. 199. In the event, transport problems meant that Bigod was unable to move all the meat and wine across the Irish Sea.
9. *Description*, II, 8, pp. 267–8.
10. *Welsh Wars*, p. 156.
11. *Great and Terrible*, p. 179.
12. *Welsh Wars*, p. 161.
13. It is unlikely that the fortifications at either of these locations were seriously defended by the Welsh.
14. *LapG*, p. 519.
15. A. Taylor, *The Welsh Castles of Edward I* (London, 1986), p. 15.
16. *LapG*, p. 522.
17. *Acts*, p. 240.
18. *Calendar of Ancient Correspondence Concerning Wales*, ed. J.G. Edwards (Cardiff, 1935), pp. 131–2.
19. *Acts*, pp. 617–18.
20. *Calendar of Ancient Correspondence Concerning Wales*, ed. J.G. Edwards (Cardiff, 1935), p. 129.
21. *LapG*, pp. 515–17.
22. *War, Politics and Finance*, p. 106.
23. Over a thousand years earlier, the Romans had similar reservations about crossing the treacherous river near its estuary. Their chosen location was upstream to the south, where they built the fort of Canovium (now known as Caerhun) on the western bank.
24. *Acts*, pp. 617–18.
25. T. Herbert and G.E. Jones (eds), *Edward I and Wales* (Cardiff, 1988), p. 60; C.T. Martin (ed.), *Registrum Epistolarum fratris Johannis Peckham*, Rolls Series, 3 vols (London, 1882–5), II, p. 467.
26. See *Welsh Wars*, p. 179.

27. *LapG*, pp. 537–40. On balance, I am inclined to accept Bangor as the crossing point. When the pontoon bridge was rebuilt in early 1283, this was the stepping-off point.

28. Quoted from *LapG*, p. 537.

29. *Acts*, pp. 626–7.

30. *Acts*, p. 627.

31. *Acts*, pp. 653–4.

32. *Acts*, p. 654.

33. C.T. Martin (ed.), *Registrum Epistolarum fratris Johannis Peckham, Rolls Series*, 3 vols (London, 1882–5), pp. 473–7.

34. In the years to come, Pecham would instruct his clergy to re-educate the people of Wales to remove their belief in Trojan heritage and their hope of a messiah-like deliverer who would help them reclaim the rule of all Britain; C.T. Martin (ed.), *Registrum Epistolarum fratris Johannis Peckham, Rolls Series*, 3 vols (London, 1882–5), pp. 741–2.

35. T. Herbert and G.E. Jones (eds), *Edward I and Wales* (Cardiff, 1988), p. 56; *Calendar of Welsh Rolls*, pp. 275–6.

36. *War, Politics and Finance*, p. 170.

37. *Edward I*, pp. 238–9.

38. *Great and Terrible*, p. 185.

39. This was part of an escalating row between the king and Archbishop Pecham.

40. *Brut (Pen. 20)*, 1282.

41. *Calendar of Ancient Correspondence Concerning Wales*, ed. J.G. Edwards (Cardiff, 1935), p. 129.

42. *Calendar of Ancient Correspondence Concerning Wales*, ed. J.G. Edwards (Cardiff, 1935), p. 129.

43. *LapG*, pp. 566–7.

44. *Calendar of Ancient Correspondence Concerning Wales*, ed. J.G. Edwards (Cardiff, 1935), pp. 83–4.

45. Printed and translated in A.J. Taylor, *Studies in Castles and Castle-Building* (London, 1985), pp. 229–31.

46. www.british-history.ac.uk/lancs-ches-record-soc/vol14/pp102-121.

47. F.C. Suppe, 'The cultural significance of decapitation in high medieval Wales and the Marches', *BBCS*, 36 (1989), 147–60.

48. J.P. Clancy, *The Earliest Welsh Poetry* (London, 1970), p. 173.

49. J.P. Clancy, *The Earliest Welsh Poetry* (London, 1970), pp. 172–3.

50. *Welsh Wars*, pp. 188–9.

51. *Calendar of Welsh Rolls*, p. 281.

52. *Age*, p. 318.

53. *Brut (Pen. 20)*, 1275.

54. The men of Lincoln incurred the displeasure of the king when they refused to accept any part of Dafydd's body. They were eventually made to pay a fine for this behaviour.

Chapter 10: Castles, Colonisation and Rule

1. Town charters were granted to Harlech, Cricieth, Castell y Bere, Caernarfon, Conwy, Rhuddlan and Flint between September and November 1284.

2. *Edward I*, p. 216.

3. It is possible that the idea to build Beaumaris on Anglesey was also conceived at this time but not followed through; the final link in Edward's chain would not be started until 1295.
4. Master Bertram had travelled to Caernarfon after being present at the siege of Castell y Bere, but he passed away on 29 February 1284.
5. See *Edward I*, p. 231.
6. Sioned Davies, *The Mabinogion* (Oxford, 2007), p. 104.
7. A. Taylor, *The Welsh Castles of Edward I* (London, 1986), p. 78. Abigail Wheatley agrees that the banded masonry is in imitation of Roman construction, but doubts the explicit connection to Constantinople; see D.M. Williams and J.R. Kenyon (eds), *The Impact of the Edwardian Castles in Wales* (Oxford, 2010), p. 131.
8. The king's statue and the stone eagles were not added until the reign of Edward's son, Edward II. As well as the obvious imperial correlation of the eagle as the standard of the Roman legions, the symbol could also be related to the Welsh name for Snowdonia, *Eryri*, which was traditionally translated as 'the land of the eagles' from the Welsh word for eagle, *eryr*. However, it is more likely that *Eryri* should be generically translated as 'highlands' from the Latin verb *oriri* ('to rise'). Edward's well acknowledged love of falconry may also have played a part in the choice of decoration.
9. *War, Politics and Finance*, p. 171.
10. See *War, Politics and Finance*, p. 111.
11. *Edward I*, p. 215.
12. See *Age*, p. 255.
13. *Edward I*, p. 204.
14. *Welsh Wars*, p. 202.
15. Edward had been presented with the Croes Naid while at Conwy in 1284 by Hugh ab Ithel, a former clerk of Llywelyn's. In return, Hugh was given a robe worth 20 shillings and the funds to enable him to study at Oxford.
16. *Great and Terrible*, pp. 202–3.

Chapter 11: Resistance and Submission

1. For full treatment of this revolt, see R.A. Griffiths, *Conquerors and Conquered in Medieval Wales* (Stroud, 1994).
2. Other leftovers from the siege that have been recovered include a large number of smaller stones that were thrown at the castle, links of chain mail, arrowheads, slingshots and a spearhead. Over a hundred arrowheads were recovered, many with long, sharp points designed to penetrate armour and chain mail.
3. *Edward I*, p. 218.
4. *Edward I*, p. 219.
5. J. Given, *State and Society in Medieval Europe: Gwynedd and Languedoc Under Outside Rule* (New York, 1990), p. 150.
6. J. Given, *State and Society in Medieval Europe: Gwynedd and Languedoc Under Outside Rule* (New York, 1990), p. 151.
7. *Edward I*, p. 406.
8. G. Rex Smith, 'The Penmachno Letter Patent and the Welsh Uprising of 1294–95', *CMCS*, 58 (2009), 49–67.
9. At Flint at the start of the revolt, the English burgesses deliberately set fire to their town as they fled from the Welsh to take shelter in the castle.

10. The king's relationship with the Riccardi of Lucca bankers was in its death throes at this time because of their loss of £66,666 he had entrusted to their care; see *Great and Terrible*, pp. 270–1.
11. *Edward I*, p. 224.
12. *Great and Terrible*, pp. 284–5.
13. G. Rex Smith, 'The Penmachno Letter Patent and the Welsh Uprising of 1294–95', *CMCS*, 58 (2009), 49–67, esp. 63.
14. For further discussion of this battle, see M. Prestwich, 'A new account of the Welsh campaign of 1294–95', *WHR*, 6 (1972), 89–92; R.F. Walker, 'The Hagnaby Chronicle and the battle of Maes Moydog', *WHR*, 8 (1976), 125–38; J.G. Edwards, 'The Battle of Maes Moydog and the Welsh campaign of 1294–5', *EHR*, 39 (1924), 1–12.
15. *Edward I*, p. 223.
16. Quoted from *Edward I*, p. 223.
17. For full discussion, see R.F. Walker, 'The Hagnaby Chronicle and the battle of Maes Moydog', *WHR*, 8 (1976), 125–38.
18. T. Herbert and G.E. Jones (eds), *Edward I and Wales* (Cardiff, 1988), p. 65.
19. In 1296 the enormous, mounting cost of Edward's Scottish wars meant that all royal building work was cancelled, excepting only expenditure on Beaumaris and Caernarfon.
20. At the time no specific reference was made to the titles 'prince' or 'principality', but it became common to refer to young Edward as Prince of Wales.

Chapter 12: A United Kingdom?

1. *Edward I*, p. 225.
2. *The Chronicle of Pierre de Langtoft*, ed. T. Wright, 2 vols (London, 1866–8), II, pp. 264–7.
3. R.R. Davies, *The First English Empire: Power and Identities in the British Isles, 1093–1343* (Oxford, 2000), pp. 87–8.
4. *Edward I*, pp. 375, 564.
5. *Great and Terrible*, p. 346.
6. R.R. Davies, 'Llywelyn ap Gruffudd, Prince of Wales', *Journal Merioneth Hist. Soc.*, 9 (1983), 264–77, esp. 275.
7. *Mountain People* by the Super Furry Animals (Huw Bunford, Cian Ciaran, Dafydd Ieuan, Guto Pryce, Gruff Rhys). Copyright © Universal Music Publishing Group.

Bibliography

Abbreviations

AC – *Annales Cambriae*

Acts – H. Pryce (ed.), *The Acts of Welsh Rulers, 1120–1283* (Cardiff, 2005)

Age – R.R. Davies, *The Age of Conquest: Wales, 1063–1415* (Oxford, 1991)

Arch. Camb. – *Archaeologia Cambrensis*

BBCS – *Bulletin of the Board of Celtic Studies*

BIHR – *Bulletin of the Institute of Historical Research*

Bren. – *Brenhinedd y Saeson or The Kings of the Saxons*, ed. and trans. T. Jones (Cardiff, 1971). All year references are to the amended dates given by Jones.

Brut (Pen. 20) – *Brut y Tywysogyon or The Chronicle of the Princes, Peniarth MS. 20 Version*, ed. and trans. T. Jones (Cardiff, 1952). All year references are to the amended dates given by Jones.

Brut (RBH) – *Brut y Tywysogyon or The Chronicle of the Princes, Red Book of Hergest Version*, ed. and trans. T. Jones (Cardiff, 1955). All year references are to the amended dates given by Jones.

CMCS – *Cambrian/Cambridge Medieval Celtic Studies*

Description – Gerald of Wales, *The Description of Wales*, ed. and trans. L. Thorpe (Harmondsworth, 1978)

Edward I – M. Prestwich, *Edward I* (London, 1988)

EHR – *English History Review*

FH – *Flores Historiarum*, ed. H.R. Luard, 3 vols (Rolls Series, London, 1890)

Great and Terrible – M. Morris, *A Great and Terrible King: Edward I and the Forging of Britain* (London, 2009)

HW – J.E. Lloyd, *A History of Wales from the Earliest Times to the Edwardian Conquest*, 2 vols (3rd edn, London, 1939)

Journey – Gerald of Wales, *The Journey Through Wales*, ed. and trans. L. Thorpe (Harmondsworth, 1978)

LapG – J.B. Smith, *Llywelyn ap Gruffudd, Prince of Wales* (Cardiff, 1998)

MP – *Matthew Paris' English History*, ed. and trans. J.A. Giles, 3 vols (London, 1852–4)

NLWJ – *National Library of Wales Journal*

P&P – *Past and Present*

PBA – *Proceedings of the British Academy*

TCHS – *Transactions of the Caernarfonshire Historical Society*

THSC – *Transactions of the Honourable Society of Cymmrodorion*

TRHS – *Transactions of the Royal Historical Society*

TWNFC – *Transactions of the Woolhope Naturalists Field Club*

War, Politics and Finance – M. Prestwich, *War, Politics and Finance Under Edward I* (London, 1972)

Welsh Wars – J.E. Morris, *The Welsh Wars of Edward I* (Oxford, 1901; new edn Stroud, 1996)
WHR – *Welsh History Review*

Printed sources

Annales Cambriae, ed. J. Williams ab Ithel (Rolls Series, London, 1860)
Annales Monastici, ed. H.R. Luard, 5 vols (Rolls Series, London, 1864–9)
Bosco, N., 'Dafydd Benfras and his *Red Book* poems', *Studia Celtica*, 22 (1987), 49–117
Brenhinedd y Saeson or The Kings of the Saxons, ed. and trans. T. Jones (Cardiff, 1971)
Breuddwyd Maxen, ed. I. Williams (3rd edn, Bangor, 1928)
Brut y Tywysogyon. Peniarth Ms. 20 version, ed. T. Jones (Cardiff, 1941)
Brut y Tywysogyon or The Chronicle of the Princes. Peniarth Ms. 20 Version, ed. and trans. T. Jones (Cardiff, 1952)
Brut y Tywysogyon or the Chronicle of the Princes. Red Book of Hergest Version, ed. and trans. T. Jones (Cardiff, 1955)
Calendar of Ancient Correspondence Concerning Wales, ed. J.G. Edwards (Cardiff, 1935)
Calendar of Ancient Petitions Relating to Wales in the Public Record Office, ed. W. Rees (Cardiff, 1975)
Cartae et alia Munimenta de Glamorgan, ed. and trans. G.T. Clark, 6 vols (Talygan, 1910)
Charters of the Abbey of Ystrad Marchell, The, ed. G.C.G. Thomas (Aberystwyth, 1997)
Cronica de Wallia, in T. Jones (ed.), '*Cronica de Wallia* and other documents from the Exeter Cathedral Library Ms. 3514', *BBCS*, 12 (1946–8), 27–44
Cyfres Beirdd y Tywysogion, ed. R.G. Gruffydd, 7 vols (Cardiff, 1991–6)
Dickinson, J.C., and P.T. Ricketts, 'The Anglo-Norman chronicle of Wigmore Abbey', *TWNFC*, 39 (1969), 413–45
Facsimile of the Chirk Codex of the Welsh Laws, ed. J. Gwenogvryn Evans (Llanbedrog, 1908)
Flores Historiarum, ed. H.R. Luard, 3 vols (Rolls Series, London, 1890)
— ed. and trans. C.D. Yonge, 2 vols (London, 1853)
Geoffrey of Monmouth, *The History of the Kings of Britain*, ed. and trans. L. Thorpe (Harmondsworth, 1968)
Gerald of Wales, *Journey through Wales, Description of Wales*, ed. and trans. L. Thorpe (Harmondsworth, 1978)
'*Historia Brittonum*' and the '*Vatican*' Recension, The, ed. D.M. Dumville (Cambridge, 1985)
John of Salisbury, *Historia Pontificalis*, ed. M. Chibnall (Edinburgh, 1956)
— *The Letters of John of Salisbury, Volume One: The Early Letters (1153–61)*, ed. and trans. W.J. Millor and H.E. Butler (Edinburgh, 1955)
— *The Letters of John of Salisbury, Volume Two: The Later Letters (1163–80)*, ed. and trans. W.J. Millor and C.N.L. Brooke (Oxford, 1979)
— *Policraticus*, ed. C.J. Nederman (Cambridge, 1990)
Jones, G., *The Oxford Book of Welsh Verse in English* (Oxford, 1983)
Jordan Fantosme, *Jordan Fantosme's Chronicle*, ed. and trans. R.C. Johnston (Oxford, 1981)
Latin Redaction 'A' of the Law of Hywel, ed. and trans. I.F. Fletcher (Aberystwyth, 1986)
Latin Texts of the Welsh Laws, ed. H.D. Emanuel (Cardiff, 1967)
Law of Hywel Dda, ed. and trans. D. Jenkins (Llandysul, 1986)
Laws of Hywel Dda, ed. and trans. M. Richards (Liverpool, 1954)
Liber Eliensis, ed. E.O. Blake (London, 1962)
Littere Wallie preserved in Liber A in the Public Record Office, ed. J.G. Edwards (Cardiff, 1940)
Llandaff Episcopal Acta, 1140–1287, ed. D. Crouch (Cardiff, 1988)

Llyfr Blegywryd, ed. S.J. Williams and J.E. Powell (3rd edn, Cardiff, 1961)

Llyfr Colan, ed. D. Jenkins (Cardiff, 1963)

Llyfr Iorwerth, ed. A.R. Williams (Cardiff, 1960)

Mabinogion, ed. and trans. J. Gantz (Harmondsworth, 1976)

Matthew Paris, *Chronicles of Matthew Paris*, ed. and trans. R. Vaughan (Gloucester, 1986)

— *English History*, ed. and trans. J.A. Giles, 3 vols (London, 1852–4)

— *Mattoei Parisiensis, Monachi Sancti Albani, Chronica Majora*, ed. H.R. Luard, 7 vols (Rolls Series, London, 1872–83)

Nennius: British History and the Welsh Annals, ed. and trans. J. Morris (London, 1980)

New Translated Selections from the Welsh Medieval Law Books, ed. and trans. D. Jenkins (Aberystwyth, 1973)

Orderic Vitalis, *Historia Ecclesiastica*, ed. and trans. M. Chibnall, 6 vols (Oxford, 1969–80)

'Owein' or 'Chwedyl Iarlles y Ffynnawn', ed. R.L. Thomson (Dublin, 1968)

Owen, A., *Ancient Laws and Institutions of Wales*, 2 vols (London, 1841)

Patent Rolls, 1216–32 (London, 1901–3)

Pedeir Keinc y Mabinogi, ed. I. Williams (Cardiff, 1930)

Penguin Book of Welsh Verse, The, ed. and trans. A. Conran (Harmondsworth, 1967)

Registrum Epistolarum fratris Johannis Peckham, ed. C.T. Martin, 3 vols (Rolls Series, London, 1882–5)

Roger of Howden, *Annals of Roger de Hoveden*, ed. and trans. H.T. Riley, 2 vols (London, 1853)

— *Magistri Rogeri de Houedene*, ed. W. Stubbs, 4 vols (Rolls Series, London, 1868–71)

Roger of Wendover, *Flores Historiarum*, ed. H.G. Hewlett, 3 vols (Rolls Series, London, 1886–9)

— *Flowers of History*, ed. and trans. J.A. Giles, 2 vols (London, 1849)

Rotuli Parliamentorum, 7 vols (Record Commission, 1783–1832)

Rowland, J., *Early Welsh Saga Poetry* (Cambridge, 1990)

Salmon, M., *A Source Book of Welsh History* (Oxford, 1927)

The Chronicle of Pierre de Langtoft, ed. T. Wright, 2 vols (London, 1866–8)

Thomson, D.S., *Branwen Uerch Lyr* (Dublin, 1961)

Thomson, R.L., *Pwyll Pendeuic Dyvet* (Dublin, 1957)

Vegetius, *De Re Militari*, ed. C. Lang (Leipzig, 1885), partial trans. in T.R. Phillips, *The Roots of Strategy* (London, 1943), trans. in full, N.P. Milner, *Vegetius: Epitome of Military Science* (Liverpool, 1993)

Walter Map, *De Nugis Curialium/Courtiers' Trifles*, ed. and trans. M.R. James, C.N.L. Brooke and R.A.B. Mynors (Oxford, 1983)

Welsh Assize Roll, 1277–84. Assize Roll No.1147, ed. J.C. Davies (Cardiff, 1940)

Welsh Poems, Sixth Century to 1600, ed. and trans. G. Williams (London, 1973)

Welsh Verse, ed. and trans. T. Conran (2nd edn, Southampton, 1986)

William of Malmesbury, *Gesta Regum Anglorum/The History of the English Kings*, ed. and trans. R.A.B. Mynors, R.M. Thomson and M. Winterbottom (Oxford, 1998)

— *Historia Novella*, ed. and trans. K.R. Potter (Edinburgh, 1955)

Williams, D.H., *Welsh History through Seals* (Cardiff, 1982)

Secondary works

Alcock, L., 'Excavations at Degannwy Castle, Caernarfonshire, 1961–6', *Archaeological Journal*, 124 (1967), 190–201

Arnold, C.J. and J.W. Huggett, 'Pre-Norman rectangular earthworks in mid Wales', *Medieval Archaeology*, 39 (1995), 171–4

Arnold, C.J., J.W. Huggett and H. Pryce, 'Excavations at Mathrafal, Powys, 1989', *The Montgomeryshire Collections*, 83 (1995), 59–74

Avent, R., *Castles of the Princes of Gwynedd* (Cardiff, 1983)

— 'Castles of the Welsh princes', *Château Gaillard*, 16 (1992), 11–20

Bachrach, B.S., 'Military Logistics During the Reign of Edward I of England, 1272–1307', *War in History*, 13 (2006), 423–40

— 'The practical use of Vegetius' *De Re Militari* during the Middle Ages', *The Historian*, 27 (1985), 239–55

Barrow, G.W.S., 'Wales and Scotland in the Middle Ages', *WHR*, 10 (1980–1), 302–19

Barry, T.B., R. Frame and K. Simms (eds), *Colony and Frontier in Medieval Ireland* (London, 1995)

Bartlett, R., *Gerald of Wales, 1146–1223* (Oxford, 1982)

— 'Technique militaire et pouvoir politique, 900–1300', *Annales: Economies-Sociétés-Civilisations*, 41 (1986), 1135–59

— *The Making of Europe* (London, 1993)

— and A. Mackay (eds), *Medieval Frontier Societies* (Oxford, 1989)

Bartlett, T. and K. Jeffery (eds), *A Military History of Ireland* (Cambridge, 1996)

Bartlett, W.B., *The Taming of the Dragon: Edward I and the Conquest of Wales* (Stroud, 2003)

Bennett, M., '*La Regle du Temple* as a military manual, or how to deliver a cavalry charge', in Harper-Bill, *Studies*, pp. 7–20

— 'The medieval warhorse reconsidered', *Medieval Knighthood*, V (1994), 19–40

Blair, C., *European Armour* (London, 1958)

Bloch, M., *Feudal Society* (2nd edn, London, 1965)

Boussard, J., 'Les mercenaires au XIIe siècle', *Bibliothèque de l'École des Chartres*, 106 (1945–6), 189–224

Bradbury, J., *The Medieval Archer* (Woodbridge, 1985)

— *The Medieval Siege* (Woodbridge, 1992)

Brodie, H., 'Apsidal and D-shaped towers of the princes of Gwynedd', *Arch. Camb.*, 164 (2015), 231–43

Bromwich, R. and R. Brinley Jones, *Astudiaethau ar yr Hengerdd* (Cardiff, 1978)

— *Medieval Welsh Literature to c.1400 including Arthurian Studies* (Cardiff, 1996)

— A.O.H. Jarman and B.F. Roberts (eds), *The Arthur of the Welsh* (Cardiff, 1991)

Brown, S.D.B., 'The mercenary and his master', *History*, 74 (1989), 20–38

Burgess, E.M., 'The mail-maker's techniques and further research into the construction of mail garments', *Antiquaries Journal*, 33 (1953), 48–55, 193–202

Caple, C., 'The castle and lifestyle of a thirteenth-century independent Welsh lord; excavations at Dryslwyn Castle, 1980–8', *Château Gaillard*, 14 (1990), 47–59

Carpenter, D.A., *The Struggle for Mastery: Britain 1066–1284* (London, 2003)

Carr, A.D., 'A debatable land: Arwystli in the middle ages', *Montgomeryshire Collections*, 80 (1992), 39–54

— 'The last and weakest of his line: Dafydd ap Gruffudd, the last Prince of Wales,' *WHR*, 19 (1999), 375–99

— 'Welshmen and the Hundred Years War', *WHR*, 4 (1968–9), 21–46

Charles-Edwards, T.M., *Early Irish and Welsh Kinship* (Oxford, 1993)

— *The Welsh Laws* (Cardiff, 1989)

— *Wales and the Britons, 350-1064* (Oxford, 2013)

— M.E. Owen and P. Russell (eds), *The Welsh King and his Court* (Cardiff, 2000)

Church, S.D., 'The rewards of royal service in the household of King John: A dissenting opinion', *EHR*, 110 (1995), 277–302

— 'The 1210 campaign in Ireland: Evidence for a military revolution', *ANS*, 20 (1997), 45–57

Clancy, J.P., *The Earliest Welsh Poetry* (London, 1970)

Contamine, P., *War in the Middle Ages* (London, 1984)

Conway-Davies, J., 'A grant by David ap Gruffudd', *NLWJ*, 3 (1943–4), 29–32, 158–62

Corfis, I.A., and M. Wolfe (eds), *The Medieval City Under Siege* (Woodbridge, 1995)

Coulson, C., 'Fortress policy in Capetian tradition and Angevin practice', *ANS*, 6 (1983), 13–38

Cowley, F., *Gerald of Wales and Margam Abbey*, Friends of Margam Abbey Annual Lecture (1982)

— *The Monastic Order in South Wales, 1066–1349* (Cardiff, 1977)

Cox, D.C., 'The battle of Evesham in the Evesham chronicle', *BIHR*, 63 (1990), 337–45

Critchley, J.S., 'Military organisation in England, 1154–1254' (unpublished Ph.D. thesis, University of Nottingham, 1968)

Crouch, D., *The Beaumont Twins* (Cambridge, 1986)

— 'The earliest original charter of a Welsh king', *BBCS*, 36 (1989), 125–31

— *The Image of Aristocracy in Britain, 1000–1300* (London, 1992)

— 'The last adventure of Richard Siward', *Morgannwg*, 35 (1991), 7–30

— 'The slow death of kingship in Glamorgan', *Morgannwg*, 29 (1985), 20–41

— *William Marshal* (London, 1990)

Curry, A., 'Review article: Medieval warfare, England and her continental neighbours, eleventh–fourteenth centuries', *Journal of Medieval History*, 24 (1998), 81–102

Davidson, H.R.E., *The Sword in Anglo-Saxon England* (Oxford, 1962)

Davies, R.R., *Domination and Conquest* (Cambridge, 1990)

— 'Llywelyn ap Gruffudd, Prince of Wales', *Journal Merioneth Hist. Soc.*, 9 (1983), 264–77

— *The Age of Conquest: Wales 1063–1415* (Oxford, 1991)

— (ed.), *The British Isles 1100–1500: Comparisons, Contrasts and Connections* (Edinburgh, 1988)

— *The First English Empire: Power and Identities in the British Isles, 1093–1343* (Oxford, 2000)

— 'The peoples of Britain and Ireland, 1100–1400', *TRHS*, 4–7 (1994–7)

— *The Revolt of Owain Glyn Dŵr* (Oxford, 1995)

Davies, Sean, 'Anglo-Welsh warfare and the works of Gerald of Wales' (unpublished MA thesis, University of Wales Swansea, 1996)

— 'The Battle of Chester and Warfare in Post-Roman Britain', *History*, 95 (2010), 143–58

— *The First Prince of Wales? Bleddyn ap Cynfyn, 1063–75* (Cardiff, 2016)

— 'The *teulu* c.633–1283', *WHR*, 21 (2003), 413–54

— *Welsh Military Institutions, 633–1283* (Cardiff, 2004); reprinted in paperback as *War and Society in Medieval Wales, 633–1283* (Cardiff, 2014)

Davies, Sioned, *The Four Branches of the Mabinogi* (Llandysul, 1993)

— *The Mabinogion* (Oxford, 2007)

— and N.A. Jones (eds), *The Horse in Celtic Culture: Medieval Welsh Perspectives* (Cardiff, 1997)

Davies, T.M., 'Gruffudd ap Llywelyn, King of Wales,' *WHR*, 21 (2002), 207–48

— and Sean Davies, *The Last King of Wales: Gruffudd ap Llywelyn, c.1013–1063* (Stroud, 2012)

Davis, P., *Castles of Dyfed* (Llandysul, 1987)

— *Castles of the Welsh Princes* (Swansea, 1988)

Davis, R.H.C., *The Medieval Warhorse* (London, 1989)

Delbrück, H., *History of the Art of War*, trans. W.J. Renfroe, 4 vols (London, 1982)

DeVries, K., 'Catapults are not atomic bombs: Towards a redefinition of "effectiveness" in premodern military technology', *War in History*, 4 (1997), 454–70

Duby, G., *Chivalrous Society* (London, 1977)

Duffy, S., 'King John's expedition to Ireland in 1210: The evidence reconsidered', *Irish Historical Studies*, 30 (1995), 1–24

Dumville, D.M., *Histories and Pseudo-Histories of the Insular Middle Ages* (Aldershot, 1990)

— 'Nennius and the *Historia Brittonum*', *Studia Celtica*, 10–11 (1975–6), 78–95

— 'review of K. Hughes, *The Welsh Latin Chronicles*,' *Studia Celtica*, 12–13 (1977–8), 461–7

— 'Sub-Roman Britain: History and legend', *History*, 62 (1977), 173–92

Edwards, J.G., 'The Battle of Maes Moydog and the Welsh campaign of 1294–5', *EHR*, 39 (1924), 1–12

Ellis, T.P., *Welsh Tribal Law and Custom in the Middle Ages*, 2 vols (Oxford, 1926)

Finberg, H.P.R. (ed.), *The Agrarian History of England and Wales*, I (Cambridge, 1972)

Fox, C., *Offa's Dyke* (Oxford, 1955)

France, J., 'The military history of the Carolingian period', *Revue Belge d'Histoire Militaire*, 26 (1985), 81–99

— *Victory in the East* (Cambridge, 1994)

— *Western Warfare in the Age of the Crusades, 1000–1300* (London, 1999)

Garnett, G., and J. Hudson (eds), *Law and Government in Medieval England and Normandy: Essays in Honour of Sir James Holt* (Cambridge, 1994)

Gillingham, J., 'Conquering the barbarians: War and chivalry in twelfth-century Britain', *Haskins Soc. Journal*, 4 (1992), 67–84

— *Richard Coeur de Lion: Kingship, Chivalry and War in the Twelfth Century* (London, 1994)

— 'The beginnings of English imperialism', *Journal of Historical Sociology*, 5 (1992), 392–409

— 'The context and purposes of Geoffrey of Monmouth's *History of the Kings of Britain*', *ANS*, 13 (1990), 99–118

— 'The travels of Roger of Howden and his views of the Irish, Scots and Welsh', *ANS*, 20 (1997), 151–69

— and J.C. Holt (eds), *War and Government in the Middle Ages: Essays in Honour of J.O. Prestwich* (Woodbridge, 1984)

Given, J., *State and Society in Medieval Europe: Gwynedd and Languedoc Under Outside Rule* (New York, 1990)

Golding, B., 'Gerald of Wales and the monks', *Thirteenth-Century England*, 5 (1993), 53–64

Grabowski, K., and D.M. Dumville, *Chronicles and Annals of Medieval Ireland and Wales* (Woodbridge, 1984)

Gresham, C.A., 'Aberconway charter', *BBCS*, 30 (1982–3), 311–47

Griffiths, R.A. (ed.), *Boroughs of Medieval Wales* (Cardiff, 1978)

— *Conquerors and Conquered in Medieval Wales* (Stroud, 1994)

Harper-Bill, C. (ed.), *Studies in History Presented to R. Allen-Brown* (Woodbridge, 1989)

Hawkes, S.C. (ed.), *Weapons and Warfare in Anglo-Saxon England* (Oxford, 1989)

Herbert, T., and G.E. Jones (eds), *Edward I and Wales* (Cardiff, 1988)

Higham, R., and P. Barker, *Timber Castles* (London, 1992)

Hill, D., 'The construction of Offa's Dyke', *Antiquaries Journal*, 65 (1985), 140–2

Hogg, A.H.A., and D.J. Cathcart King, 'Early castles in Wales and the Marches', *Arch. Camb.*, 112 (1963), 77–124

Holden, B.W., 'The Making of the Middle March of Wales, 1066–1250,' *WHR*, 20 (2000), 207–26

Hollister, C.W., *Anglo-Saxon Military Institutions* (Oxford, 1962)

— *The Military Organisation of Norman England* (Oxford, 1965)

Holt, J.C., *Magna Carta* (Cambridge, 1965)

— 'The end of the Anglo-Norman realm', *PBA*, 61 (1975), 223–66

— *The Northerners* (Oxford, 1961)

Hooper, N., 'Anglo-Saxon warfare on the eve of the Norman Conquest', *ANS*, 1 (1978), 84–93

— and M. Bennett (eds), *The Cambridge Illustrated Atlas of Warfare: The Middle Ages, 768–1487* (Cambridge, 1996)

Hopkinson, C., 'The Mortimers of Wigmore, 1086–1214', *TWNFC*, 46 (1989), 177–93

— 'The Mortimers of Wigmore, 1214–82', *TWNFC*, 47 (1993), 28–46

Hughes, K., 'The Welsh-Latin chronicles: *Annales Cambriae* and related texts', *PBA*, 57 (1973), 233–58

Hyland, A., *The Medieval Warhorse from Byzantium to the Crusades* (Stroud, 1994)

Jarman, A.O.H., and G.R. Hughes (eds), *A Guide to Welsh Literature* (Cardiff, 1992)

Jobson, A., *The First English Revolution: Simon de Montfort, Henry III and the Barons' War* (London, 2012)

Johnstone, N., '*Llys* and *Maerdref*: The royal courts of the princes of Gwynedd', *Studia Celtica*, 34 (2000), 167–210

Jones, G.R.J., 'Multiple estates perceived', *Journal of Historical Geography*, 11 (1985), 352–63

— 'The defences of Gwynedd in the thirteenth century', *TCHS*, 30 (1969), 29–43

— 'The distribution of bond settlements in north-west Wales', *WHR*, 2 (1964–5), 19–36

— 'The military geography of Gwynedd in the thirteenth century' (unpublished MA thesis, University of Wales Aberystwyth, 1949)

— 'The models for organisation in *Llyfr Iorwerth* and *Llyfr Cyfnerth*', *BBCS*, 39 (1992), 95–118

— 'The pattern of settlement on the Welsh border', *Agricultural History Review*, 8 (1960), 66–81

— 'The tribal system in Wales', *WHR*, 1 (1960–3), 111–32

Jones, W.R., 'England against the Celtic fringe: A study in cultural stereotypes', *Journal of World History*, 13 (1971), 155–71

— 'The image of the barbarian in medieval Europe', *Comparative Studies in Society and History*, 13 (1971), 376–407

Jones, W.R.D., 'The Welsh rulers of Senghennydd', *Caerphilly*, 3 (1971), 9–19

Jones-Pierce, T., *Medieval Welsh Society*, ed. J.B. Smith (Cardiff, 1972)

Keegan, J., *A History of Warfare* (London, 1993)

— *The Face of Battle* (Harmondsworth, 1983)

Keen, M., *Chivalry* (London, 1984)

Kenyon, J.R. 'Fluctuating frontiers: Normano-Welsh castle warfare, *c.*1075–1240', *Château Gaillard*, 17 (1996), 119–26

— and R. Avent (eds), *Castles in Wales and the Marches* (Cardiff, 1987)

King, A., *Edward I: A New King Arthur?* (London, 2016)

King, D.J. Cathcart, 'Henry II and the fight at Coleshill', *WHR*, 2 (1964–5), 367–75

— 'The defence of Wales, 1067–1283: The other side of the hill', *Arch. Camb.*, 126 (1977), 1–16

Kirby, D.P., 'Hywel Dda: Anglophile?', *WHR*, 8 (1976–7), 1–13

Knight, J.K., 'Welsh fortifications of the first millennium AD', *Château Gaillard*, 16 (1992), 277–84

Koch, H.W., *Medieval Warfare* (London, 1978)

Latimer, P., 'Henry II's campaign against the Welsh in 1165', *WHR*, 14 (1988–9), 523–52

Lewis, C.W., 'The treaty of Woodstock, 1247: Its background and significance', *WHR*, 2 (1964–5), 37–65

Lloyd, J.E., *A History of Wales from the Earliest Times to the Edwardian Conquest*, 2 vols (3rd edn, London, 1939)

— 'The Welsh chronicles', *PBA*, 14 (1928), 369–91

Lloyd-Jones, J., 'The court poets of the Welsh princes', *PBA*, 34 (1948), 167–97

Loyn, H.R., *The Vikings in Wales* (London, 1976)

— 'Wales and England in the tenth century: The context of the Athelstan charters', *WHR*, 10 (1980–1), 283–301

Ludlow, N., 'The Castle and Lordship of Narberth,' *The Journal of the Pembrokeshire Historical Society*, 12 (2003), 5–43

McGeer, E., 'Byzantine siege warfare in theory and practice', in Corfis and Wolfe, *Medieval City*, pp. 123–9

McGlynn, S., 'The myths of medieval warfare', *History Today*, 44 (1994), 28–34

McNeill, T., *Castles in Ireland: Feudal Power in a Gaelic World* (London, 1997)

Mann, K.J., 'King John, Wales and the March' (unpublished Ph.D. thesis, University of Wales Swansea, 1991)

Maund, K.L., *Handlist of the Acts of Native Welsh Rulers, 1132–1283* (Cardiff, 1996)

— *The Welsh Kings: The Medieval Rulers of Wales* (Stroud, 2000)

Mayr-Harting, H., and R.I. Moore (eds), *Studies in Medieval History Presented to R.H.C. Davis* (London, 1985)

Morillo, S., 'review of Suppe, *Military Institutions,*' *Trans. Shropshire Arch. and Hist. Soc.*, 70 (1995), 218–19

Morris, J.E., *The Welsh Wars of Edward I* (Oxford, 1901, new edn Stroud, 1996)

Morris, M., *A Great and Terrible King: Edward I and the Forging of Britain* (London, 2009)

Nicolle, D., *Medieval Warfare Source Book: Vol. 1, Warfare in Western Christendom* (London, 1995)

Oakeshott, R.E., *The Sword in the Age of Chivalry* (London, 1964)

Oman, C., *A History of the Art of War in the Middle Ages, 378–1485* (Oxford, 1991)

Owen, D.H. (ed.), *Settlement and Society in Wales* (Cardiff, 1989)

Parker, G., *The Cambridge Illustrated History of Warfare* (Cambridge, 1995)

Pierce, G.O., 'The evidence of place-names', in *Glamorgan County History*, III, pp. 456–92

Pierce, I., 'Arms, armour and warfare in the eleventh century', *ANS*, 10 (1987), 237–58

— 'The knight, his arms and armour in the eleventh century', *Medieval Knighthood*, I (1986), 157–64

Powicke, M.R., *Military Obligations in Medieval England* (Oxford, 1962)

Prestwich, M., 'A new account of the Welsh campaign of 1294–95', *WHR*, 6 (1972), 89–92

— *Edward I* (London, 1988)

— *The Three Edwards* (London, 1980)

— *War, Politics and Finance Under Edward I* (London, 1972)

Pryce, H., 'Ecclesiastical wealth in early medieval Wales', in Edwards and Lane, *Early Church*, pp. 22–32

— 'In search of a medieval society: Deheubarth in the writings of Gerald of Wales', *WHR*, 13 (1986–7), 265–81

— 'Owain Gwynedd and Louis VII: The Franco-Welsh diplomacy of the first Prince of Wales', *WHR*, 19 (1998), 1–28

— (ed.), *The Acts of Welsh Rulers, 1120–1283* (Cardiff, 2005)

— 'The church of Trefeglwys and the end of the "Celtic" charter tradition in twelfth-century Wales', *CMCS*, 25 (1993), 15–54

Rees, S.E., and C. Caple, *Dinefwr Castle and Dryslwyn Castle* (Cardiff, 1996)

Rees, W., *A Historical Atlas of Wales from Early to Modern Times* (Cardiff, 1951)

Remfry, P.M., 'Cadwallon ap Madog, Rex de Delvain, 1140–79, and the re-establishment of local autonomy in Cynllibiwg', *Trans. Radnorshire Soc.*, 65 (1995), 11–32

— 'The native Welsh dynasties of Rhwng Gwy a Hafren, 1066–1282' (unpublished M.Phil. thesis, University of Wales Aberystwyth, 1989)

Rex Smith, G., 'The Penmachno Letter Patent and the Welsh Uprising of 1294–95', *CMCS*, 58 (2009), 49–67

Roderick, A.J., 'Feudal relations between the English crown and the Welsh princes', *History*, 37 (1952), 201–12

Rogers, R., 'Latin siege warfare in the twelfth century' (unpublished D.Phil. thesis, Oxford University, 1984)

Rowlands, I.W., 'The 1201 peace between King John and Llywelyn ap Iorwerth', *Studia Celtica*, 34 (2000), 149–66

— 'The making of the March. Aspects of the Norman settlement in Dyfed', *ANS*, 3 (1980), 142–58

— 'William de Braose and the lordship of Brecon', *BBCS*, 30 (1982–3), 123–33

Ryan, J., 'A study of horses in early and medieval Welsh literature, *c.*600–1300 AD' (unpublished M.Phil. thesis, University of Wales Cardiff, 1993)

Salzman, L.F., *Edward I* (London, 1968)

Schubert, H.R., *History of the British Iron and Steel Industry* (London, 1957)

Seebohm, F., *The Tribal System in Wales* (2nd edn, London, 1904)

Simms, K., *From Kings to Warlords* (Woodbridge, 1987)

Simpkin, D., *The English Aristocracy at War: From the Welsh Wars of Edward I to the Battle of Bannockburn* (Woodbridge, 2008)

Smail, R.C., *Crusading Warfare* (Cambridge, 1956)

Smith, J.B., 'Land endowments of the period of Llywelyn ap Gruffudd', *BBCS*, 34 (1987), 150–64

— 'Llywelyn ap Gruffudd and the March of Wales', *Brycheiniog*, 20 (1982–3), 9–22

— *Llywelyn ap Gruffudd, Prince of Wales* (Cardiff, 1998)

— 'Llywelyn ap Gruffudd, Prince of Wales and Lord of Snowdon', *TCHS*, 45 (1984), 7–36

— 'Magna Carta and the charters of the Welsh princes', *EHR*, 99 (1984), 344–62

— 'Owain Gwynedd', *TCHS*, 32 (1971), 8–17

— 'The kingdom of Morgannwg and the Norman conquest of Glamorgan', in *Glamorgan County History*, III, pp. 1–44

— 'The lordship of Glamorgan', *Morgannwg*, 9 (1965), 9–38

— 'The middle March in the thirteenth century', *BBCS*, 24 (1970), 77–93

— and T.B. Pugh, 'The lordship of Gower', in *Glamorgan County History*, III, pp. 205–83

Smith, L.B., 'Llywelyn ap Gruffudd and the Welsh historical consciousness' *WHR*, 12 (1984), 1–28

— 'The death of Llywelyn ap Gruffydd: The narratives reconsidered', *WHR*, 11 (1982), 200–13

— 'The *gravamina* of the community of Gwynedd against Llywelyn ap Gruffudd', *BBCS*, 31 (1984), 158–76

Squatriti, P., 'Digging ditches in early medieval Europe', *P&P*, 176 (2002), 11–65

Stephenson, D., 'A reconsideration of the siting, function and dating of Ewloe castle', *Arch. Camb.*, 164, (2015), 245–53

— 'Empires in Wales: From Gruffudd ap Llywelyn to Llywelyn ap Gruffudd', *WHR*, 28 (2016), 26–54

— *Political Power in Medieval Gwynedd: Governance and the Welsh Princes* (Cardiff, 2014)

— *The Last Prince of Wales* (Buckingham, 1983)

— 'The politics of Powys Wenwynwyn in the thirteenth century', *CMCS*, 7 (1984), 39–61

Strickland, M. (ed.), *Anglo-Norman Warfare* (Woodbridge, 1992)

— 'Military technology and conquest: The anomaly of Anglo-Saxon England', *ANS*, 19 (1996), 353–82

— *War and Chivalry: The Conduct and Perception of War in England and Normandy, 1066–1217* (Cambridge, 1996)

Suppe, F.C., *Military Institutions on the Welsh Marches: Shropshire, AD 1066–1300* (Woodbridge, 1994)

— 'The cultural significance of decapitation in high medieval Wales and the Marches', *BBCS*, 36 (1989), 147–60

Taylor, A.J., 'Master Bertram, *Ingeniator Regis*', in C. Harper-Bill (ed.), *Studies in History Presented to R. Allen-Brown* (Woodbridge, 1989), pp. 289–304

— *Studies in Castles and Castle-Building* (London, 1985)

— *The Welsh Castles of Edward I* (London, 1986)

Thordemann, B., *Armour from the Battle of Wisby, 1361*, 2 vols (Stockholm, 1939)

Toy, S., *A History of Fortification, 3000 BC–1700 AD* (2nd edn, London, 1966)

Treharne, R.F., 'The Franco-Welsh treaty of alliance in 1212', *BBCS*, 18 (1958–60), 60–75

Turvey, R., 'The defences of twelfth-century Deheubarth and the castle strategy of the Lord Rhys', *Arch. Camb.*, 144 (1995), 103–32

— *Llywelyn the Great* (Llandysul, 2007)

— *Owain Gwynedd: Prince of the Welsh* (Talybont, 2013)

Verbruggen, J.F., *The Art of Warfare in Western Europe in the Middle Ages* (New York, 1977)

Wainwright, F.T., 'Cledemutha', *EHR*, 65 (1950), 203–12

Walker, R.F., 'Hubert de Burgh and Wales, 1218–32', *EHR*, 87 (1972), 465–94

— 'The Anglo-Welsh wars, 1217–67; with special reference to English military developments (unpublished D.Phil. thesis, Oxford University, 1954)

— 'The Hagnaby Chronicle and the battle of Maes Moydog', *WHR*, 8 (1976), 125–38

— 'The supporters of Richard Marshal, Earl of Pembroke, in the rebellion of 1233–4', *WHR*, 17 (1994), 41–65

— 'William de Valence and the army of west Wales, 1282–3', *WHR*, 18 (1997), 407–29

Warren, W.L., *Henry II* (London, 1973)

White, L., *Medieval Technology and Social Change* (Oxford, 1962)

Wiedemann, B.G.E., ' "Fooling the court of the lord Pope": Dafydd ap Llywelyn's petition to the Curia in 1244', *WHR*, 28 (2016), 209–32

Williams, A.R., 'Methods of manufacture of swords in medieval Europe', *Gladius*, 13 (1977), 75–101

— 'The knight and the blast furnace', *Metals and Materials*, 2 (1986), 485–9

— 'The manufacture of mail in medieval Europe: A technical note', *Gladius*, 15 (1980), 105–34

Williams, D.M. and J.R. Kenyon (eds), *The Impact of the Edwardian Castles in Wales* (Oxford, 2010)

Williams, J.E. Caerwyn, *The Poets of the Welsh Princes* (Cardiff, 1994)

Williams-Jones, K., 'Llywelyn's charter to Cymer Abbey in 1209', *Journal Merioneth Hist. Soc.*, 3 (1957), 45–78

Willoughby, R., 'The shock of the new', *History Today*, 49 (1999), 36–42

Index